DUBLIN•7•

DUBLIN •7•

ASHTOWN ❖ BROADSTONE ❖ CABRA ❖ CHURCH STREET
ELLIS & ARRAN QUAYS ❖ OXMANTOWN ❖ PHIBSBOROUGH
ROYAL CANAL ❖ SMITHFIELD ❖ STONEYBATTER

Bernard Neary

THE LILLIPUT PRESS
DUBLIN

First published 2016 by
THE LILLIPUT PRESS
62–63 Sitric Road, Arbour Hill
Dublin 7, Ireland
www.lilliputpress.ie

ISBN 978 1 84351 6811

10 9 8 7 6 5 4 3 2 1

Set in 11.5 pt on 16 pt Fournier with
Brandon Grotesque display by Marsha Swan
Printed in Spain by GraphyCems

Contents

Preface

My Reasons for Writing
a History of Dublin 7

I grew up in the suburb of Cabra West, which I have always thought of as my village; I regarded Dublin 7 as my town. Children had incredible freedom and we explored way beyond the confines of our area from an early age. When President John F. Kennedy came to Ireland in 1963 and was presented with the Freedom of the City, my pal Daithí Roach said, 'Sure we all have that.' And we did – in spades.

I began a lifetime association with 'the Naller' when my sister Anne brought me, in my pram, to see the steam trains as they puffed their way along the banks of the Royal Canal. Later, with pals, we would spend long summer days and weekends walking along the banks of the canal as far as Dorset Street or out to Ashtown. During these summer months we looked for nests, caught pinkeens and tadpoles, tore down branches to make bows and arrows, collected bamboo to make peashooters and hard berries for ammunition; we rowed along the canal on roofs hacksawed off cars lying in the city dump on Ballyboggan Road. We joined the big lads who retrieved scrap metal from the canal for Beano, who lived in one of the big houses then dotting the fields around Cabra. Some of us even had tea and biscuits in Beano's house. Our childhood was one of adventure and the world we explored was that which encompassed the town of Dublin 7.

Along with some of my pals, my first job was helping 'the slop-man' Whacker with his horse. He kept pigs in a yard off a lane in Bridgefoot Street in Dublin 8. We were all aged around eight, and initially helped Whacker when his horse and cart turned onto our road; soon we were meeting him on Carnlough Road, later walking down to Old Cabra to meet him. We noted the direction from which his cart came, and soon our meeting point took us first to Rathdown Road and then Charleville Road; eventually, early one morning, we met him outside his yard on Bridgefoot Street. Going through Annamoe, we watched and listened to the banter between Whacker and his customers; from observing Whacker I learnt to build up longlasting friendships with people of all ages, who shared their life experiences with someone like me who enjoyed their stories.

As young explorers we ventured beyond the Navan Road to the great expanse of the Phoenix Park, entering it through Cabra Gate or one of the turnstiles along Blackhorse Avenue. Sometimes we'd stop at one of the small shops on the way to buy sweets. On Saturday or Sunday afternoons we'd go to the pictures, to the Cabra Grand or the Plaza Cinema, just off Dorset Street. We spent the bus fare on sweets and walked through Phibsborough, then along the linear park beside the State picturehouse, through the Basin and into Blessington Street, then down towards Dorset Street. After the pictures we sometimes walked home via Broadstone Station and Phibsborough, or else down Bolton Street, North King Street, Manor Street, Prussia Street and Old Cabra Road. Many a time we stopped at the lock-ups behind Hanlon's pub and gawked at the fancy cars as they returned from their Sunday afternoon runabout.

From an early age we went down to Dalymount Park to see the Bohs playing. We used to climb over the wall using a telegraph pole on the laneway parallel to the houses on Connaught Street. One Sunday the pole was smeared with tar and we had to pay in at the schoolboy entrance. At ten I was going to International matches with my pals – I remember attending a sell-out Ireland *vs* Austria tie in 1962 and becoming separated from the others; undaunted, I watched the match on my own.

Each September, from about 1959 until 1964, a gang of us went up to the haybarn on Bellevue Farm, sitting in the hay and eating the jam sandwiches we made for the adventure; we would hide in the straw and have fights with the hay. The adventure ended at sunset, when we slung home, exhausted but excited. I left all this, and my association with Whacker, behind when I started secondary school in September 1964.

I had started a paper round for Alfie and Rose Groves of Killala Road a couple of years previously and I kept this up. This provided me with pocket money for the five years I spent at St Declan's CBS, as well as a deep understanding of and a connection to the people, young and not-so-young, of Cabra West. On Sunday mornings I did my round, calling out '*Press Indo People Express*' as I walked the roads of Cabra West with Yanny Groves and the box-cart. After then enjoying a fry-up in Rose's kitchen, I relieved Alfie for the last Mass on the Navan Road. For a soccer-mad teenager, it was exciting when Nobby Stiles was staying in the Giles' house on Navan Road as he bought all the papers and gave a good tip. When I finished up, I generally called into the lounge of the Oasis on Fassaugh Avenue at around half-one to hand over the takings to Alfie, who always bought me a lemonade.

It was a common pastime, not only in my teens but into my twenties, to walk along the canal or through the Phoenix Park or into Cardiffsbridge with my friends, and we would chat with whoever happened to be standing outside their gate, in their garden or fishing by the Naller or the Tolka. I developed such a deep interest in the area that one day my friend Mick Doyle suggested I write a history of Cabra. I set about the task in 1975 and in 1976. The encouragement and assistance of Dermot Bolger and his Raven Arts Press led to the next stage, the publication of *A History of Cabra*, launched in the Grapevine Arts Centre, North Great George's Street, in the autumn of 1976. The print run of 800 copies sold out within two months.

Dermot's huge interest in Francis Ledwidge from Slane, County Meath, fascinated me, particularly when he marvelled that the First World War poet walked through Finglas on his journey home from the city; I thought that Ledwidge also must have walked through Broadstone and Phibsborough. Further support from Dermot led to more research and in 1982 *A History of Cabra and Phibsborough* was launched in the City Arms Hotel, Prussia Street, which went to three editions. Finally, after a number of years of further research, a history of Dublin 7 was published in 1992. It sold 4000 copies and also became a collectors' item. These books can be accessed through the Library Service.

I am often accused of seeing things through rose-tinted glasses, but I have always thought of myself as fortunate to have been brought up among the people of Cabra West and of Dublin 7. I feel privileged to have been asked by The Lilliput Press to write this volume on Dublin 7, woven from research and the reminiscences and recollections of honest, hardworking extraordinary people, all with one thing in common: roots in a unique part of this capital city of ours.

Their toil, effort and integrity, as in similar communities throughout the State, have been overlooked; if their traits had been instilled in some of those in positions of power and trust over recent decades, Ireland today would be a better place.

Welcome to my Dublin 7. The many people I encountered here during my formative years have long since passed away. In my experience and in that of many of my generation, they created a strong sense of community in the villages and towns of Dublin 7. An example of this is the development of the Credit Union movement in the district, with its unique voluntary community input.

I have written the book in what I hope is an easy-to-follow format, treating it as an informal walking guide through the district. I have tried to include as much information as possible. Given the size of Dublin 7 and the wealth of its history, its people and places, it is perhaps time for a Dictionary of Dublin 7 Biography. Until then, welcome to my world of Dublin 7. Enjoy the read.

Bernard Neary
Cabra, Dublin, November 2016

1 | A General Introduction

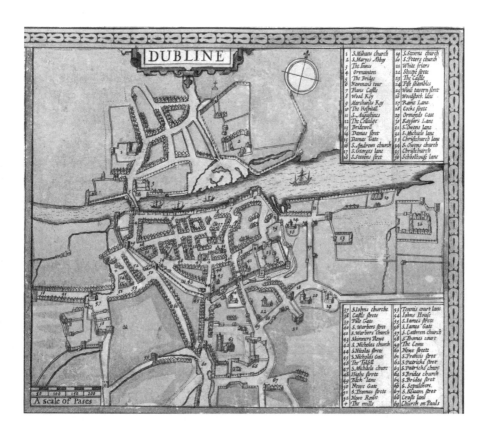

The postal district of Dublin 7 encompasses a significant area and is one of the oldest inhabited regions of Ireland's capital city. It is home to some of the finest buildings in the country, including the Four Courts, Broadstone Railway Station, Kings Inns, the Incorporated Law Society, Mater Hospital and St Peter's Church. The area enclosed by the postal boundary includes Ashtown, Cabra, Grangegorman, Phibsborough and Smithfield. In pre-Christian times the district witnessed cavalcades passing from the north, over the ford on the River Liffey at Átha Cliath and on into Wicklow. For many centuries one of the great roads from the royal seat of Tara, County Meath to the monastic city of Glendalough in County Wicklow, passed through Cabragh, over Bóthar na gCloch, the Stony Road, now Stoneybatter, into Fercullen and on to the Dublin and Wicklow mountains. Stoneybatter is one of the oldest highways in Europe.

Cabra formerly covered a vast area, stretching from present-day North Circular Road to Glasnevin in the east, Castleknock and Blanchardstown to the west and Fingal to the north. It comprised two districts, Much Cabragh and Little Cabragh and was divided by the great forest Salcock's Wood, which extended west from Dalymount Park to Infirmary Road and north to Cabra Cross, at the city end of Ratoath Road. It was here in Salcock's Wood that the O'Toole clan, on their return home after a marauding expedition to Finglas, were intercepted and attacked by the citizens of Dublin. The citizens, well-armed but ill-trained, were routed by the O'Tooles. From the eleventh to the thirteenth century Cabragh was well outside the city boundary and was not populated to any great extent, with only a few families living in the area.

At the close of the thirteenth century King Edward I granted the 'ploughland of Ballygossan alias Cabragh Hill' to the Prior of Holmpatrick. From an early period the Prior of Ballybogan possessed several lands and tenements here, which the king then presented to William Stockenbregge of Dublin 'for many favours received'. In 1609 Henry Pierse had a grant of the towns, villages and lands of Much and Little Cabragh, containing 240 acres and therein stated to have been 'parcel of the possessions of St Mary's Abbey'.

The failed Fenian revolt of 1867 resulted in the trial of those leaders taken prisoner, at Green Street Courthouse. Many were deported to Australia. Following those trials, over 300,000 people took part in a mass meeting at Cabra in October 1869, in a field between the Royal Canal and Finglas Road. It was called to demand the release of Fenian prisoners. Isaac Butt chaired the meeting, and at that time he lived in 64 Eccles Street. The following account of that public meeting is taken from the *Illustrated London News* of 23 October 1869:

> Fenian Amnesty Meeting at Dublin: The great open-air meeting got up by the 'Amnesty Association' of Dublin to pass resolutions demanding the liberation of the Fenian conspirators and insurgents now in prison was mentioned in our last week's news. It was held in a field in a place named Cabra, in the neighbourhood of the city, on Sunday week, at two o'clock in the afternoon. The Dublin Police Commissioners had issued a notice that no party procession through the streets would be allowed; in consequence of which the managers of Amnesty Association determined to give up their plan of a general demonstration within the city and directed that the flags and banners should not be displayed 'til the place of meeting was reached. But this order was imperfectly observed.
>
> Trade Unions and various other societies marched separately from Ormond Quay or Sackville Street, through Cavendish-row, Frederick-street and Berkeley-street and along the North Circular Road, with their banners and bands of music, all the people wearing green sashes and rosettes, or green hat-bands, while some had green mixed with

Monster Meeting at Cabra, 1869 (Courtesy *London Illustrated News*)

orange colour. Each trade guild was headed by an open carriage or car, drawn by four horses, and about thirty trades were represented. They began to come on the ground and at ten o'clock the whole number of people was reckoned by tens of thousands. Mr Isaac Butt, Q.C., was in the chair; and the speakers were Mr G.H. Moore, M.P. for Mayo; Mr Hickey of Castlebar; the Rev. Mr Leverett of Tyrone; Mr G. Russell of Limerick; and Mr Hugh O'Donnell, President of the Dublin Trades Association. The proceedings were orderly and quiet.

The monster meeting had a significant political and historical impact in that it turned the nation against the long-established British practice of forced deportation. Although public opinion in the eastern states of Australia had brought about the demise of deportation by the early 1860s, the western seaboard of that vast continent had, by a State government policy decision of 1860, decided to open its doors to deportees. It was to here, the remote and barren lands of Western Australia, that John Boyle O'Reilly and other Fenians of the failed Rising of 1867 were sent. The turning of the tide following the massive show of support at the Cabra meeting sounded the death knell for forced deportation and a few years later the State Government of Western Australia reversed its policy of accepting convict labour, the last of the Australian States to so do.

The area covered by the Dublin 7 postal district figured prominently in the years of unrest leading up to the granting of Irish independence in 1922. The collapse of decrepit tenement houses in Church Street in early 1913, though not a catalyst for the strikes and historic Lockout of that year, provided a backdrop to it. The trade union leader James Larkin, a key figure in events of that year, was then living at 27 Auburn Street, Phibsborough with his wife and three sons, paying a weekly rent of nine shillings out of a salary of £2 2s. 0d. a week. Of even greater significance was the part played by many in the district, and the events occurring there, during the Easter Rising of 1916.

Easter Rising 1916

During the Easter Rising many locations were taken over by insurgent forces, with military engagements taking place at Bolton Street, Church Street, the Four Courts, North King Street, Phibsborough and Cabra. Broadstone Railway Station also figured and on the morning of the Rising Seán Harling, who lived in Cabra, was selling racecards outside the station for the Fairyhouse race meeting on Easter Monday morning, 1916. He later took part in the fighting and in the War of Independence, and took the anti-Treaty side in the Civil War.

On the morning of Easter Monday, 24 April 1916, men of the First Battalion, under the command of Commandant Edward 'Ned' Daly, paraded with their arms and equipment before taking up positions in the Four Courts, Church Street, North King Street, Phibsborough and other areas in the district. The Four Courts secured, the Nationalist forces now occupied a strategic point dominating the approaches along the north quays to Kingsbridge Railway Station and the rail line to the Curragh Military Camp, County Kildare, where the main concentration of British troops in Ireland was stationed. Captain Denis O'Callaghan, along with Gerry Holohan and Eamonn Martin, who were detailed to capture Broadstone railway station, failed in their mission but went to the nearby Linenhall police barracks where they captured some arms and set fire to the building. Sam O'Reilly was in charge of a detail that blew up the rails near the station on Easter Monday; they destroyed the signal system and cut through the telegraph lines before reporting to the General Post Office (GPO) the following day.

Also on Easter Monday the Lancers of the 6th Reserve Cavalry, based in Marlborough (now McKee) Barracks on Blackhorse Avenue, were escorting an ammunition convoy from Dublin docks and passed by O'Connell Street before coming under fire near the Four Courts, losing three dead and two wounded. Their five ammunition wagons remained pinned down in nearby Charles Street West for the next three days. Later that same day the Lancers made the failed sortie down O'Connell Street against the insurgent position in the GPO. Four of their number were killed in this sortie. They then retreated to Rutland Square, now Parnell Square, staying there for a short time before returning to their barracks. That was the only attempt to use cavalry in a traditional role during Easter week. For the remainder of the Rising the cavalry acted only in a dismounted capacity or for the transport of military supplies and equipment.

As a result of the failed attempt by the rebels to capture the telephone system at Crown Alley, the British authorities were able to call up reinforcements from the Curragh, Athlone, Belfast and Templemore. On Tuesday 25 April the British forces struggled to break into the entrenched insurgent posts, attacking positions in Cabra, North Circular Road and the Four Courts. Nationalist forces held off these attacks, with British forces suffering heavy losses, particularly in the Kingsbridge area. The hundreds of British reinforcements arriving into the general district saw Tuesday closing with the insurgent forces retiring to their strong city-centre positions and with the sound of gunfire ringing out all over the capital.

On Wednesday 26 April the rebel strongholds at the Four Courts, North King Street and Church Street held out under heavy British gunfire. This was the day of the battle of Mount Street Bridge, when seven men at Clanwilliam House held off superior British forces, until forced to retire after a nine-hour assault. The British General Maxwell subsequently reported on this engagement as follows: '... the battalion charging in successive waves carried all before them, but, I regret to say, suffered severe casualties in doing so. Four officers were killed, fourteen wounded, and of the other ranks 216 were killed and wounded'. During this day the lines of communication between Seán Heuston at the Mendicity Institute and the Four Courts were cut, and with more than half of his men without ammunition, Houston was forced to surrender his small garrison at Kingsbridge, now present day Houston Station. Seán Heuston had connections with the district; born on 21 February 1891, he was the eldest son of John Heuston and Maria (*née* McDonald) of 24 Lower Gloucester Street. At the time of the Rising he was a clerk in the Great Southern and Western Railway and his mother was living at 20 Fontenoy Street; he left this address for his posting at the Mendicity Institute. Successive *Thom's Directory* editions, up to the 1930s, show Mrs Heuston as residing at this address.

On Thursday 27 April the British shelled insurgent positions in the Four Courts and Phibsborough, occupied Bolton Street Technical Schools and attacked posts in North King Street. The Phibsborough defenders were shelled by heavy guns, which were horse-drawn from Smithfield to a nearby position. A shell fell beside the small Baptist church in Phibsborough and tore a hole in the perimeter railing surrounding the church. Heavy fighting took place in the distillery building off North King Street. On Friday the GPO was shelled and by nightfall the entire building was in flames. In Church Street and North King Street the British launched heavy infantry attacks.

On Saturday 29 April the British launched a dawn attack with bayonets in the entire Church Street and North King Street area; this attack was repulsed and British arms captured. Fighting continued in many parts of the city, including the Four Courts. Thomas Clarke, Seán Mac Diarmada, Padraig Pearse, James Connolly and Joseph Plunkett held council in 16 Moore Street and decided to surrender, sending Elizabeth Farrell as envoy to the Crown forces. The insurgents were forced to accept unconditional surrender, bringing an end to the Easter Rising. Large-scale arrests throughout the country followed, with deportations to England and Wales and executions the aftermath of a heroic stand for Irish self-determination. Between 4 and 12 May 1916, eleven of the leaders of the Rising were executed in Dublin. Ned Daly, Commander of the 1st Battalion forces deployed in the area now covered by Dublin 7, was among the first of the leaders to be executed, on 4 May 1916. The brother-in-law of Thomas Clarke, he was born in Limerick in 1891 and was just twenty-five years old.

Postcard of the aftermath of the 1916 Rising in Church Street
(Courtesy http://www.islandireland.com/)

8

Michael O'Hanrahan was also executed on the same day; the third in command at Jacob's Mill, prior to his execution he was in cell number sixty-seven in Kilmainham Gaol and was seen by his three sisters, and attended by Fr Albert, the Church Street Capuchin. Born on 16 January 1877 in New Ross, County Wexford, Michael O'Hanrahan moved to Dublin with his family as a young man. A journalist and author, he secured employment as a proofreader at the Cló Cumann printing works, which published for the Gaelic League, and lived with his mother, his brother Henry and his sisters Áine, Marie and Eily in a staunchly republican household at 67 Connaught Street, Phibsborough. This house became a storage centre for weapons in the weeks leading up to the Easter Rising. His brother Henry saw action too in Jacob's and was subsequently sentenced to death, commuted to a prison sentence. His sister Eily was also in Jacob's factory when the Rising broke; Thomas McDonagh sent her back to her house as there were arms hidden there, and directed her to give them out to the men he sent with her. Con Colbert, from Newcastlewest, County Limerick, who came to Dublin at an early age to live with his sister, was also executed at Kilmainham. He went to the national school at St Mary's Place, off Mountjoy Street, and later attended O'Connell's.

On Easter Week an incident took place on Cabra Road, where the shops, known locally as the Seventeen Shops, were built in the 1930s. A car approached Phibsborough from the west with two occupants inside. They had hired it in Mullingar as the train line to Dublin had been pulled up to impede the dispatch of troops and artillery. In the taxi were Oliver St John Gogarty and Laurence Ginnell, MP for Westmeath, whose green bedspread was even then flying over the GPO. He was keen to be at the House of Lords for a closed emergency session. The car's windscreen was shattered by a bullet on Cabra Road. A sixteen-year-old youth stood in front of the car. On seeing that it was not a military vehicle, he said: 'Sorry, I was told to shoot at British vehicles and I thought you were a military car 'cos your headlights were blazing.' 'But you could have killed us,' said an irate Gogarty. 'Like I said,' replied the boy, 'I thought you might have been British, so I gave you the benefit of the doubt.' The car continued its journey without further incident.

Research by Glasnevin Cemetery shows that 485 people were killed in the Easter Rising; the majority of casualties were civilians, with 184 killed in Easter week; a quarter (107) were soldiers, many of whom were Irish, with fifty-eight insurgent deaths; thirteen policemen died. Almost one in five of those killed was under the age of nineteen. One of those killed was Seán Healy, shot dead by British forces. A bronze plaque on the footpath at Doyle's Corner, directly opposite the old Allied Irish Bank building on Phibsborough Road, marks where he fell. Commissioned by Coiste Cuimneacháin Náisiúnta, it reads: '*In memory of Seán Healy, Na Fianna Éireann, aged 15 years. Mortally wounded by British forces at this spot during the Easter Rising April 1916. Fuair sé bás ar son na hÉireann.*' In his book *Children of the Rising*, RTÉ broadcaster Joe Duffy tells the story of the forty children killed.

In what became known as 'the North King Street murders' George Ennis, who lived at 174 North King Street, was among those who were rounded up and shot dead during an unprovoked rampage by members of the South Staffordshire Regiment. The atrocity occurred on the last day of fighting and the circumstances of his death, and those of others on that street on Saturday 29 April 1916, were shocking even by the standards at that time. Paul Taylor, who grew up in Black Street, states that, 'he [George Ennis] was a coachbuilder by trade and then aged fifty-one. Helena, the sister of George Ennis, was my great-grandmother and my dad Frank told me that the word in the family was that George was bayoneted to death, and the floor boards in the hallway were bloodstained for many years afterwards.' Number 174 was a tobacconist and newsagent's shop and the proprietor Michael Noonan was also shot dead in the massacre. Other civilians were murdered in the Louth Dairy at number 27, and at numbers 170, 172 and 177 North King Street. Max Caulfield, the author of *The Easter Rebellion*, puts the figure at 'no less than fifteen innocent civilians'. The names of the victims of the North King Street murders and the locations of the killings are outlined in *Dublin in Rebellion* by Joseph E.A. Connell Junior; they also appear on a commemorative plaque, erected as part of the 1916/2016 Centenary Programme, on a wall outside Kevin Barry House on the corner of North King Street and Coleraine Street.

War of Independence

The first time that Ned Broy met Michael Collins was in a house on the Cabra Road; a member of the Royal Irish Constabulary and the Dublin Metropolitan Police and based in Dublin Castle in 1918, the following is an extract from a witness statement, which he made in 1955 for the military archives:

I was filled with curiosity. Would this Michael Collins be the ideal man I had been dreaming of for a couple of years? There was no photograph of him at that time in the record book. So, steeped in curiosity, I went to 5 Cabra Road and was received in the kitchen by the Foleys, a place where every extreme nationalist visited at some time or another. I was not long there when Greg Murphy and Michael Collins arrived. He was dressed in black leggings, green breeches and a trenchcoat with all the usual buttons, belts and rings. The Foleys went away and I had a long talk with Mick from about 8:00 pm until midnight. He thanked me for all the documents I had sent and all the information and said it was of the utmost assistance and importance to them. We discussed why so many arrests took place and, particularly, the German Plot information – why that went wrong, especially the arrest of de Valera. He said at a few minutes before train-time de Valera looked at his watch and announced that, notwithstanding the threatened arrests, he was going home. They had dissuaded him, but he insisted on going home and left the station, travelling on the pre-arranged train.

The house referred to is directly across from St Peter's Church, on New Cabra Road; there is a large holly tree in the garden and granite steps lead up to the front door. The present owner acquired the house thirty years ago, and a friend of his collects the berries from the holly tree in wintertime. It was once the home of Michael Foley and his wife Máire (*née* Smart).

Ned Broy also met Michael Collins in the home of Dilly Dicker on Mountjoy Street; he left and received messages from Collins there, and in Capel Street Library and other houses in the area, including 44 Mountjoy Street and Foley's Typing Agency on Bachelor's Walk. Arrested and imprisoned in Arbour Hill, under sentence of death, Ned Broy was released when the Truce with Britain was agreed and acted as bodyguard to Michael Collins during negotiations in London. He married in 1923 and joined the ranks of An Garda Síochana. He became a Chief Superintendent in 1925 and was appointed Garda Commissioner in 1933, retiring in 1938. He died on 22 January 1972; his surviving daughter Áine lives in Rathfarnham.

After the London negotiations, Irish independence followed in the form of a partitioned country, with twenty-six counties making up the Irish Free State and the remaining six forming the Northern Ireland Stormont administration. Despite ratification of the Treaty by Dáil Éireann and by the majority of the people of Ireland in a subsequent plebiscite or referendum, a short and bitter civil war ensued between the pro-Treaty or Free State side and the anti-Treaty or Republican side. It was not uncommon for members of families to take different sides in the conflict, causing heartache and bitterness. Michael O'Neill of Cabra Park and his brother Sam fought on opposing sides; subsequently Michael never ever spoke to his family about these turbulent times. During hostilities two IRA members, Christopher Breslin and Joseph Kernan, died following an exchange of gunfire with pro-Treaty forces at Cabra Cross on 3 April 1923, just at the corner of Rathoath Road and New Cabra Road. A simple memorial set in the wall commemorates the incident.

Handball and Dublin 7

Handball was introduced to Dublin 7 in the late nineteenth century by the Irish Christian Brothers when they erected a long single-walled ball alley in the playground of the grounds of St Joseph's School for the Deaf. Three matches could be played simultaneously in the court, thus bringing twelve boys into action at the same time. Handball was very popular in those days, and players from outside the district were regularly invited in for a game with enthusiasts like Brothers Dalton, Johnston and their fellow contemporaries, several of whom were notable exponents of the sport. Famous players came in from different parts of the city to engage in exhibitions for the entertainment of both the Brothers and pupils. In one such exhibition, played in the early 1920s, four of Ireland's then leading professionals took part – J.J. Kelly, Andy Durkin, Jack Brady and James 'Clarke of the Boot'. Jim Clarke of Prussia Street and his sons John, Jim, Austin and Frank also played there, Jim in the 1920s and his sons in later years. Jim regularly organized tournaments for the youth of Aughrim Street parish, noted at that period for its array of competent and exciting handball players, including P.J. O'Neill, Con Healy, M. Reid, J.W. and C. Clarke.

When the Dublin Primary Schools Handball Competitions were inaugurated in 1954 St Joseph's was represented by one of its finest schoolboy handball players of all time, Frank Flynn. From the west of Ireland, Frank proved a very popular competitor. Handballers living in Dublin 7 included Tim Hurley, an old-time professional who took part in tournaments at the Green Street alley during the

1940s; Oliver Noonan, winner of Dublin titles around the same period, and Austin Clarke, winner of many Dublin, Leinster and Irish Championships. Austin Clarke was recognized as the 1953 World Champion by the American Handball Union; he lived at 45 Cabra Road for many years prior to his death in 1963. Dermot McDermot, of Skreen Road, Cabra, a former Chairman of the Labour Court, was a contemporary of the great Austin Clarke and is yet another winner of several Dublin titles. A Cabra family called the Robinsons were well known in soccer circles, but were also noted handballers, along with several of their contemporaries including P. Scannel, an Army and Dublin Champion.

In the early years handball was played at St Joseph's and the Ball Alley, Manor Street, which was in the old stable yard at the rear of number 42; the house once served as a coachhouse and later as a garda station. Many of the games in the Metropolitan Club's Murphy Cup Competition of 1924, won by the legendary Stephen Quirke, were played here. Local Gardaí attached to the barracks took up the sport and became noted exponents, including B.J. Daly and T.J. O'Reilly, who both became World Police Champions in 1924. The alley was responsible for the huge popularity of the game in the surrounding district, where every gable end was used to good effect.

St Joseph's Cabra. Boys assembled in front of school
(Courtesy Lawrence Collection, NLI)

During the early 1920s Aughrim Street was noted for the number of family groups comprising three or more handball players from the same family, such as the Carberys, Clarkes, Fitzsimons, Hudsons, Kanes, O'Briens, Quirkes and Sheridans. Handball was extremely popular throughout the district, to its extreme borders – there was a ball court in operation at the turn of the twentieth century at Ashtown, behind the Halfway House. Famous handballers played major contests on the court here, including old-time professionals like T. Aldridge and G. Robinson of Athy, County Kildare; James Clarke of Aughrim Street and US-born John Lawlor. Patrick Lyons and Tim Hurley of Dublin played in the Irish Doubles Championships at Ashtown in 1912. The Ashtown ball court was closed down for some years but reopened in the 1930s; it was demolished during the early 1960s.

Handball proved to be a popular pastime in the new housing developments of the 1930s and 1940s. From this time a number of new handball alleys served the district such as those located at Fassaugh Road and Ventry Park Play Centres (three courts and one court respectively) and the Bogeys (two courts). These complemented the older alleys, such as those mentioned above and others at St Peter's and Brunswick Street National Schools and the army barracks at Arbour Hill (two courts). The court at Ventry Park was dismantled in 1981 and those in the Bogeys were demolished around 2003.

Credit Union Movement

Dublin 7 is undoubtedly the cradle of the Credit Union Movement in Ireland, for it was from here that Miss Nora Herlihy sowed the first seeds of what was to become one of the great success stories of twentieth-century Ireland. Born in Ballydesmond, County Cork, on 27 February 1910, she qualified as a teacher and moved to Dublin in 1936, securing a position in Basin Lane National School. In 1943 she settled in Phibsborough, renting a house at 50 Shandon Park. In 1955 she was appointed to West Liffey Street National School, located beside Benburb Street; the building was burned down by an arsonist in the early 1970s. An apartment complex now occupies the site, facing onto the Esplanade.

The twin evils of unemployment and emigration, which she saw first hand in her native Ballydesmond during the 1930s and in the Dublin of the 1940s and 1950s, left a lasting impression on her. She developed a lifelong interest and passion for the idea of cooperative credit as a means of developing local initiatives to combat unemployment and emigration and end the corrosive effect they had on the quality of Irish life. Immersing herself in local and national efforts to set up a cooperative movement, in June 1957 she acted as Secretary to the first meeting, which led to the establishment of an entity called the Credit Union Extension Service, and subsequently to the foundation of the Credit Union Movement in Ireland. Attending that first meeting with Nora were Sean Forde, Miss Gilvarry, Michael Callanan, Seamus MacEoin and Tomas MacGabhann.

The close of 1957 saw the formation of Dun Laoghaire and Donore Avenue Credit Unions and in that same year, thanks to the work of the Credit Union Extension Service and Nora in particular, the government set up a Consultative Committee to examine the question of legislation on cooperative efforts in the community. Nora, nominated by the Irish Countrywomen's Association, was appointed a member of that committee, which deliberated for five years and produced its report to government in 1963. Everyone, including politicians, senior civil servants and voluntary organizations, acknowledged her tremendous hard work. Three years later the efforts of the Committee bore fruit with the passing of the Credit Union Act 1966. Nora's ability, drive, honesty and commitment to the ideals of the Credit Union Movement were recognized and honoured when the President of Ireland, Eamonn de Valera, requested her presence when he signed the Credit Union Act on 29 August 1966. From 1957 until the signing of the Act, she devoted all her spare time and energies to the growth of the movement. On many occasions she used all her teacher's salary to assist a fledgling Credit Union.

Shandon Park was the unofficial headquarters of the Credit Union Extension Service until it moved to premises in North Frederick Street in 1967. All correspondence emanated from her home, her postman being often heavily burdened with incoming mail. She travelled to America and extensively throughout Ireland to foster the growth of the movement, anxious that it not be confined to Dublin and its environs. The Derry MEP John Hume was an early admirer and often visited her, even after her retirement from active life in 1986, when she bade farewell to her rented house at Shandon Park and moved into her newly purchased home in Dalkey. She died there in February 1988. She is buried in her native Ballydesmond. A book on her life by Brother A.T. Culloty gives an excellent insight into the foundation of the movement and to the background that encouraged its roots. Her dedication and commitment to Irish life was recognized by the people of Dublin 7 in 1984, when she officially opened the new purpose-built offices of West Cabra Credit Union on Kilkiernan Road, named Nora Herlihy House in her honour.

The Credit Union Movement has long since come of age and in 2002 it boasted over one million members with savings in excess of five billion euro. It survived the economic crash of 2008, the effects of the subsequent downturn leading to consolidation in the Credit Union industry. Dublin 7 has seen its share of consolidation, with the amalgamation of Premier Navan Road and District Credit Union with West Cabra Credit Union to form Community Credit Union. Other credit unions operating in the area include Aughrim Street Parish and District Credit Union, 44 Manor Street; Halston Street Credit Union, 145 Capel Street, Dublin 1 (it was originally located in Beresford Street, Dublin 7); and Phibsborough and District Credit Union, 392 North Circular Road. In 2004 St Raphael's Garda Credit Union (called Uncle Raphael by its members) moved from 81 Upper Dorset Street to the Naas Road.

City Arms Hotel, Prussia Street, early 1900s
(Courtesy Seamus Kearns Postcard Collection)

James Joyce and Dublin 7

James Joyce was born on 4 February 1882 at 41 Brighton Square, Rathgar, and died in 1941. Dublin 7 is fortunate in that it enjoys strong Joycean connections. In late 1901 the Joyce family moved to 32 Glengarriff Parade, which lies off the North Circular Road and adjacent to Mountjoy Prison; it is the first house with steps leading up to the hall door, on the left hand side of the road. It was here that George, the gifted younger brother of James Joyce, died on 9 March 1902, aged just fourteen years. In October 1902 the Joyce family were once more on the move, this time to 7 St Peter's Terrace. The street name and house numbers were changed some years ago and it is now 5 St Peter's Road. In December of that same year James Joyce was living at this address when, on an impulse, he left home and went to live in Paris. He returned in April 1903 after receiving a telegram from his father telling him that his mother was dying. She died at home here on 13 August 1903.

The following year the family was once again on the move, to 44 Fontenoy Street, off Mountjoy Street, adjacent to St Mary's church. This was the smallest house his family had lived in and his father John Joyce was still living here in 1931; he died in December of that year. Joyce's sister Margaret Alice, born in 1884, was educated by the family governess Mrs Elizabeth Conway and later at the Dominican College in nearby Eccles Street. Known as 'Poppie', she ran the Joyce household for six years before leaving Fontenoy Street in August 1905 to become a nun. She took the name Sister Mary Gertrude and went to New Zealand, where she died in 1964; she is buried in Waimairi Cemetery in Christchurch. The house does not appear to be that much different today from what it looked like in 1905; it is single-storey to the front, with the rear being two-storey. The family spent an unusually long spell at this house, and in July 1909 James Joyce, by this time living in Trieste with Nora, paid a visit to Dublin accompanied by his infant son Giorgio, lodging at 44 Fontenoy Street. He stayed with his family here until January 1910. The fine two-storey house at the rear of Number 44, and also the three single-storey cottages in tiny St Michael's Place beside it, are interesting as they are not at first visible to passers-by, being nestled behind the houses on Fontenoy Street.

Doyle's Corner in Phibsborough was formerly called Dunphy's Corner and is referred to by this name in Joyces's *Ulysses*, as Paddy Dignam's funeral passes on its way to Glasnevin Cemetery: 'Dunphy's Corner. Mourning coaches drawn up drowning their grief. A pause by the wayside. Tiptop position for a pub.' The Ormond Hotel on Upper Ormond Quay is where Bloom pens a letter, under the pen name of Henry Flower, as he sits in the bar: 'Blot over the other so he can't read. Something detective read off blotting pad. Letters read out for breach of promise. From Chickabiddy's owny Mumpsypum. Laughter in Court. Henry. I never signed it.'

Barney Kiernan's licensed premises were situated on the corner of Green Street and Little Brittain Street. This is where the 'Cyclops' episode of *Ulysses* is set; it is around the corner that Bloom ascends from a coach 'to the glory of the brightness at an angle of forty-five degrees over Donohoe's in Little Green Street'. It is in Kiernan's pub that the topic of hanging is discussed in all its gory details, including that of Robert Emmet following his conviction for treason in Green Street Courthouse nearby. Kiernan's was a fixture here for many years, and *Thom's Directory* of 1870 records 'Bernard Kiernan, Tea, Wine and Spirit Merchants' as occupying 8, 9 and 10 Little Brittain Street.

James Joyce lived for a spell at 4 Eccles Street, and number 7 was where his friend J.F. Byrne lived. This house, with its low railings, became the setting for the residence of the *Ulysses* characters of Leopold and Molly Bloom. The houses on this side of Eccles Street, adjacent to Dorset Street, including number 7, were demolished and the Mater Private Hospital is now located on the site. The original front door is on display in the James Joyce Museum in North Great George's Street, where it is on loan from Marks & Spencer's.

James Joyce frequented the City Arms Hotel when he lived in St Peter's Terrace, and he placed the premises on the Joycean trail by immortalizing it in *Ulysses*: when Leopold Bloom 'worked with the cows', he stayed at the hotel: 'I was up at that meeting in the City Arms ... Cattle traders, says Joe, about the foot and mouth disease' (*Ulysses*, p. 288, 664/5). In the 1880s it was Miss Eliza Dowd who called 'time' here. Broadstone Railway Station also has a Joycean connection, for in the summer of 1900 his father John was employed in Mullingar, County Westmeath on the revision of the electoral list; he took James and other family members with him. They travelled by train to and from Broadstone Station. Joyce's *Stephen Hero* contains a tract on that time spent in Mullingar. It was here also where Nora Barnacle, his future partner and wife, first arrived in Dublin when she left her home in Galway to start a new life in early 1904.

The influence of Joyce's suburban life in the district can be found in the poem 'Tilly', which appears in a thin volume of his poetry called *Pomes Penyeach* (1927):

He travels after a winter sun,
Urging the cattle along a cold red road,
Calling to them, a voice they know,
He drives his beasts above Cabra.

Green Street Courthouse (Bernard Neary)

Finally, the Four Courts and Green Street Courthouse have a huge significance in *Ulysses*. According to the Honourable Mr Justice Adrian Hardiman, Judge of the Supreme Court, legal topics and characters appear in it much more frequently and more significantly than literary criticism has so far acknowledged. He cites the thirty-two court cases, both civil and criminal, eleven named and eight unnamed judges, thirteen barristers, eleven named and more unnamed solicitors plus a struck-off solicitor, two Taxing Masters, a cost accountant and others. In the chapter 'Wandering Rocks', the Four Courts is visited; at that time the Round Hall was festooned with statues of former luminaries of the legal profession: 'lawyers of the past, haughty, pleading, beheld pass from the Consolidated Taxing Office to *Nisi Prius* Court Richie Goulding carrying the costbag of Goulding, Collis and Ward and heard rustling from the Admiralty Division of Kings Bench …'. According to Adrian, 'the lawyers of the past were Lord Chancellor Plunkett, Sir Michael O'Loughlen, Master of the Rolls; Chief Baron Joy, Chief Justice Whiteside, Richard Lalor Sheil and Lord Chancellor O'Hagan. All the statues were erected between 1851 and 1887. The appetite of the profession and the judges for statuary seemed to have been satisfied in that year because two niches left vacant were still unfilled when the rest were destroyed by the bombardment of the Four Courts by Free State forces during the Civil War in 1922.' A respected and noted Joycean scholar, Mr Justice Adrian Hardiman died in March 2016, aged sixty-four years.

Joyce's masterpiece also includes some celebrated murder trials, including the Childs murder case. Thomas Childs was charged with the murder of his brother, at his brother's own home in Bengal Terrace on Finglas Road, near Glasnevin Cemetery. The trial, in which the defendant was acquitted, was a sensational one during that time when Joyce was at University College Dublin. Indeed, he attended the trial himself in Green Street Courthouse, while an undergraduate in 1899.

Nature and Dublin 7

The district boasts a variety of wildlife; the fox and the spiky hedgehog can often be seen. The badger is not an uncommon sight in the area today, along with the pipistrelle bat. The well-known Dublin 7 ornithologist Fergus Fitzgerald, from Carnlough Road, Cabra West, is a longtime activist of BirdWatch Ireland and has seen mink along the banks of the Royal Canal near Ashtown. Daubenton's bats feed above the surface of the duck pond in the Phoenix Park near Ashtown Castle. Cormorants can be spotted at Ashtown, on the old mill rooftop, and along the Tolka river around Cardiffsbridge. The elusive and colourful kingfisher can sometimes be seen flying along the Royal Canal or the Tolka river, particularly around the parkland at Cardiffsbridge.

With regard to birdlife the district offers a wide variety to the amateur or professional birdwatcher, who can indulge in this great pastime at the many fine, well-maintained public parks and open spaces in Dublin 7, including the Basin and Linear Park at Phibsborough, Great Western Square, John Paul II Park (the Bogeys), Oxmantown and the Royal Canal. Many species live and feed in the district. BirdWatch Ireland is a national voluntary organization for the conservation of wild birds and their habitats. Research and survey, management of reserves and species protection and education are among its main activities. Its Tolka Branch meets in the Botanic Gardens on the third Thursday of every month at 8 pm, with a day outing the following Saturday. Children, accompanied by adults, are always most welcome.

Blessington Basin in the 1980s, before restoration

An Teanga Gaeilge

The Irish language is alive and well in the district, and both Cabra Library and Phibsborough Library offer Irish conversation classes; they also run special events each year during Seachtain na Gaeilge, held every year in March. Gaelscoil Bharra opened its doors in 1996 in prefabricated units situated beside Naomh Fionnbarra GAA Club on Quarry Road. It currently consists of eight classrooms and there is a Naoinra attached to the school; there were 280 children on the rolls in March 2016 and the principal then was Seán Ó Donaile. A new, purpose-built school is presently being built on the site and the Gaelscoil is due to transfer to the new building in September 2017.

The all-Irish, Roman Catholic Volunteer Co-educational Secondary School, Coláiste Mhuire, relocated from Parnell Square to Cabra West in 2008, housed in temporary accommodation in the grounds of St Joseph's, Cabra. A secondary school for boys, it became co-educational. In September 2012 it moved into a new, purpose-built second-level school building on Ratoath Road, on land formerly within the walled grounds of St Joseph's next to St Declan's College;

it had 250 pupils on its rolls in February 2016 and the principal then was Tomás Ó Murchú.

There are numerous occasions and events that afford the use of the native tongue throughout the district; there are also evening classes in Irish from beginner level in Gaelscoil Bharra for those wishing to learn the language. Comhaltas Ceoltóirí Éireann, which is the largest group involved in the preservation and promotion of Irish traditional music, has branches throughout Ireland. The Dublin 7 Comhaltas branch, Craomh Paddy Bawn Ó Broin, is based in St John Bosco school on Navan Road, where it meets on Friday evenings; in April 2016 it introduced Irish language lessons to its schedule.

2 | Ashtown and Navan Road

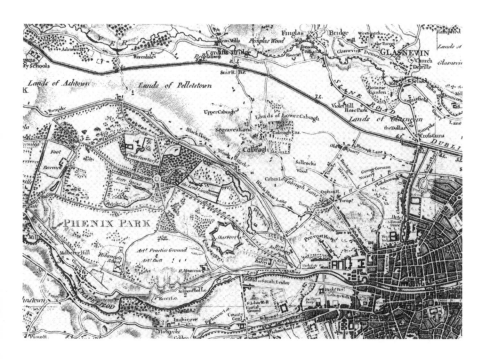

Ashtown is the name from which the Anglo-Norman Trench family took the title of baronet in 1800 before the Act of Union. The Priory of St John the Baptist once possessed a large part of 'the land at Ashtowne'. Old deeds show that 152 acres of land at Ashtown were purchased in 1663 from John Connel of Pelletstown 'to be annexed to the Phoenix Park'. The remainder of the Ashtown lands, inherited by John's heir Maurice, were forfeited to the Crown and subsequently granted to Thomas Keightly in 1688. Present-day Ashtown stretches from the Ashtown Gate at Phoenix Park to River Road, which runs by the Tolka.

The 1841 population Census lists forty-one houses in Ashtown with a population of 238. By 1851 the number of houses had increased to seventy-eight, housing a population of 422, probably as a result of the influx of people in the wake of the Famine. By 1861, in the first of many waves of emigration during the post-Famine years, the number had dropped to sixty-three houses with a population of 366, a figure that was to remain static until the end of the nineteenth century.

The major local landmark at Ashtown is the Halfway House. There has been an inn on this site for over two hundred years and it was located on what was then a small, quiet, country crossroads, called Kelly's Corner, from the name of the family who owned the premises. Peter Kelly was the proprietor during the 1920s and 1930s; Giles was the last of the family to manage the pub. The premises boasted a bagatelle table that was popular with locals during the 1940s through to the 1960s. It still survives and is stored somewhere on the premises. The old inn was demolished in 1946 and rebuilt, extended and renovated over the years. The present proprietor Con Treacy acquired the premises in November 1987. Michael Mullane is the manager; John Dwyer is the assistant manager and calls 'time' when Michael is off duty. Christy McGovern, of 278 Navan Road, was a long-time regular here; he often stopped by on the way back from Cavan with his wife Annie (*née* Gillick), who would have a glass of De Kuyper, a Dutch gin that came in a distinctive green bottle. Philip Gillick, retired Court Tipstaff to Mr Justice Paul Butler, recalls that Annie (his auntie) had to drink her gin in the snug while Christy had his tipple in the bar. Christy died in 2009 aged ninety-two years.

Kelly's Inn provided the setting for an ambush on the official car of Sir John French (1852–1925), the British Lord Lieutenant in Ireland, who had fought in the Boer War and seen military service in Sudan and with the British Expeditionary Force in Europe during the First World War. On Friday, 19 December 1919 a small group of IRA volunteers led by Dan Breen and acting on information received, lay in wait behind a hedge in the grounds of the pub. Shortly after midday the train from Galway carrying the Lord Lieutenant from his home in the west of Ireland stopped at the little Ashtown Railway Station. He was accompanied by his aide-de-camp, secretaries and an armed escort; a military guard of honour welcomed him.

As the convoy of three cars set off for the Viceregal Lodge in the Phoenix Park with John French in the leading vehicle, the attackers put their plan in train. Just before Ashtown Cross volunteer Martin Savage pushed a cart across the road in front of the second car and the ambushers then opened fire on French's vehicle. The escort returned fire. A member of the escort and Martin Savage were fatally wounded in the exchange. Two bullets hit French's vehicle but it increased speed and reached the safety of the Phoenix Park. The attackers then fled the scene across open fields, leaving their comrade's body behind.

Following an inquest in Bessborough Police Barracks, Phoenix Park, Martin Savage's body was returned to his family and subsequently brought to

Aerial view of Ashtown, late 1940s (Courtesy Ashtown Tinbox Co.)

Sligo for burial. A stone memorial, erected in 1948 to his memory at Ashtown Cross, was removed and relocated beside the roundabout directly opposite the Halfway House following the completion of the Navan Road dual carriageway and Blanchardstown bypass in 1991. He is commemorated locally by the naming in his honour of the housing complex at Martin Savage Park, Ashtown. One of his comrades in the operation was Vincent 'Vinny' Byrne, who lived for many years at 59 Blessington Street, Dublin 7, before moving to Drimnagh and later to Artane. Born in 1900, he joined the Irish Volunteers at fourteen, and served with the 2nd Battalion at Jacob's Mill during the Easter Rising 1916. On Bloody Sunday, 21 November 1920, he commanded an IRA detail that killed two of the 'Cairo Gang', British intelligence agents, in their lodgings at 38 Upper Mount Street, and he took part in the Custom House raid on 25 May 1921. He was the last surviving member of Michael Collins' feared special squad, and died on 13 December 1992.

Adjacent to Kelly's Inn was St Patrick's Home for Mothers and Babies, at 381 Navan Road, which opened in 1910 as part of a social programme run by the Dublin Public Assistance District, and was later placed under the direction and management of the Sisters of Charity of St Vincent de Paul (now called the Daughters of Charity). Over the years, unmarried mothers who found themselves pregnant were lodged here to have their babies, which were generally placed for adoption. According to the writer Mike Millotte in his book *Banished Babies*, St Patrick's was involved in the secret export of 254 children, born in the home, to the USA for adoption from the 1940s to the 1970s. St Patrick's was closed down in 1985 and was sold. The present-day Kempton housing development was built on the site. The records of the home are held by the Health Service Executive, Northern Area Child Care Services, Park House, North Circular Road, Dublin 7. *Banished Babies* was expanded, updated and re-issued by New Island Books in 2011.

St Patrick's also featured in an RTÉ *Prime Time* documentary on 9 June 2014 with regard to the conducting of medical tests on children there, and with anatomical tests of infants who died at the home, from the 1940s up to the 1960s. For anyone wishing to read more on St Patrick's, there is an excellent article on www.thejournal.ie by Paul Redmond, who was born there.

Kelly's Halfway House, Ashtown, 1936 (Courtesy Kelly's)

Rathborne Candles

Ashtown's most notable inhabitants were undoubtedly the Rathborne family, famous Dublin candle manufacturers. Rathborne Limited, their successors, can lay claim to being the oldest continuing manufacturing company in Ireland and one of the oldest in Europe. The Rathborne family established their trade in Ireland when their original factory in Chester, England, closed down as a result of the silting-up of the River Dee. The candlemaking business was originally located in the Liberties, adjacent to Christ Church Cathedral, and the firm's traditional establishment date is 1488, although the name appears in the *Dublin Assembly Rolls* for 1455. In 1650, in what was probably the first relocation of a business from the south to the north side of Dublin, it set up business first in Pill Lane (Chancery Street), later moving to St Mary's Lane, in 1723; it then moved to Cabragh Lane (Prussia Street) in 1738. Finally, in 1742, William Rathborne leased a large tract of land in Dunsink from the Right Honourable William Conolly, beginning the manufacture of candles on Mill Lane, beside the Canal bridge at Ashtown (outlined on the 1838 Ordnance Survey map) and at another location beside present-day Dunsinea House. This was before the construction of the Royal Canal, which began in the 1790s. Dunsinea House, the seat of the family for over one hundred years, was built in 1810 by William's successor, Henry Rathborne.

Candle manufacturing was a lucrative business and the Rathbornes conducted a thriving trade at Ashtown, giving employment down the years to hundreds of people from the village and from places as far away as Blanchardstown and Cabra. The family was so wealthy that when William's daughter Anne married one Mungo Campbell in 1740, she was described in the *Dublin Gazette* as 'a young lady possessed of beauty, merit and a considerable fortune'. During the latter part of the nineteenth century they concentrated the bulk of their operations at Dunsinea.

In 1817 a bill was tabled in Parliament to introduce gaslighting to the city of Dublin; at that time the humble candle was the source for street lighting. Henry Rathborne successfully petitioned Henry Grattan and the bill was shelved; however, progress could not be held back, and within a few years gaslight came to the city when the Act of Lighting the City and Suburbs of Dublin with Gas (George IV) came into force in 1821; in 1844 even the Mansion House itself was gaslit. The economic effect of this on the candle-manufacturing industry was somewhat mitigated by the repeal of the Candle Tax, which had been introduced in 1709 under an Act that also banned the widespread practice of making candles in the home.

In 1850 Rathborne's secured the contract for the provision of candles to the new prison at Mountjoy, which opened in March of that year; around this time they moved all their production to Dunsinea, vacating the old mill building on Mill Lane, Ashtown. In 1866 the firm, with John G. Rathborne at the helm, purchased a lease at North Lotts, on Wharf Road, now East Wall Road, and constructed a storage depot there for the import of paraffin wax and oils. The company was reorganized, with production and packaging concentrated solely at Dunsinea; office and city dispatch was placed at a premise the company had at 44 Essex Street and rural dispatch at East Wall. In the late 1800s the company was a noted supplier of light to the vehicular trade – carriage and bicycle lights were candle-powered then. In 1895 a fire at the Dunsinea factory destroyed many of the firm's records and during that year the innovative John G. Rathborne died; his son Henry Burnley inherited the firm but around 1912 could not get either of his own two sons to take over the business, so he decided to sell it. His sons Henry Barton and Charles John thought that electricity was going to wipe out the candle trade, telling their father that 'even the *Titanic* is all-electric' and had no interest in taking over what they considered a dying enterprise.

The Rathborne family sold its interest in their company John G. Rathborne Ltd to E. Ryan & Company, a subsidiary of Lever, a soap-manufacturing company, in 1920; in 1923 it was sold again, to Candles Ltd, a London candle manufacturer and a subsidiary of Shell, the petroleum company. It subsequently ceased operations at Dunsinea and relocated to East Wall Road in 1925, where the storage depot had been redeveloped during 1924 into a storage and manufacturing centre. In 1966 it amalgamated with Lalor Candles Ltd. It later opened a shop on the site for the retail of its products, and this became a regular stopping-point for thousands of Dublin commuters who took time out from their commute, particularly around Christmas time, to purchase candles. William Gavin Clarke started working in East Wall in 1981 and recalls that at that time the company was still producing tallow candles for export to Madagascar.

Finally, in 2002 the company made its last move, relocating from East Wall to new factory premises in Rosemount Business Park, Ballycoolin Industrial Estate, Blanchardstown, ironically just a stone's throw from Dunsinea, where it operated in the 1700s. The company is still engaged in the age-old craft of candlemaking and celebrated 500 years of manufacturing in Ireland in 1988. It employs a staff of sixteen. Its biggest market is that of the Church and the company turns out twenty million two-hour votive lights each year; the plastic cup used to hold the votive candle is manufactured by a company in Bray, County Wicklow.

Besides catering to the Church and a thriving mass market, in recent years it has successfully gained access to high-end retailing outlets: in 2015 Brown Thomas in Grafton Street started to sell the company's scented candle range. A book on the history of Rathborne's, entitled *The Candle Factory* and published in 1998 by The Lilliput Press, outlines in detail the long and chequered history of this famous chandler. The present managing director of the company is Vincent Brady, who grew up on Dingle Road, Cabra West.

The Old Mill, Ashtown

The old building on Mill Lane served many manufacturing purposes over the years and is described on the Ordnance Survey map of 1870 as a polish factory. The firm of Ronuk Ltd manufactured polish at the mill at the end of the nineteenth century and up until the late 1990s traces of that firm's old machinery were still visible on the grassland by the Royal Canal. There was a clock on the outside wall of the mill, the face and the minute hand of which could still be seen by passers-by until 2008, when it was removed by the present owners for renovation and repair, which has not been possible to date. In addition, a small part of the old machinery is still in the attic of the building. It is said that this clock came from Newgate Prison, on Green Street, Dublin 7.

In the late 1900s the mill was used for storage by the Ashtown Wholesale Trading Company, which was acquired by Burke Brothers Son and Company Ltd in 1976; in the mid-1980s Burke Brothers constructed a huge warehouse on the site, which was then one of the largest of its kind in the country. During excavations for this project large copper pots used by Rathborne's for the melting of wax were found; the company later disposed of these. Also discovered were shafts, bear-blocks and some of the old bottling plant used by Ronuk. In recent years Burke Brothers expanded their operations with the construction of a new, modern warehouse, completed in 2008. They also put a new roof on the old mill in an effort to preserve the integrity of the structure. At the canal side of the mill one can easily see the mill race leading from the Royal Canal, which provided power to the building; the remains of the workings for the mill wheel are also clearly visible.

Burke Brothers was founded by Thomas Burke, who was born at 19 Goldsmith Street, Phibsborough, in April 1916. When he was just twelve years old he started work in Guinness Brewery where he later became a nightwatchman. He moved to Phibsborough Road as a young adult and in the mid-1940s, in order to scrape a living, he started making concrete blocks in the back yard of his home at weekends and during the day; at night he worked away at 'the day job' in the brewery. There was a huge demand for concrete blocks after the war and he rented an adjoining yard at the back of the present day Cesar's Palace premises to cater for the growing business. He called the business 'Burke Brothers'; he did not have any brothers but was afraid of losing his job if it was found out that he was running the enterprise. By the time he retired from his job in the brewery his part-time business had expanded so much that it was now a leading building materials and hardware supplier in the city; evidence of this is borne out by the fact that in 1965 the rateable valuation of the Phibsborough premises was £110. Today the firm is a major supplier to the building trade and to hardware businesses and is a large local employer; the current Managing Director is Tom Burke, son of the founder.

Ashtown Level Crossing

The Ashtown railway level crossing, which is manually operated, is now the only one remaining in the district. An interesting part of Dublin street architecture was located here up until the early 1990s. A letterbox bearing the crest of King George was set into the stone pillar at the entrance to the former stationmaster's house. In what some locals termed an apparent 'officially sanctioned act of vandalism' it was removed in late 1995. John Malone, originally from Connemara, came to live in the stationmaster's house with his parents when he was just seven years of age. He recalls coming home from town in October 1995 and seeing metal pieces from the letterbox scattered on the ground. On making enquiries he discovered that it was the postal authority who removed it. John's father, also John Malone, worked on the old Galway to Clifden railway line and when it closed down he was transferred to Ashtown, being employed as a signalman at Liffey Junction, Cabra. He recalls those early days:

> The last Station Master to live in the house here was 'old Rock', the grandfather of the singer from Cabra West, Dickie Rock. I remember the barges used to ply the canal when I was young; Jemmy Leech, Bill Malinn and the Caffrey's, who came from Athlone, all had barges running along the canal then. My father worked for CIE until he retired in 1960. He died on 29 September 1965, the day of the All-Ireland. I remember the two houses across the road; Ted Galway's father built the two-storey one. The last residents here were Tilly, who lived in the big house, and Olga, who lived in the cottage. I woke up one morning and they were gone. Just like that.

The houses mentioned, comprising a two-storey and a single-storey residence, were located on the towpath beside the city side of the bridge at Ashtown, where the present sculpture of a lock-gatekeeper and lock is set. The owners lived in the houses for a number of years prior to their sale. The developers considered that the success of the project depended upon the acquisition and demolition of the two homes; they also depended upon the access that the houses and gardens afforded to their adjoining bank of land, which was rezoned for commercial and housing purposes.

Ashtown Cross and Environs

At Ashtown Cross, now the Ashtown Roundabout, stood the manufacturing works of Ashtown Tinbox Company Ltd. Built in 1930, the factory was named Saint Eloi Works, after Saint Eloi, the patron saint of tinsmiths. It remained in production for over sixty years. The factory provided long-term full-time jobs in the locality; in addition it offered summer work for hundreds of second-level schoolchildren over the years.

Due to competition from cheap imports it closed its doors in 1991, when the factory was purchased by the Blanchardstown-based Crest Foods. The last production manager at the plant was Noel Noonan, who later established a small tin-packaging business, Ashtown Packaging Ltd, in nearby Broombridge Industrial Estate, Cabra.

Ashtown Tln Box Factory, *circa* 1940 (Courtesy Ashtown Tinbox Co.)

The tinbox factory site was subdivided and sold, and the Opel Car show-rooms, formerly situated at Cabra Garage, near the junction of Cabra Road and Carnlough Road, now occupies part of the site. A five-storey over-basement office block, with the Revenue Commissioners as a tenant, was completed in early 2002, towering over the nearby Halfway House. Next door to the tinbox factory was the glove-manufacturing firm of George Horne. It closed down in the mid-1960s and the building was taken over by the tinbox company, which expanded its oper-ations. Gilt Edge, who moved into the new industrial complex nearby, continued the tradition of textile industry at Ashtown established by George Horne until 2006, when it closed down its manufacturing business as it was unable to compete with overseas competition. Gilt Edge Distribution Ltd is managed by the Grogan Brothers. Balfour, distributors of uniforms to the public sector for over seventy years, moved to Ashtown in 2000. It provides a small number of jobs with its alteration service.

Directly opposite the car showrooms, in the corner of the former Phoenix Park Racecourse, stood a distinctive redbrick Victorian structure built in the

Tudor style by Lord Arnott in the final years of the nineteenth century. This was Ashtown House, destroyed by fire during the mid-1980s over a number of quiet bank holiday weekends; the burnt-out ruin became a familiar landmark for many years. No sign of it remains today.

The *Education Report* of 1826 refers to 'a Protestant Free School as then existing at Ashtown, attended by fifty pupils and supported by an income of £100 per annum, defrayed by the Trustees of the will of Mr Morgan'. This was Morgan's Boys' Endowed Boarding School, founded in 1813 for 'boys of respectable Protestant parentage' and it was situated between Navan Road and the Royal Canal, near the present-day Topaz garage; permanent Traveller accommodation now occupies the site. In 1912 it had forty boys on the roll, of whom fifteen paid a fee of £24 yearly; the education of the remainder was provided free of charge. The school Governor was Henry B. Rathborne JP, owner of the Rathborne candle factory nearby; the Matron was Mrs Jeffers and her husband Robert was the Headmaster.

Mercer's Endowed Girls' School was located on the same site and there is a memorial tablet in St Brigid's Church, Castleknock, dedicated to the memory of Miss Kate Curtis, who for thirty-eight years was a Matron and teacher here. She died in 1899 aged seventy-four and the plaque was erected by some of her former pupils and a few other friends. It too catered for those of 'respectable Protestant parentage' and in 1912 it had thirty-six girls on the roll of which six were fee-paying, the fee being £15 a year; Miss Frances Smith was the Matron and Headmistress. Both schools, Morgan's in 1956 and Mercer's in 1966, were taken over by King's Hospital School, which at that time was located in Blackhall Place.

At the Ashtown Gate, Phoenix Park, stood the old Belleville farm; two housing complexes and an apartment development now occupy the site; the original lodge was restored for habitation and is accessed from Blackhorse Avenue. The old house, Belleville House, adjoining the Navan Road boundary, had a door set in the stone perimeter wall to allow pedestrian access; that door still exists, next to the bus stop at the roundabout at Ashtown. Marion Hendron is listed as occupier of Belleville House in the 1985 edition of *Thom's Directory*. It was sold in the late-1980s and the site, including old stable buildings and sheds, lay derelict for a number of years prior to redevelopment. It was in one of those derelict outhouses, which had an entrance off Blackhorse Avenue, where the family of banker Jim Lacey (Managing Director of National Irish Bank) was held during a kidnap for ransom in November 1993.

A criminal gang entered his home in Blackrock, County Dublin, tied up his wife Joan, their two young children and their babysitter, Tanya Waters. During a subsequent criminal trial in October 1997, Mrs Lacey described how she, her children and Ms Waters were 'put in a van and driven to stables in Blackhorse Avenue and put lying down upstairs and tied and gagged'. She said that they 'were left at the stables all day while the gang listened to Garda messages on their walkie-talkies' and that one of the gang told her that they would be 'freed at six o'clock if everything went okay. If not, we would each be kneecapped in both knees'. Over £300,000 was handed over at the bank headquarters in Dame Street. The family were freed later that day by An Garda Síochána. The prosecuting Garda was Detective Superintendent Felix McKenna. Only one person was convicted in the case.

Blackhorse Avenue

The Hole in the Wall is located on Blackhorse Avenue, formerly Blackhorse Lane, not far from the junction with Baggot Road; a turnstile into the Phoenix Park adjoins the entrance to the premises, which is claimed to be the longest pub in Ireland. It was licensed around the early 1600s, although the first documented evidence is the renewal of the licence granted by decree of Charles II in 1668. Originally known as 'Ye Signe of Ye Blackhorse', it became known to Dubliners of the late-1700s as Nancy Hand's Tavern, from the name of a popular hostess of that time. Francis Gardiner took over from Nancy Hand following her death in 1822 and he was succeeded by Michael Kennedy in 1857. After Michael Kennedy's death in 1885 his widow ran the premises, renaming it Nancy Hand's Blackhorse Tavern. In 1902 Levinus Doyle became the proprietor, renaming it the Black Horse Tavern; he is said to have served members of the British military through a hole in the park wall, located outside the entrance to the pub. Levinus died in 1915 and his wife Catherine then ran the business, until it was bought by Jim Clancy in 1943. The present proprietor is P.J. McCaffrey, who acquired the premises in 1970.

Not far from the pub, between Nephin Road and Cabra Gate, was an old well, known in the late 1800s as the 'Poor Man's Well'. This wild corner of Blackhorse Avenue was cleared by Dublin City Council during 2015 as part of the road improvement scheme for Blackhorse Avenue. The old well was rediscovered during these works and can now be clearly seen by passers-by; the works revealed the existence of a badger set. In a secluded spot near the corner of Nephin Road and Blackhorse Avenue stood Villa Park, built by a Mr Goggins: the house gave its name to the surrounding housing development. It lay derelict until its demolition in the late 1990s; two apartment blocks now occupy the site. One of the few remaining old houses in the area, situated on the corner of Villa Park Road and Blackhorse Avenue, it was let out for bedsit accommodation during the 1980s. Devlin's panel beater and car repair business occupied a site on the corner of the garden. The last resident was Mrs Norton, a friendly lady who did voluntary work with the Royal British Legion. The house was vacated in the 1990s and was unoccupied and derelict for a number of years. It was demolished in 2006 and the site lay vacant in 2016.

Hole in the Wall, Blackhorse Avenue, 1930 (Courtesy P.J. McCaffrey)

Poor Man's Well, 2016 (Bernard Neary)

Elmgrove House, on Blackhorse Avenue, was built in 1880 by Henry Baggot; Baggot Road is called after the family. The last residents of this old house were Peter Baggot, a member of the old North Dublin Rural Council, who died on 16 April 1941 and his wife Harriett, who died on 20 October 1964. The house was acquired by Ned Cumiskey in the early 1960s and opened as a pub. Originally called The Elmgrove Inn, over the following years it was enlarged and altered. In the early 1970s there was a skittle alley at the back of the pub, demolished during one of the subsequent renovations. In 1990 the entire structure was gutted, to be replaced by a purpose-built public house. Now called The Turnstile, it was again redeveloped in 2000 and renamed Ned's Bar in memory of Ned Cumiskey, long remembered by locals for annoyingly, and nightly, hammering at each table with a small mixer bottle to signal drink-up time. A cluster of small workers' cottages located within the present-day carpark were boarded up and derelict for many years; they were removed at the end of the last century. Nearby Conor Clune Road, off Baggot Road, is called after the young patriot from County Clare who was murdered by the British military on Bloody Sunday, 21 November 1920, along with Dick McKee and Peadar Clancy. Maurice Daly, who played for Wolverhampton Wanderers and who later took up coaching in Sweden, lived on this road; his brother Brian played League of Ireland football with St Patrick's Athletic.

Edmund Terence 'Terry' Murphy (1917–95) started work in Dublin Zoo in 1943 in an administrative capacity and three years later moved to Blackhorse Avenue to be closer to his job. Having a natural sympathy for animals, he was appointed Superintendent of Dublin Zoo in 1957. He compiled the *Official Guide to the Dublin Zoo* in 1960 and published his autobiography *Some of my Best Friends are Animals* in 1979; his enthusiasm informed his later RTÉ series *Animal Trail*. His main achievement was the transfer of animals from cages to open-plan environments, culminating in the creation of Fota Wildlife Park, County Cork, in 1979. A joint project with University College Cork, it opened to the public in 1993 just two years before he died on 29 July 1995.

Between Nephin Road and Skreen Road stood Park Stores, which closed down in 1995; an apartment block was built on the site. During the 1970s Jack O'Driscoll, a member of An Garda Síochána, lived above the shop; he kept bees in the back garden of the shop and in Blanchardstown. Former bee-keeper Matt Leech, who grew up in Inchicore and now lives in Kilbarrack, recalls Jack as 'a great experimenter in bee-keeping'. The Park Stores was one of many dairy shops dotting the local landscape up to the late-1900s. Tom Treacy was born in Capel Street and lived over McNeill's, a small music shop there, for most of his life. He once worked with HB ices and delivered to all the shops, newsagents and dairies in Dublin 7: 'I remember all the shops there; there was the Post Office and the shop beside it in Villa Park, the Grove on Navan Road, the Highway on Skreen Road and Park Stores, to name a few. The children used call me 'funny feet' because at that time one of the products I delivered was called Funny Feet and was an ice-pop with the shape of toes on it.' Tom now lives in Aughrim Court.

The writer Mary Russell grew up around the corner from Blackhorse Avenue, on Skreen Road: her family lived on the crescent there, facing the old tennis court, now a fenced-in garden. She attended the Dominican Convent on Ratoath Road and went to a boarding school in Athlone aged thirteen. Her published works include *The Blessings of a Good Thick Skirt*, *Please Don't Call it Soviet Georgia* and *Journeys of a Lifetime*. More recently her travels have taken her to Iraq and Syria; she is known for her writings in the *Irish Times* and the *Guardian* on Baghdad and Damascus. She now lives in Portobello.

At one point the city boundary was marked by a stone in the wall of the Phoenix Park, opposite Springfield Estate, next to Skreen Road. This small estate is built on the grounds of an old manor called Springfield House; a former resident here was a Mr Sherlock, a city stockbroker. In the early part of the last century it was the home of Annie and Patrick Sheridan; Annie died in January 1942 and Patrick died in June 1952. There was a small gate lodge attached to Springfield and in the 1870s Michael Kennedy, a land steward, lived here and ran the Black Horse Tavern on Blackhorse Lane.

Navan Road

The main road from Dublin to the provincial town of Navan, County Meath, was formerly called the Great Navan Road, and it begins at Cabra Cross. It cuts through the districts of Cabra and Ashtown in Dublin 7. The stretch of the road between Cabra Cross and Nephin Road was formerly called Windy Harbour.

St Vincent's Centre is on Navan Road, past the junction with Baggot Road, on a large site backing onto Blackhorse Avenue. It was built in the 1800s as a Poor Law School known as Cabra Auxiliary of the North Dublin Union, and the children were originally taught by the Dominican nuns of Cabra. This task was then handed over to the Daughters of Charity in September 1892, with 118 children, classed as 'sick' to 'feeble-minded', on the roll. In 1925 the nuns started a school for those with learning disabilities after a request from the Irish Free State government. In 1928 they started to take in children from all over Ireland. Catering for those with special needs, the complex includes a Child Study Centre, opened in 1969, a national school and the de Paul swimming pool, which was opened in 1972 and totally revamped in 2015. The pool was a popular venue with people living beyond the surrounding area, and many of the district's children first learned to swim here. Bungalows were constructed in the grounds between 1989 and 1992, with an entrance off Blackhorse Avenue; these offered independent living to clients of St Vincent's. Dwellings were also purchased nearby, enabling clients to live normal lives in society.

The Premier Credit Union, Villa Park Gardens, Navan Road, was founded in 1962 by Mr and Mrs Joe Costello, Walter Cullen, Mrs Dolan, Jackie Doyle, Michael McGuinness, Kathleen Matthews and Stephen Monaghan. Michael McGuinness, a Garda based at the Bridewell Garda Station, told me that they 'started it off with £1, a half-crown from each of the eight of us'. The Credit Union began business in the skittle alley at the back of Cumiskey's pub on Blackhorse Avenue. They later operated from a pre-fabricated building at the back of the church on Navan Road before purchasing their present headquarters in Villa Park. In 1988 they extended and modernized their premises to facilitate the growing demand for their services in the area. In the first thirty years of the life of the Credit Union it made loans totalling IR£26 million, had savings in excess of IR£5 million and boasted 4500 members.

Villa Park Avenue was built in the late 1940s and was home to William 'Bill' Shanahan, a native of County Tipperary and a member of An Garda Síochána. Born in 1897, in his day he was a famous athlete: he won the Munster and Irish high jump championship in 1918 and in 1922 won the Irish long jump championship. A notable achievement was winning the high jump event in the 1926 Triangular International, which featured teams from Ireland, England and Scotland, at Hampden Park, Glasgow. He served with distinction as a Garda and in October 1940 was presented with the Scott Medal for Valour after an attempted armed robbery at Holles Street on 7 May 1940, when he received five bullet wounds in the chest. His wife Josephine (*née* Bulfin) had passed away two weeks before the incident. He lived at 4 Villa Park Avenue and died on 20 May 1954, aged fifty-seven.

Villa Park Gardens was constructed during the 1950s and initially called Villa Park Crescent. Tony Behan is a retired legal cost accountant and well known in the area. A former President and the current Vice-President of the Old Dublin Society, he moved into his new home in Park Crescent in 1957; it was renamed Villa Park Gardens in 1959. A trove of knowledge on local history, Tony wrote a book on the first fifty years of the Navan Road parish.

During the 1940s the city boundary was expanding towards Cabra and Ashtown and new residents of the Roman Catholic persuasion living in the Navan Road area walked across the Phoenix Park to attend Mass in the village of Chapelizod. They began to look towards building their own parish church and plans were drawn up for a church and school on a site belonging to the Dominican Convent. The site was purchased in 1947 for the sum of £500 and a condition of the sale was a requirement that the parish construct a seven-foot boundary wall, together with the replacement of a then-existing concrete animal watering trough on a field belonging to the convent, bordering Ratoath Road. The replacement trough could still be seen though vegetation in recent years, to the rear of Convent View Cottages on Ratoath Road. After completion of these works by a local contractor, Mr Delaney, of 74 Navan Road, at a cost of £1270, building began on the Church of Our Lady Help of Christians.

Designed by the architect Simon Aloysius Leonard and built by Murphy Brothers of Rathmines, the project was completed in December 1951 and officially opened the following year, at a cost of £62,500. An interesting fundraising initiative to furnish the new church was the purchase by donors of mahogany benches, complete with an inscribed family memorial plate, at a cost of £15 each. A bungalow at 6 Villa Park Avenue was bought to serve as a presbytery; this was named St Philomena's. Subsequently, in 1956, two houses were acquired on Park Crescent estate, on sites 11 and 12, now 192 and 194 Navan Road, for use as residences and a presbytery for the new parish. In 1965 the parish team comprised Fr Peter Maguire (Parish Priest), Fr Maurice Courtney, Fr Donal Coghlan and Fr James Toohey. Many weddings have taken place in the church over the years, one of the most celebrated being that of Ann Giles to Nobby Stiles, the famous Manchester United player. Ann's brother Johnny, a much-capped Irish International footballer and well-known television soccer pundit, is from the district. A former Manchester and Leeds United player, he successfully managed the English League side West Bromwich Albion during the 1970s and the Irish Senior International team in the mid-1970s.

St John Bosco Boys' National School was built in 1955 and Michael Rowan was the first school principal. Girls were educated in the Phoenix Park School, the name of which is cut into the granite wall of the façade; called St Philomena's at that time, it has an entrance off Blackhorse Avenue. In 1969 the pupils moved into new premises beside the church, called Our Lady Help of Christians Girls' National School. Today the little school in the Phoenix Park serves as a special primary school for children aged between four and twelve. It is co-educational with a maximum enrolment of eighteen; a placement school, it provides for children who have the potential to return to mainstream education.

Shortly after the foundation of the State, the former Under Secretary's house at Ashtown in the grounds of the Phoenix Park, built in the 1750s, was made available as the residence and headquarters of the first Papal Nuncio. During the mid-1970s the building was found to have dry rot. A site was secured in the grounds of the Dominican Convent, Cabra, with an entrance fronting onto Navan Road. A new Papal Nuncio's house was inaugurated on 5 September 1978. When the old building at Ashtown was subsequently demolished, it revealed within its walls a medieval castle, which was preserved and renovated and is now a visitor attraction at Ashtown Visitor Centre with a magnificently refurbished Victorian walled garden and adjoining yard.

A lifelong trade unionist, Michael 'Mickey' Mullen lived at 202 Navan Road. From 1961 until 1969 he served as a Dáil TD, and later as a Senator from 1973 to 1977. He was the General Secretary of the Irish Transport and General Workers Union, now part of SIPTU, from 1969 until his death in November 1982.

St Oliver Plunkett GAA Club was founded in 1960 catering for various age categories, including school, juvenile, junior, intermediate and senior, in football, hurling and camogie. The most notable club achievement was the winning of Intermediate Hurling League and Championship honours in 1984. The completion of their own purpose-built premises, Áras Pluncéid, during 1990, marked a milestone in the history of the club and the official opening by President Mary Robinson took place in May 1991. At this time the management committee consisted of Tom Walsh, Castleknock (Chairperson); Paul Dwyer, Villa Park (Vice-Chairperson) and Denis Carr, Kinvara Road (Treasurer). John 'Johnny' McGreevy of Glendhu Road, a well-known figure in the district, has been deeply involved in club management in various categories over the years – as chairperson, vice-chairperson and secretary. The clubhouse has since undergone further development and expansion, with a new gym and weights room and a large function room. Recent successes include the 2006 Dublin AFL Division 2 title and the 2007 Dublin AFL Division 1 title.

In the late 1990s the club amalgamated with Eoghan Ruadh GAA Club; founded in 1917, Eoghan Ruadh catered for hurling in the parish of Aughrim Street and it enjoyed a proud tradition in Dublin hurling, contesting several county finals before winning the Dublin title in 1951. The club's Camogie section, founded in 1937, won its first Dublin Senior Camogie Championship in 1953. The glory years for the section came in the late 1960s, when it won three in a row All Ireland Senior Club Camogie Championships, in 1967, 1968 and 1969. Two presidents (Pat Rafferty and Phyllis Breslin) and a Dublin chairperson (Anne Ashton) of the Camogie Association played on the 1967 winning team. The club played its home matches on pitches in the Phoenix Park. Due to the general demographics in its own catchment area, it found it difficult to field full teams and in the late 1990s it amalgamated with Plunkett's, becoming St Oliver Plunkett-Eoghan Ruadh GAA Club.

3|Broadstone

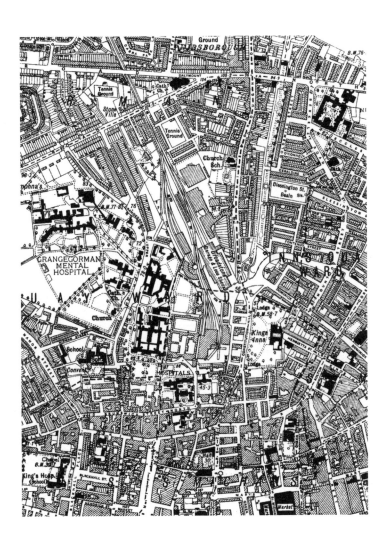

B roadstone seems to be a name that is purely English in origin but is in fact derived from the Norse Bradog-Steyn, the stone of the Bradoge. It was here at Broadstone that the Bradoge Water flowed over a stone bottom on its way to the River Liffey. The road between Broadstone and Glasnevin, known of old as Finglas Road, though called 'the road to Phibsborough', was for a portion of its length known as Glasmanogue, the high road passing through a village or district of that name. Glasmanogue is marked on most of the old Dublin maps and here in 1575 the mayor and sheriffs of the city held their courts during the outbreak of a great plague which, it is stated, 'carried off 3000 persons, depopulating the city to such an extent that grass grew on the streets'. Constitution Hill, formerly called North Townsend Street, was a busy and prosperous place during the early days of the Royal Canal, containing 'many good inns for the entertainment of man and beast'. The name is an imitation of Constitution Hill in London and not from the fact that the Lord Mayor held court here on the occasion of the aforementioned plague in Dublin city.

There were many tenement houses between Constitution Hill and Prebend Street, which ran along the railway yards of the Broadstone Railway Station.

These were demolished after the Emergency and the placenames disappeared: Farrell's Lane, St Thomas Avenue, Shaw's Lane, Monck Cottages and Nugent's Lane. Dublin Corporation built a complex of flats on the site. A turntable was located in the railway yard, near to Monck Cotttages.

Before the inception of the Midland and Great Western Railway (MGWR) in the early 1840s, Broadstone was a very busy place, being the point of departure for the canal 'fly boats' – fast passenger boats – to Mullingar, the River Shannon and several places in between. The Broadstone branch of the Royal Canal was a cut of nearly a mile and a half from the direct line. It ran from a cut in the main canal, near Mountjoy Prison, under Blacquire Bridge, and ended at docks and stores at the rear of Constitution Hill, where the barges of several merchants were loaded and unloaded. The property of the New Royal Canal Company was taken over by the MGWR following its establishment pursuant to an Act of Parliament. On the opening of the railway line all passenger boats stopped plying but the canal continued to be used for goods traffic. The old approach to the new railway station, through Dominick Street Upper, was a rather beautiful spot in the late 1800s and the surroundings, including King's Inns with its spacious grounds, were most appealing to the eye. The area was reaping the benefits of the many building developments of the early and middle 1800s, including the railway station itself.

Foster Aqueduct

For nearly 150 years the Foster Aqueduct at Broadstone was a unique Dublin landmark. The Royal Canal Company constructed the aqueduct at Constitution Hill to allow the transport by water of goods and passengers to the Canal Harbour, over what was then the main road to the villages of Phibsborough, Glasnevin, Finglas, Ashbourne and Slane. In the 1950s it was removed for a somewhat similar reason – to ease the passage of public road passenger vehicles along what became a key city traffic artery.

The aqueduct, locally called the 'ache-a-dock', was originally a stone structure carrying the canal over Phibsborough Road to the docks in the terminus of the Royal Canal on the west side of Constitution Hill, between the House of Industry, later the Richmond and Whitworth Hospital, and the Registry of Deeds. It was built by Miller and Ruddery around 1800 in the Egyptian Revivalist style,

View of the City of Dublin, Foster Aqueduct, 1831 (*Ireland Illustrated*, Courtesy NLI)

with an arch thirty feet wide and fifteen feet high, and two small arched passages on each side for pedestrian traffic. On the south side, over the arch, there was an inscription on a stone tablet: *Foster Aqueduct. Serus in coelum redeas, diuque, populo Hiberniae intersis.* It was named in honour of John Foster, Baron Oriel and Speaker of the Irish Parliament in 1710, a staunch opponent of the relaxation of the Penal Laws. Roughly translated, the inscription expressed a wish that death would not intervene to deprive him of a long life among the people of Ireland. There was a tablet on the opposite side but it bore no inscription. Foster was born in 1667, and in 1695 married Rebecca, daughter of Henry and Sarah (*née* Stanley, daughter and heir of Sir Thomas Stanley of Grangegorman) Monck. He was appointed Lord Chief Justice of the Common Pleas in 1714, a position he held until his death on 2 July 1720.

According to Brendan Fitzgerald, who was attached to the City Engineering Department of Dublin Corporation in the early 1950s, every effort was made to save the tablet but unfortunately it was lost as the workman taking the panel down thought it was in one piece. (On the application of the cold chisel it proved to be made up of three pieces, which fell down and were broken.) Like the aqueduct to which his name was given, Foster's residence at 50 Fleet Street, the former ESB office and retail outlet, also disappeared.

Although the aqueduct now lies buried in the new roadway constructed to facilitate the traffic along this northeastern highway, we are not without pictorial records of it. The earliest of these is 'A view of the City of Dublin from the Foster Aqueduct, looking southward' (M. Craig, del. T. Dixon, sculp). According to Harvey, in his publication entitled *Dublin* the date of the print is 1816 but in the *Elmes Catalogue of Irish Topographical Prints* published by the National Library of Ireland, no date is given. The aqueduct was considered a clever architectural and engineering feat. After the purchase of the New Royal Canal Company by the MGWR, the aqueduct was filled in and used as a road entrance into the railway station forecourt.

Buses or large trucks regularly became trapped under the bridge. Pat McCaffrey from Cabra West recalled an exciting event in 1950, when a truck driver transporting apples heading for the fruit markets lost part of his load while travelling under the aqueduct: 'Apples were flying everywhere and we just couldn't believe it. We filled our jumpers to bursting. It was great.' However, it was a headache for the city traffic authorities and in 1951 this unique part of old Dublin vanished forever.

Broadstone Railway Station

In October 1836 a Royal Commission was set up to consider the future development of railways in Ireland. In 1838 the Commission recommended two mainline railways, one to the northwest and one to the southwest; it held that the west was adequately served by the existing canal structure. However, opinions soon changed and in the early 1840s the MGWR was established. On 21 July 1845 a Dublin to Mullingar main line, with a branch to Longford, a total distance of seventy-six miles, was sanctioned. Ceremonial cutting of the first sod took place in June 1846 and within ten months the twenty-six miles to Enfield were completed. Services on this first stage of the MGWR railway line began on 28 June 1847. A short time later, services were extended to Kinnegad and on 2 October 1848 the first train reached Mullingar to tremendous local excitement; on 1 August 1851 the seventy-six-mile section to the western terminus at Galway was opened. Its inauguration was the longest stretch of railway line opened at the same time in Ireland. This section had only one significant engineering feat, the Shannon Bridge at Athlone.

The engineer responsible for the laying of the line was George Hemans, who later became Dublin City Engineer. He was the son of Captain Alfred and Felicia Dorothea (*née* Browne) Hemans. Felicia was born in Liverpool on 25 September 1793 and enjoyed immense popularity as a poet. *Poems*, which was published in 1808, was written when she was between eight and thirteen, and was the first in a series of twenty-four volumes of verse. At nineteen Felicia married Captain Hemans; they separated in 1818. Her prolific literary output helped to support her five children, including George. She became a literary celebrity, admired by such famous older writers as William Wordsworth and Sir Walter Scott. Her poems include 'The Landing of the Pilgrim Fathers', 'Dirge' and the well-known 'Casablanca', which opens with the line 'The boy stood on the burning deck …'

The MGWR established its headquarters at its newly purchased Royal Canal Depot at Broadstone. It was to become the third largest of the pre-amalgamation railway networks in Ireland with 538 route miles. The headquarters of the Royal Canal Company served as a temporary railway terminal while an extensive railway

Broadstone Railway Station, early 1900s (Courtesy Seamus Kearns Postcard Collection)

terminus was constructed. When the new station opened the Royal Canal building was converted to dormitory accommodation, first for country rail drivers and later for country bus drivers staying overnight in Dublin. It served as the headquarters of Color Me Beautiful Ltd during the late 1900s but is currently vacant. The fine imposing houses facing onto Phibsborough Road, known as Royal Canal Terrace, were built in 1826.

In 1849 the building of the Broadstone Railway Station, designed by architect John Skipton Mulvany, was completed: in the 1850 Valuation List it is described as having a valuation of £1000 'including stores, offices and coach factory'. The only large Graeco-Egyptian building in Dublin, this magnificent structure is now preserved, a reminder of the halcyon days of railways in Ireland. In 1982 I was given a detailed tour of the complex by Tommy Thornton of CIE and was pleasantly surprised to find that the building contained a fine dome, which is not visible from the roadside. From the rooftop marvellous panoramic views of the city can be had. As the station was constructed within the old canal harbour, a floating pontoon was constructed in front of the new building to enable road traffic to gain access to the terminus. In 1879 this pontoon was removed when the aqueduct and harbour docks were filled in, providing an impressive new vehicular entrance to the railway station.

Broadstone Railway Station, early 1900s (Courtesy Irish Railway Record Society)

Just eleven years after the station was built extensive alterations were made to the terminus, including the erection of a classical-style colonnade, supported by metal pillars, which cannot today be easily viewed by passers-by. These developments raised quite a few eyebrows at the time as people wondered why the alterations were being undertaken on a comparatively modern building; if deemed necessary, they should have been made in the first place. The *Dublin Builder* edition of 1 April 1861 raised this issue and published the following extract from the *Freeman* newspaper, which highlights the extent of the alterations carried out:

> Today or tomorrow the alterations which have been for some months in course of preparation, come into effect at Broadstone Terminus. To avoid the inconvenience and possible dangers of changing rails as hitherto in leaving or arriving the trains were compelled to do, the platforms have been altered from one side of the building to the other. The south-west will, in future, be the departure side, the north-east the arrival; the travellers leaving Dublin passing the front of the terminus and reaching this platform by a handsome collonade, supported with metal pillars, and through a spacious ticket office. On this the departure platform will now be found with waiting rooms and in an additional storey the offices of the traffic manager, engineer, the auditor, also spare rooms, suitable for branch company's uses, all to the number of nine, opening on a corridor 300 feet in length.
>
> On the opposite side the arrival platform has now been formed. It opens on a magnificent collonade, about fifty feet in width by 600 feet in length. This is appropriated to vehicles of every description, which can leave its inclosure with the utmost celerity. The alterations are decided improvements. They have, we understand, been carried out under the supervision of Mr C. Wilkinson, of Westland-row. The interior of the station is being further beautified by the painting in bright colours of the roof, pillars and delicate iron work of the spacious and graceful shed – the building, altogether, presenting a railway terminus in every way worthy of a great and enterprising company.

In 1879 further major developments were completed, including the filling in of the canal harbour to facilitate the construction of a carriage shop and the conversion of the harbour goods store into a wagon depot. The wharfage store where boats used to load and unload became a timber store. The approach to the station was improved by the building of a new roadway through a portion of the

Blessington Estate, beginning at Broadstone, sweeping around the rear of Middle Mountjoy and Fontenoy Streets and terminating in Mountjoy Street at St Mary's Chapel of Ease. The sidewalks of this new street were planted with trees, giving a prosperous appearance to this new approach to the terminus. Other developments carried out at this time included the erection of a fitting shop allowing the company to build their own locomotives and carriages. The following brief extract from the *Irish Builder* of 15 February 1879 gives a description of the type of railway carriage built at the new complex:

> We were shown an excellent specimen of what may be termed a 'family first-class carriage', fitted with couches, arm-chairs, separate servants' compartment, and provided at the other end with a lavatory and other sanitary and travelling requisities. This carriage is fitted with Cleminson's patent frame and axles. The works carried out at the Broadstone Terminus of the Midland Railway indicate the fastly-growing wants of the company in connection with their inland and cross-channel trade.

A sad incident occurred near the station in 1854, as the following extract from the *Journal of the Irish Railway Record Society* (No 16, Spring 1955) records:

> On April 20 1854 a regrettable accident occurred on the MGWR near the Broadstone Station. Mr Charles Tarrant, Engineer of the Royal Canal, was walking down the line to the terminus when he was knocked down and fatally injured by the Fairy engine which was returning from the coke ovens. It seems that Tarrant, who was in the habit of travelling on engines returning to Broadstone, signalled to the crew of the Fairy that he wished to board the engine. He then crossed the track to mount a wooden ticket platform situated just south of the North Circular Road bridge. As he was doing so, his hat blew off and he foolishly tried to retrieve it, with fatal results. The coke ovens referred to were situated near the first milepost between the line and the Royal Canal. Coal was brought to the site by lighters from the canal basin at the North Wall.

The Coke Ovens, marked on the Ordnance Survey map of 1838, was the site of a signal cab in 1872 and a playground, albeit a somewhat dangerous one, for generations of children during the early 1900s. It was where the cinders and ashes from the steam engine era were dumped and covered over with clay and by grass and weeds. They are still remembered in the locality; the Coke Ovens

Cottages are situated on the towpath not far from Des Kelly's Carpets at Cross Guns Bridge. Another building, named Coke Ovens Lodge, was near the line leading into the station and this is delineated on the Ordnance Survey map of 1870. It was demolished in the mid-1950s, although the remains were still visible in the thick overgrowth up to early 1985.

Leaving Broadstone Railway Station, 1920s (Courtesy Irish Railway Record Society)

An outbreak in 1887 of fire in the engine paints shop, a single-storey building with a roof of glass and wood, gives an insight into the cost of dealing with a call-out from the fire brigade. The shop contained paints, oils, turpentine and one train-engine. The alarm was raised at 9.25 on the morning of 7 April 1887 and the fire brigade was notified by police telegraph. Before the arrival of the brigade, staff removed the engine from the paints shop. The fire spread to the machinery section, but was quickly brought under control. Paints and oils were destroyed, along with thirty feet of roof and some wooden panelling. The machinery, stated to be 'costly and valuable', was undamaged. The fire brigade estimated the damage at £220 6s. 7d., and their expenses at twenty-six shillings and recouped the sum of thirteen shillings from the MGWR under Section 10 of the Fire Brigade Act. In that particular year the Dublin fire service expenses 'for turning out to fires, horsing engines, etc.' amounted to £141 11s. 6d. Of this, they recouped £24 19s. 0d. under Sections 9 and 10 of the Fire Brigade Act. Their total wages bill that year came to £2130 7s. 5d.

Train Ticket MGWR (Courtesy Tommy Thornton, CIE)

A number of those employed at Broadstone Railway Station took part in the Easter Rising, including Gerald 'Gerry' Boland of the well-known republican family, a brother of Harry Boland. He worked here as an apprentice, joining Dublin Corporation upon qualifying as a fitter.

The MGWR was absorbed into the Great Southern Railway in the amalgamation of the railways during the 1920s. At that time trains from Mullingar to Broadstone, with thirteen stops on route, were allowed two hours and ten minutes for the journey. The journey time had been reduced considerably by the time the station stopped operating as a passenger terminus. The Great Southern Railway continued to use Broadstone as a passenger train station until 1937, when all passenger traffic ceased. It was then used solely as a rail goods depot. When diesel locomotives were introduced around 1950, none were allocated to Broadstone. In November 1954 the locomotive depots in the Dublin area were reorganized, with Inchicore becoming a diesel-only depot (with the exception of the works pilots, which were steam-driven). All steam engines transferred to Broadstone, which became the sole steam depot for Dublin.

Towards the late 1950s steam locomotion began its rapid demise in Ireland, and around this time Broadstone Railway Station was closed; however, the complex continued to play a major role in the area of public transport and it became an important garage for buses serving both city and provincial routes, and a key centre for Bus Éireann's road haulage activities. The engineering division of Bus Éireann is located just inside the Phibsborough Road entrance. In 2016 the station was enjoying a renaissance, as the works on expanding the LUAS tram network began; the line will extend from the city centre, into Broadstone and along the former railway line to Liffey Junction; the work when completed will breathe new life into this historic part of the City of Dublin.

Disused Water Tower, 2016 (Bernard Neary)

Highfield House

Highfield House was situated on North Circular Road, just past the railway bridge in the direction of the Phoenix Park. Set in approximately three acres of gardens, this imposing building was constructed by the MGWR to accommodate management staff at Broadstone; *Thom's Directory* for 1917 records Percy Alexander Hay, Company Secretary and William Purcell O'Neill, Chief Engineer, as living here. Originally two semi-detached houses, it was altered to serve as a single unit and for many years it was an administrative centre for the Irish Christian Brothers, who purchased the building from CIE, the successors to the MGWR, in 1939 and renamed it Cuan Mhuire. Initially, half of the building was let to a Mrs Kennedy, who provided student lodgings for many years until the Brothers required possession of both dwellings. A small granite cottage at the entrance, 274 North Circular Road, became a gate lodge; one Mrs Mangan lived here during the 1920s. From the 1960s until the early 1990s it served as a security lodge; there is presently a planning notice for a mixed housing and apartment development on the site, dating from 2012. The two granite entrance pillars to the old house still stand: on one 'High' is carved and on the other 'Field'. Nearby, at the railway bridge, are two small railway cottages.

A large granite and concrete water tower in the grounds of Highfield House was supplied by an underground pipe running along the railway track from the Royal Canal at Liffey Junction, providing water to both Broadstone and Amiens Street Railway Stations for many years. Until the early 1980s it was used to wash the buses at the Broadstone depot but became obsolete; it was still there in July 2016, though not visible from the North Circular Road anymore due to heavy overgrowth. Opposite Highfield House is the little housing development on Cherrymount Road; this gets its name from Cherrymount House, on the left as one enters the cul-de-sac, and clearly shown on the 1876 Ordnance Survey map. At that time it was the residence of one Matthew J. Mooney, a surname then common in the district.

King's Inns

King's Inns and the Registry of Deeds are opposite Broadstone Station, although the Inns can also be accessed from Henrietta Street, where King's Inns Library is located. This is James Gandon's last great architectural work; he was aided by his pupil Henry Aaron Baker. The foundation stone was laid by the Earl of Clare, Lord Chancellor of Ireland, on 1 August 1795. The main construction did not take place until 1802; Gandon retired to England in the wake of the 1798 rebellion and only returned when the nationalist aspirations had been suppressed. There is no evidence that the Inns possessed a library prior to 1787, when a nucleus collection was formed through the purchase of the private library of Mr Justice Robinson.

The present Library building in Henrietta Street was completed in 1827 and houses 117,000 volumes, of which half are purely law books. The main Library and Reading Room is of immense architectural interest, with a fine stained-glass window. Another stained-glass window, on the stairs leading to the Reading Rooms, depicts the arms of the Benchers and has the following inscription: *Erected at the private expense of the Benchers of the Honorable Society of the Kings Inns. M. O'Connor, 80 Dame Street.* The building can best be viewed from the lawn facing onto Constitution Hill; the grounds are open to the public and serve as a park, maintained by Dublin City Council. The Bradoge river runs beneath. Next to King's Inns is Temple Cottages, a quiet cul-de-sac. This is home to Robert Ballagh, the prominent artist and designer. He has lived in the district for many years, having moved here from Ballsbridge, Dublin 4. He designed the twenty-pound note, made obsolete by the introduction of the euro, which depicted the Great Liberator, Daniel O'Connell.

Mountjoy Street and Environs

St Mary's Church of Ireland, fronting onto Mountjoy Street at its junction with St Mary's Place, was designed and built by the architect John Semple in 1830. Born in 1801 and a grand-nephew of the famous architect George Semple of Queen Street, he also designed Grangegorman and Tipperkevin churches. St Mary's was photographed by William Henry Fox Talbot, the pioneer of photography, as early as 1845 and the playwright Seán O'Casey was christened here. It was deconsecrated some years ago and in the 1980s the building served as the headquarters for the Dublin Corporation Traffic Warden service; it now functions as offices for a number of commercial enterprises. Called the 'Black Church' by northsiders due to the fact that its dark calpstone gives it a black hue after rain. Local folklore has it that if you run around the church three times at midnight, you will see the devil. Poet Austin Clarke was born at 83 Manor Street on 8 May 1896; in 1899 his family moved to 15 Mountjoy Street, where he grew up. His autobiography *Twice Around the Black Church*, published in 1962, recalls this superstition. His other works include *Collected Plays* (1963) and *First Flight to Africa* (1964) which won the Denis Devlin Memorial award for poetry from the Irish Arts Council. He died on 19 March 1974 and his private papers are with the University of Austin, Texas and the National Library of Ireland.

Madeline 'Dilly' Dicker, a girlfriend of Michael Collins' before Kitty Kiernan, lived at 30 Mountjoy Street, one of a number of 'safe houses' used by him. It was an ideal safe house as a laneway runs alongside it, leading from Mountjoy Street down into Dorset Street and Dominic Street, with another laneway running along the back of the house. Doors in the garden's side and back wall afforded a quick exit, if such was necessary. Dilly Dicker was an ardent nationalist and a member of Cumann na mBan and Sinn Féin. During the War of Independence she undertook many risky tasks for Michael Collins. The house was sold and renovated in 2010; however, an outdoor toilet at the side of the house survives and remains in the same condition as it was in 1920. Another girlfriend of Michael Collins', Susan Killeen, lived at 19 Mountjoy Street with the family of her uncle, Patrick.

The Munster Private Hotel, also known as Arás na nGael or Grianán na nGaedheal, was owned by Myra T. McCarthy, a staunch republican from County Kerry. Across the road from the home of Dilly Dicker, it has long ceased to be a hotel or lodging house and is now divided into two separate properties, 44 and 44A Mountjoy Street. Seán MacDermott stayed here during the week before the 1916 Rising, and it was there that he briefed the Volunteers who were to travel to the Wireless College at Caherciveen, County Kerry to obtain equipment and broadcast news of the insurrection to the outside world. The mission failed as three of the volunteers were killed when their car drove off Ballykissane Pier on the way to Cahirciveen. Michael Collins lived here for a spell in 1917, as did Fionán Lynch. Even after Michael Collins went on the run, he still left his laundry in the hotel and picked it up on Saturdays. In 1918 the British spy Timothy Quinlisk was also a guest. Myra took a neutral stance during the Civil War, and catered for both sides. An interesting example of this can be found in the book *Kerry's Fighting Story*, which states that Michael Collins and Richard Mulcahy often called in for breakfast and collected laundry or messages, to be later followed by Eamonn de Valera and Cathal Brugha, on the same business.

The An Óige International Youth Hostel is on the corner of Mountjoy Street and Upper Wellington Street. The headquarters of the organization, it provides low-cost accomodation to visitors from all over the world. It was previously a convent and school run by the Sisters of Charity. The oldest orphanage in Dublin, called St Joseph's Girls' Orphanage, was founded here in 1770; by 1912 it had come under the care of the Sisters of Charity who in that year appealed for donations that would be 'most thankfully received by the Very Rev. D. Downing P.P. Berkley-street'.

Middle Mountjoy Street, which joins Palmerston Place to Upper Dominick Street, is interesting with regard to the number of well-kept family homes; the houses on the right-angled corner as one turns into Palmerston Place are quite distinctive. John O'Leary, born in Tipperary town on 23 July 1830, came to Dublin in 1847 and got involved with the Young Ireland movement. James

Stephens recruited him into the Irish Republican Brotherhood in 1858 and in August 1863 he became editor of the new Fenian newspaper, the *Irish People*. He was living at 16 Middle Mountjoy Street when he was arrested in the early hours of 16 September 1865, during a large-scale rounding-up of Fenian activists; a plaque on the wall of the house commemorates this fact. He was sentenced to twenty years' penal servitude with hard labour on 7 December 1865 and imprisoned in Portland Prison. He was released early on condition that he leave Ireland; he went to live in Paris in January 1871. He returned to Ireland in 1885 and lived with his sister Ellen in Rathmines. He became friends with William Butler Yeats, whose genius he recognized, giving the poet access to his personal library; for his part Yeats accepted O'Leary's criticism of his work. John O'Leary is immortalized in the Yeats poem 'September 1913':

> Romantic Ireland's dead and gone,
> It's with O'Leary in the grave.

St Mary's Place National School is close to the Black Church; it is a modern five-storey building catering for 209 children. The principal is Éadaoin Kelly and the deputy principal is Bríd Brophy. It is the result of the amalgamation of several local schools over the years, beginning in the 1970s and including Scoil Mhuire (a girls' national school formerly on King's Inns Street), Plás Mhuire Boys' National School and St Joseph's National School, Upper Wellington Street. St Joseph's formerly housed a FÁS community training programme: in recent years the Roman Catholic social and community services organization, Crosscare, have occupied the premises. The name of the school is in granite over the doorway of the redbrick building. The former Christian Brothers Boys' National School at St Mary's Place, built in 1854, was taken over by the Catholic Youth Council in the mid-1970s and operated as the Young Traveller Hotel. Today it too is occupied by Crosscare, which provides accommodation for the homeless.

Wellington Street Upper and Lower intersect with Mountjoy Street. Seán Thomas O'Kelly was born at 4 Lower Wellington Street on 25 August 1882, and the house is listed as a tenement at this time in *Thom's Directory*. He was the eldest son of Samuel O'Kelly, a master boot- and shoemaker, who had a shop at 1 Berkeley Road. Educated at the Sisters of Charity National School on Mountjoy Street (1886–90) and St Mary's Place (1890–4), he then continued his secondary education at O'Connell's CBS, North Circular Road, where he acquired his love of Irish. He was a founding member of the Irish Volunteers and supervised the landing of arms at Kilcoole, County Wicklow, in August 1914. He worked closely with the Roman Catholic bishops in the drafting of the Criminal Law Amendment Act 1935, which outlawed contraception. In 1945 he won the first contested presidential election held in Ireland, and was re-elected in 1952 for a further seven-year term. He died on 23 November 1966 in the Mater Private Nursing Home. Lower Wellington Street has changed dramatically in the intervening years and all the houses date from the late 1900s.

4 | Cabra

C alled Cabragh until the early twentieth century, the district lay within the boundary of the former barony of Nethercross and meant thicket, moor, waste or bad land. The old approach to Cabra from the city, before the construction of North Circular Road in 1800, was via Stoneybatter, Cabragh Lane and Old Cabragh Road. Cabragh Lane was renamed Prussia Street after Frederick the Great, King of Prussia, in 1765. At Cabra Cross the road swung north and descended along present-day Ratoath Road until it reached the sleepy village of Cardiffsbridge. In time the area became divided up into what was called Much or Greater Cabragh (Castleknock) and Little Cabragh (Finglas).

Between 1720 and 1850 the Industrial Revolution caused a dramatic change to the Cabra landscape with the construction of the Royal Canal in 1790 and the laying of the Dublin–Galway railway line in the 1840s, both of which ran through the heart of Cabra. From about 1880 to 1930 it became a prominent market-garden centre and one of the main vegetable-producing areas in the country. It also served as a giant lairage, where cattle being brought to market at Hanlon's Corner were kept overnight in pens and grazing fields.

Dublin grew dramatically from the late 1920s and these changes were overseen by Horace Tennyson O'Rourke, a town planner and Dublin City architect from 1922 until his retirement in 1945. He monitored the development of the city during a time when both its area and population doubled in size. The principal author of the *Dublin Civic Survey Report* of 1925, he was born on 21 March 1880 at 34 Richmond Place North, near Summerhill. Under his supervision and direction, the construction of local-authority housing throughout the city began. In the Dublin 7 area, the Dublin Corporation housing scheme at Annamoe and Cabra East began in 1930 and was followed in 1939 by the Cabra West housing scheme. These developments attracted manufacturing and service industries, resulting in the vast industrial area that now borders Bannow Road, Ballyboggan Road, Broombridge Road and Finglas Road. Horace lived at Lytleholme, 20 Cabra Road from 1914 until 1927; he died in Donnybrook in 1963. Lytleholme was built around 1912 and was damaged by fire during the 1970s. It was rebuilt and is now called Abridge House; it can be easily identified by its distinctive chimney.

Old Cabra Road

For hundreds of years the Old Cabra Road ran through quiet, peaceful farmland and not until the late 1920s did large-scale housing developments take place, culminating in the ambitious construction of Cabra West by Dublin Corporation in 1939. The house and farm of the Mooney family, called Cabra Lodge, was situated at the top of Old Cabra Road, on the left-hand side as one approaches Cabra Cross. They farmed in the area for generations, and were a notable family in the district until the 1950s. A member of this family, Joe Mooney, was described as a grazier living at Tolka Park, Broombridge, around 1918. During the great flu epidemic of 1918 Mary Mooney gave huge help to the Irish Christian Brothers in charge of St Joseph's School for Deaf Boys, which was badly hit by the outbreak. Her husband Joe was a Justice of the Peace and he contributed generously to the early 1900s development at St Peter's church, Phibsborough. A devout Roman Catholic, locals recalled him 'daily attending ten o'clock Mass in St Peter's, travelling by horse-drawn carriage and his coachman's name was Mr Kerrigan, who had a son commissioned a Lieutenant in the Irish Free State Army'. *Thom's Directory* records 'cattle lairs and grass parks' here in 1917 and again in 1946, when Mary was still living on the farm.

In the late 1940s the Mooney lands were purchased by the State; it was envisaged that a new hospital complex would be built on the site to house the Richmond hospitals on North Brunswick Street, which eventually transferred to Beaumont in 1987. For over forty years the land lay unused until the construction of a senior citizens' flats complex, a telephone exchange, a Department of Social Protection centre and the Donard mixed private and local-authority housing scheme in the 1980s and early 1990s. The remainder of the site was redeveloped with the addition of the Maple Shopping Centre, Cabra Library and Park Motors and an adjoining apartment complex in the opening two years of the new millennium. Directly across the road from the Mooney farm was Popular Lodge, which once served as a police barracks. The road forked here at the junction of Navan and Ratoath Road, not far from Cabragh House.

Cabragh House and the Seagraves

Cabragh House was on the site of the present-day Canon Burke senior citizen flats at the Ratoath Road, Nephin Road and Fassaugh Avenue roundabout. The original mansion was completed around 1590 and the house became the seat of the Segrave family for almost three hundred years. Walter Segrave was the first member of the family to take up residence in Cabragh House. The name Segrave is derived from the Scandinavian *Sio Greve* and the German *Zee Graf*, both meaning 'sea lord', and the Norman de Segrave. It is thought that the Segraves first arrived in England with Cerdic the Saxon in 519 AD, settling in Leicestershire. The Irish Segraves were one of the most important families living in Dublin and according to Professor Stokes in *Ireland and the Roman Catholic Church*, they were of Danish origin and settled around Dublin in early times, having a dominant hold on Irish affairs until the battle of Clontarf in 1014. In the aftermath of King Brian Boru's victory, many Segraves fled Ireland and those that remained settled outside the city boundaries in Oxmantown and Cabragh, which in a later century became absorbed into the English Pale.

From the late 1500s the Segraves were enmeshed in the politics of Ireland and saw military service in many conflicts, including the battle of Clontibret, County Monaghan, in 1595, during Hugh O'Neill and Hugh O'Donnell's Nine Years War against Elizabethan England. In the *Annals of the Four Masters* and in

Cabragh House, Ratoath Road, *circa* 1912 (Courtesy NLI)

a more concise form in the *Irish Literary Gazette*, there is a detailed account of this famous battle, fought on the banks of the small stream, the Oona. General Norris, commanding 3000 well-armed English troops, made two vain attempts to cross the stream. A troop of English cavalry led by Captain James Segrave of Cabragh – who was considered their chief champion and the most valiant man in the English Pale – impetuously galloped forward to engage in single combat with Hugh O'Neill, the Earl of Tyrone. The two horsemen met and the lance of each was splintered on the other's breastplate. Segrave flung himself onto the Earl and the two rolled together to the ground. Following hand-to-hand combat, the Earl succeeded in killing Captain Segrave.

Cabragh House became the pride of the Segrave family and its superiority over another family property at Finglaswood is apparent from its valuation, which was five times greater at £1400. Jacobean refinement was evident in its design and decoration. The *Commonwealth Survey* described it as 'surrounded by several gardens, orchards and parks, planted with ornamental trees'. Substantial outhouses and farm buildings, were, like the house, built of stone with tiled roofs. The outhouses consisted of a brewery, a dairy, two stables, a coach house, two barns, a malthouse and ox-house. The main rooms, including the hall, parlour and great bed-chamber, were wainscotted and some of the bed-chambers were decorated with cornices of wood from which tapestries were suspended.

In his will, executed in 1621, the devotion of Walter Segrave to the Roman Catholic faith is evidenced by a project, in his own or his wife's name, for the maintenance of candidates for the priesthood – from which he anticipated that not only 'the founder and giver under God' but also his executors 'might reap benefit'. He also directed that three of his best gowns and his wrought-velvet coat be sold and the proceeds be 'devoted for pious uses'. His generous character is further revealed by his care and compassion for the poor of the city and his assistance to St John's Hospital.

During the reign of Queen Anne, John Segrave occupied the property. He was licensed 'to carry sword and firearms'. He is believed to have carried out the reconstruction and additions at the mansion that remained in place until its demolition in 1939. A hiding chamber for a priest on the upper floor led to a vertical passage in the wall to the ground floor. It was remarkable for its fine wood panelling and an exquisitely carved late-Jacobean-style chimney-piece from one of the rooms, on loan to the National Museum of Ireland in 1900.

At the close of Queen Anne's reign John was succeeded by his son Henry, brought up in the very best traditions of the Roman Catholic faith, and according to the *Calendar of State Papers* Cabra became known as the 'resort of priests, Jesuits and friars'. When the Rising of 1641 broke out Henry was arrested and although there were various allegations that he had sympathy with the leaders of the Rising and 'ill tales told of him in the Swan of Thomas Street', no overt act was proved and he was soon released. During the Cromwell era (the Commonwealth of 1650-60) he was forced to leave Cabra for London, where he gave 'financial aid towards the Restoration'. The house became the residence of Colonel Sir Hierome Sankey, who had a flamboyant lifestyle. After the restoration of Charles II in 1660 the property was returned to John Segrave, who as 'an innocent papist' recovered all his estate. It was then rated as containing eleven hearths and a kiln.

John Segrave, a Colonel in a Volunteer corps, took over Cabra House on the death of his father Neill in 1777; after John's death the house passed to the Right Honorable Denis Daly, the father of the first Lord Dunstable, who was a gifted orator in Grattan's Parliament with few rivals. After the premature death of Daly in 1791, the property came into the possession of the extraordinary Lord Norbury, the hanging judge, whose tenure is chronicled separately. Following Norbury's death in 1831 the Segraves once more took possession of Cabragh House, although in 1870 Neill Segrave let it, along with forty-two acres of land, to Peter Henry. The house and lands were valued at £167, with the house on its own commanding £28. On the Ordnance Survey map of 1873 the Segraves are shown to own 148 acres at Broome Ville, Broome Lodge and Ballyboggan, all in present-day Cabra.

Charles Segrave, born in Wolverhampton, England, came back to Ireland following the death of his wife and lived for a short spell in the family home at Cabragh House. He later remarried (to one Jessica Stone) and settled in Kildreenan, near Kiltimon, County Wicklow. The Segrave family finally left Cabragh House in 1912. Charles' son, Henry Segrave, was born in Baltimore, USA, on 22 September 1896. Henry joined the British army at the beginning of the First World War and was injured in May 1915 while serving with the Warwickshire Regiment; the following year he joined the Royal Air Force at just nineteen years of age and was shot down twice. He resigned from military service at the end of the war and in 1920 took up motor racing, becoming a household name throughout the English-speaking world. He first travelled to Washington, where he started to drive on the racetracks. His initial venture was to put his own 60-horsepower Apperson race-car around a two-mile track at Sheepshead Bay, Long Island, reaching a speed of 82 miles per hour. In 1923 he won the French Grand Prix and in 1924 the Spanish Grand Prix; in March 1929 he became holder of the world land speed record, recording 231.21 miles per hour with his 23-litre Irving Napier Golden Arrow, in Daytona, USA. He then took up motorboat racing, winning many events in England before achieving his first major water-racing title, the German Championship, in July 1929. That September he won the European Championship, the Prince of Piedmont Cup, at Venice Lido, Italy; he raced in his boat *Miss England I* and captured the world record for water speed.

Miss England II

Henry Segrave was constantly setting world records for water speed. Ever ambitious to beat each preceding record, he bought a powerful motor racing boat, *Miss England II*, in 1930 for £25,000, a huge sum in those days. *Miss England II* was the second in the series and was originally built for a Lord Wakefield. Designed by Mr F. Cooper and built by Messrs Saunders-Roe, it had a displacement of four-and-a-half tons and was powered by two 12-cylinder Rolls-Royce 'R' engines, each developing 1850 horsepower. The quantity of instruments meant that two mechanics had to be taken on board, with seating installed.

With a new attack on the world water-speed record looming, the boat arrived at Borwick's Boathouse, Bowness, in the English Lake District, on 1 June 1930. The official launch of the vessel by Lord Wakefield took place on 5 June, to great public interest. From the outset, the propeller gave trouble. A screw-type propeller, it was fifteen inches in diameter and driven by the Rolls-Royce engines at 12,500 rpm. Unable to resist the tremendous water pressure at great speeds, three different propellers smashed. A fourth was fitted and on Friday 13 June 1930 the boat was towed into position, with Henry Segrave in his wicker chair at the centre of the controls and sitting on either side of him his trusted engineers, Michael Willcocks and Victor 'Vic' Halliwell. Disaster struck this ambitious attempt to achieve a new world record when Henry Segrave lost his life on Lake Windermere, aged thirty-four, having attained a speed of over 100 miles per hour with *Miss England II* before it went out of control. Vic Halliwell also died in the crash but Michael Willcocks, a former chief motor mechanic for the Admiralty, survived and even helped to rebuild *Miss England II*. He went on to ride with Kaye Don, who raced *Miss England II* during successful world-record attempts in Italy and Argentina.

Major Henry Segrave at Bowness (Courtesy Windemere Steamboat Museum)

Miss England II (Courtesy Windemere Steamboat Museum)

Not only was Henry Segrave a record-breaking racing driver, he was the inventor of the racing helmet as we now know it and was accepted as one of the pioneers of aerodynamics in association with racing cars. He married Doris Stocker in 1917 and they had no children.

In the early 1900s Archdeacon Segrave of St Peter's Roman Catholic Church, Drogheda, County Louth, was a distinguished member of the family and was always proud of his connections with Cabragh. There is a plaque to his honour in St Peter's with the following inscription:

> *The organ of this Church was erected by the Cardinal Primate, the priests of the Archdiocese and the people of the parish, as a memorial to the Right Reverend Monsignor Segrave, Parish Priest of St Peter's, 1900-1934, Vicar General and Archdeacon of Armagh, He died 13 February 1934. Behold a great priest.*

The Demise of Cabragh House

Phil Callaghan was the last resident before Cabragh House was demolished in 1939. He made a living allowing cattle to graze overnight on the seventy acres then attached to the property, prior to the livestock being taken along Ratoath Road and Old Cabra Road to the Dublin cattle market at Prussia Street; Mrs McCann, who lived in a nearby lodge, did Phil's housework and laundry. There was a small gate lodge at the front entrance to Cabragh House, at Cabra Cross; Jimmy Maher, who worked for the Keoghs, dairy-farmers, lived here until 1940. Attached to the main property was a small cottage, occupied by Julia Farrell until the outbreak of the Second World War. In addition a small farmhouse on six acres was attached to the estate and in 1870 this particular property was let to John O'Keeffe by O'Neill Segrave. The construction of the local authority housing scheme of Cabra West began in 1939, on the Cabra House estate and adjoining land, compulsory purchased for that purpose.

In the Segrave Papers now on deposit in the National Library of Ireland, 224 deeds dated prior to 1709 relate to lands in Ashtown, Cabragh, Castleknock and Finglaswood. The earliest deed bears the date of 1 September 1350 and is a lease by Hugh, son of Simon Laughles (Lawless) to John Seriaunt. Another lease, undated but evidently anterior to the 1350 one, is a conveyance by Hugo de Ellam to Simon Laeles of lands in Cabragh called Acketh Netithan, the names of adjoining lands being specified in detail. Later deeds include transactions with the O'Neills of Shane's Castle, County Antrim, the Sarsfields of Lucan and many well-known Dublin families. They also contain information about Dublin shopkeepers and street names of the eighteenth century. For example, there are seven rentals, on loose sheets, for the Cabragh Estate from 1753 (when 44 tenants paid £1372 in rent) to 1791 (when 38 tenants paid £2417 in rent).

Lord Norbury – the Hanging Judge

Cabragh House has left an indelible mark on the people of Cabra West in the form of the folklore about its most infamous occupant, John Toler, who came to live there in 1791. A descendant of a New Model Army soldier who had been given land in County Tipperary as part of the 'Plantation' policy of Oliver Cromwell, John Toler attained his prominent position as an assizes judge thanks to his ardent support for union with Great Britain. As a Member of Parliament he represented the borough of Philipstown and he used this position to secure his appointment as Solicitor General. Using systematic bribery and corruption, he gained the title of Lord Norbury and reached the Bench, where he became a corrupt and feared judge.

It was Lord Norbury, accompanied on the Bench by Mr Baron George and Mr Baron Daily, who tried and sentenced Robert Emmet to death on 19 September 1803. The 25-year-old Emmet had organized and led an ill-fated insurrection in the Thomas Street area of Dublin against British rule in Ireland. During the trial Norbury constantly harangued and insulted the defendant, interrupting as Robert Emmet delivered his eloquent speech from the dock of the courthouse at Green Street – 'you have endeavoured to establish a wicked and bloody provisional government' – before sentencing him to death. The metal rail of the dock that Robert Emmet held while delivering his speech is preserved in a glass showcase within the confines of the courthouse. That speech concluded with the following words: 'When my country has taken her place among the nations of the earth, then, and not 'till then, let my epitaph be written. I have done.' The trial lasted just one day and concluded with the passing of the death sentence. He was executed the following day, 20 September 1803, outside St Catherine's Church, Thomas Street. In 1914 Sidney Olcott, an Irish-Canadian, made a film on the patriot's life called *Robert Emmet, Ireland's Martyr*. The British military censors objected, claiming that it was 'interfering with the military recruitment drives in Ireland', and it was withdrawn. The Irish Volunteers in Killarney used the 'guns' which Olcott brought into Ireland to be used as film props while taking part in a ceremonial military parade in the town.

Norbury had a warped sense of humour. When asked to give a shilling subscription towards the burial of a solicitor, he responded, 'Here is a guinea, bury one and twenty of them.' Receiving a death sentence on the twentieth day of June, a defendant cried out, 'Ah, My Lord, give me a long day.' Norbury replied with a smirk: 'Your wish is granted, I will give you until tomorrow, the longest day in the year.' Where he could not in law impose a death penalty, he ordered deportation to New South Wales, Australia (Botany Bay), breaking the heart and spirit of the unfortunate defendants and their family and friends. He insulted the patriot Napper Tandy, who challenged him to a duel, which never materialized. Such was his infamy as a harsh and cruel administrator of 'justice' that Daniel O'Connell, the Great Liberator, felt bound to petition Parliament to have him removed from the Bench.

An old document that tells us that at a single assizes Norbury sentenced 198 individuals to death while wearing the black hat on his head, laughing and joking as if the whole matter were a comedy. He died on 27 July 1831. At his funeral, while the coffin was being lowered into the grave, a voice from the crowd cried out: 'Give him rope galore, boys, for when he was alive he never spared it.' The British Crown rewarded him well for his services; in addition to Cabragh House he also owned a townhouse in the city at 3 Great Denmark Street.

His legend still lives on: locals say that late at night the clatter of a horse's hooves can be heard and a cold gust of wind felt. Many older people recall seeing a dark, cloaked shape on a white horse on Ratoath Road late at night – the ghost of Lord Norbury. There were quite a number of reported sightings during the Second World War (the 'Emergency' in Ireland). Poet Rose O'Driscoll, who was born in Tipperkevin in County Wicklow in 1910, came to Cabra West in 1941 after the North Strand Bombing, settling on Carnlough Road. Well known in the district, her collection of poetry *Rose of Cabra* was published in 1993; she died in 1999. Her poem about the infamous hanging judge is entitled 'The Ghost of Lord Norbury':

> On Ratoath Road he rides along
> You can see his white knee-britches
> He hits his horse with a leather thong
> And jumps imaginary ditches
> The clatter of hoofs on the pavement
> Can be heard both loud and clear
> It is Lord Norbury out for a ride
> Complete with riding gear
>
> He sentenced men to hanging
> Evidence refused for each
> Among them Robert Emmet
> Who made that famous speech
> Napper Tandy challenged him
> Saying he was cruel
> Norbury got cold feet
> He refused the duel
>
> He still rides around Cabra West
> Or so the legend says

Cause the devil would not have him
When he heard that he was dead
If you see Napper Tandy
Shake him by the hand
He is looking for Lord Norbury
His revenge is planned.

Cabra Villa

Cabra Villa stood directly opposite Cabragh House, on the corner of present-day Fassaugh Avenue and Broombridge Road. It appears on the 1838 Ordnance Survey map. For nearly sixty years it was inhabited by the Keoghs, a noted local farming family. Christopher J. Keogh came to Cabra in 1880, along with his wife Anne (*née* Collins); he subsequently acquired three properties in the area, Broombridge House, Cabra Villa and Villa Park, none of which remain today. Christopher J. was a County Meath man who had a reputation as a good judge of the hunting horse. His son Christopher was born here on 8 May 1908; Christopher J. died at Cabra Villa on 12 April 1930. The Keoghs were instrumental in setting up the meat factory in Leixlip, County Kildare.

There were seven acres attaching to Cabra Villa and the Keoghs used this land to engage in dairying, with 'a modest trade of three hundred gallons a day'. In 1939 Cabra Villa was acquired by Dublin Corporation for the provision of local authority housing. Christopher then decided to 'move as far from Dublin so that I would never again be the subject of a compulsory purchase order' and acquired a farm at Finnstown, 'in the countryside, near the village of Lucan'; his mother Anne moved into nearby Broombridge House, where she was living prior to her death on 30 October 1945.

Beside Cabra Villa there was a small outbuilding with a pointed front and a figure over the door of a bearded face, which local people believed was that of Lord Norbury. It was not, according to Christopher Keogh, an image of the notorious hanging judge 'as he was always clean-shaven'. Peter Kearney lived in this house. When I visited Christopher Keogh at Finnstown House in 1982 before it was sold and turned into a boutique hotel, he related how he thought the head was part of what was once a crucifix and that the building might have served as a chapel, possibly a Penal chapel. Its proximity to the Segrave property at Cabragh House makes this likely. Cabra people who settled in the area recalled seeing the head, which disappeared when the old buildings were demolished. Cabra Villa was also once a Rathborne residence, and Christopher recalled a long loft at the back of the residence with the name Henry Rathborne carved out on a wooden beam over the entrance door. Christopher later retired to his daughter's home in Garristown, County Dublin, and died on 21 September 1988.

Christopher's brother Julius lived in Broombridge House, just over the canal at Broome Bridge, on the right-hand side as one heads out of Cabra West towards Ballyboggan Road and Finglas. He became the biggest salesmaster in the Dublin cattle market, selling between five- and six-hundred head of cattle on market days. This well-known character appears to be part of the local folklore of the district and was a much-liked and much spoken-about individual. He died on Christmas Day in 1980. St Joseph's School for Deaf Boys set up home on former Segrave land, near Cabra Villa and Cabragh House.

St Joseph's School for Deaf Boys

The joint efforts of Monsignor William Yore, parish priest of St Paul's Roman Catholic Church, Arran Quay and his counterpart at St Peter's, Phibsborough, Fr Thomas McNamara, resulted in the founding of deaf schools in Cabra. In September 1845 Monsignor Yore, known as the St Vincent de Paul of Ireland, took the first steps that led to their foundation. Willing helpers rallied to his call and on 22 December 1845 a preliminary meeting was held at the White Cross, 34 Upper Ormond Quay. Those present included Monsignor Yore, Fr McNamara, Rev. Dr Dowley, Redmond O'Carroll, James O'Farrell, William Kelly, Richard O'Reilly and Thomas Willis.

A committee was formed under the guiding hand of its President, Dr Murray, Archbishop of Dublin and on 5 January 1846 it met for the first time, under the chairmanship of Monsignor Yore. This committee, later known as the Catholic Institute for the Deaf, secured premises at a rental of £15 a year at Prospect, Glasnevin. This became the Monastery or Prospect Seminary, a word then used for a boarding school. It was inaugurated on 2 February 1849 and named St Joseph's, with just four boys on the roll. By 1851 thirty-five boys had enrolled,

Aerial view of St Joseph's, Cabra, early 1940s (Courtesy Irish Air Corps)

increasing to seventy in 1853: this resulted in overcrowding and led to the rental of a house in nearby Florinda Place.

To extend St Joseph's, Herculean fundraising efforts were made by the committee, aided by the decision of Dr Yore to raffle his entire library and donate the proceeds to the project, a gesture that raised £1570. The committee later opted for a new building, to be erected on a site at the junction of Great Navan Road and Old Cabra Road. Plans were drawn up by Mr Geoghegan, architect, for a school to accommodate one hundred boys with provision for future expansion. The foundation stone was laid by Archbishop Cullen on 9 June 1856 and completed at a cost of £11,000.

In November 1856 the committee secured the services of the Christian Brothers in the running of the new school, which opened in October 1857 under a blaze of publicity. Numerous reports of this historic occasion in Irish education appeared in the *Freeman's Journal* and *The Weekly Freeman* of 3 October 1857. Monsignor Yore continued as chairman of the committee until his death on 13 February 1864; he is buried in the O'Connell Circle, Glasnevin Cemetery, and his magnificent headstone was erected by the Dublin Cemeteries Committee. Although not a common name in Dublin, there are many headstones bearing the Yore surname in the small rural village cemetery at Dromiskin, County Louth. Monsignor Yore was himself a founding member of the Dublin Cemeteries Committee and like Daniel O'Connell was of the opinion that the cemetery should be available to all, irrespective of their religion; his proposal led to the Rev. William Maturin of All Saint's Church, Grangegorman, receiving a yearly stipend to officiate at the burial services of Church of Ireland members at Glasnevin, a duty discharged by William until 1853.

The lands of St Joseph's are part of the Segrave Cabragh property and through the efforts of Fr McNamara a lease forever was obtained from the land-lord, Captain O'Neill Segrave. On the Ordnance Survey map of 1873 a chapel and a small building marked 'Hospital', adjoining each other, are shown, indicating the chapel attached to St Joseph's and the school infirmary. In 1869 during the governorship of Br McDonnell, the east block of the main building was constructed and a refectory and chapel added, at a total cost of £5000. Later additions took place in the 1870s during the governorship of Rev. Brother Wickham, with the imposing West Wing. It was intended as a schoolroom and assembly hall; the schoolroom, 154 feet in length and forty feet in width, was described as 'one of the finest halls in the British Isles at this time, appropriated to educational purposes'. During this period the grounds were improved and landscaped. Other extensions and renovations followed, including the front lodge and model farmyard build-ings, constructed during the years 1886 to 1889.

In 1987 a new complex of schools and residential houses was completed on the site; there are nine separate buildings in the 'Deaf Village', including six resi-dential blocks, an assembly hall, gymnasium and offices. At this time it was one of the most modern schools for deaf boys in Europe. In 1990 the Irish Christian Brothers sold off five acres of land at the apex of the site bordering Ratoath and Navan Road and a small, compact housing development, called Pinehurst, was built on the site. The old front lodge was renovated and retained and some mature trees were incorporated into the landscape of the complex. In 1999 the Irish Christian Brothers ceased to be in charge of St Joseph's and the school got its first lay principal. Further redevelopments followed and in 2001 the old school building was demolished.

Throughout the years former pupils have made immense contributions in a variety of fields, including sport, industry and the arts. The following are just some of the many who have made their mark on the patchwork of Irish life:

William Carr: William was a pupil in St Joseph's in the early 1900s and on graduating established a lucrative tailoring business in Roscommon. During the school's Jubilee Year of 1933 he was selected by the past pupils to present an address to His Holiness, Pope Pius XI.

Peter Desmond Farrell: Born in 1922, he followed a successful career in soccer on graduating from St Joseph's and played with Shamrock Rovers, winning successive FAI Cup winners medals in 1944 and 1945; in August 1946 he moved to Everton for a transfer fee of £10,000. He became a Merseyside legend, playing 453 games for Everton; a road in Liverpool, Farrell Close, is named in his honour. Capped twenty eight times for Ireland, he featured in the historic tie against England at Goodison Park, Liverpool in September 1949, when Ireland scored a sensational 2–0 win over their hosts. He died in 1999.

Thomas Gallagher: During his school days in Cabra Thomas was outstanding among his peers with his football skills. A keen lover of Gaelic football, he joined his local GAA club on graduating from St Joseph's and soon gained the highest honours in the sport. In 1953 he was selected to play on the minor team for his native county. That same year Mayo won the Connaught Championship. With Mayo he went on to become the proud holder of an All-Ireland Championship Medal.

Michael O'Farrell: The following reference to a model of the 1921 Cork Exhibition, made by Limerick-born Michael and taken from that year's publication of the *Roman Catholic Deaf-mute of Brooklyn* indicates the ability and talent of yet another St Joseph's pupil: 'It is not often that we hear of a deaf-mute succeeding in such an undertaking as is here chronicled, and we are glad to be able to give prominence to it. Mr Michael O'Farrell, deaf-mute carpenter, has made an enviable reputation for himself by completing a model of the Cork Exhibition, according to scale. Those who have seen it say that it is perfect in every detail and it was highly commended by the Lord Mayor of Cork. It is about five feet square, and comprises seven halls or departments of the Exhibition'.

The ideals and aspirations of those early founders of St Joseph's, and the hard work of those who helped build the wonderful narrative of compassion and care for those with hearing and speech difficulties has left a lasting legacy.

However, mention should also be made of sexual abuse and rape within the confines of the complex during the twentieth century. This resulted in blighted, and in some cases destroyed, lives and constant battles with addiction and lack of confidence. The story of sexual abuse and rape is recorded in the Ryan Report, in which an entire chapter is devoted to St Joseph's; that Commission of Inquiry found that physical and emotional abuse made the school 'a very frightening place' and that 'sexual activity was ignored or tolerated for some considerable time' until the Health Board eventually intervened. The abuse was carried out by a number of Christian Brothers, and also by lay people, at the school between the 1950s and early 1990s. In later years, senior boys were also accused of abusing younger pupils. The story of the survivors of abuse was highlighted in an RTÉ documentary by Garry Keane entitled *If These Walls Could Talk*; that programme also included some positive experiences of former pupils at St Joseph's and was first aired in October 2015.

The most recent development at St Joseph's has been the construction of the Inspire Fitness Centre inside the old farm entrance on Ratoath Road. Its facilities are open to the wider public. The whole landscape of the Navan Road, as viewed from Cabra Cross, has changed considerably over the past twenty years, firstly with the demolition of the old school in 2001 and, in 2015, with the construction and inauguration of the new four-storey Primary Health Care Centre.

Opposite the original entrance to St Joseph's, on the corner of Ratoath Road and Cabra Road, stood a once-familiar landmark, Rosecourt. On one acre of rose trees and manicured lawns, Rosecourt was once the family home of the City Surveyor, father of the well-known Dr Moynihan of Phibsborough. He bought the site and built a six-bedroom home to his own specifications, designed by the President of the English College of Architects, Sir Edwin Lutyens, who was also responsible for the Whitehall Cenotaph in London. Many a Cabra person recalls the house for its beautiful, well-kept gardens. On the death of his father, Dr Moynihan came into possession of the house; however, after his own wife died he settled in Dalymount Terrace, Phibsborough. He was physician to Bohemian Football Club for many years. His son, Johnny Moynihan, is the Irish musician who in the mid-1960s was a founding member of the traditional music group Sweeney's Men; he later played with a number of well-known groups, including Planxty and Dé Dannan. Rosecourt was demolished in the late 1960s to make way for an apartment complex, constructed in 1971.

A public telephone kiosk and a letterbox were situated on the footpath outside Rosecourt, on the corner of Ratoath Road and Cabra Road; on the opposite side, at the former entrance to the farm at St Joseph's, was a water trough where market-bound cattle would drink; all features have long since disappeared.

Nephin Road

Nephin Road was called Blind Lane until the late 1940s, even though it was not a blind lane or cul-de-sac, but a complete thoroughfare connecting Ratoath Road with Windy Harbour and Blackhorse Lane (now Blackhorse Avenue). The present alignment of Nephin Road, from Navan Road to Ratoath Road, changed from the early 1940s. Nephin Park, renamed John Paul II Park after the Pope landed by helicopter there during his historic visit to Ireland in 1979, is more commonly known as 'the Bogeys'. This name may have resulted from the fact that there were disused cattle bogeys on the adjacent railway line at Reilly's Bridge during the early 1940s. The road sign on the nearby roundabout, inscribed 'The Bogeys Roundabout', alludes to the colloquial name. The popular Fianna Fáil TD Richard 'Dickie' Gogan, who represented the area in Dáil Éireann during the 1950s and early 1960s, lived at 122 Nephin Road.

Cabra Farm stood at the junction of Blind Lane and the Great Navan Road, directly opposite the present-day garda station. A long building with a thatched roof, it was the home of James Reid, a Poor Law Guardian and a member of the Board of Dublin County Council. He had about thirty horses in paddocks on the farm, which were used to plough the land and also to transport the produce to the Dublin Fruit and Vegetable Markets. He employed over thirty women from the Liberties and Gloucester Street areas of the city in the weeding and harvesting of crops; horse-drawn carts would ferry these women to and from the city. It was replaced by a more modern two-storey detached house in the first half of the last century, on the site of the original thatched cottage. This house, surrounded by a huge array of shrubs, trees (especially cherry blossoms) and bushes, was noted for the birdsong emanating from the confines of its large walled garden. The garden became silent after it was cleared following the sale and demolition of the house in 2008; the site has lain vacant and boarded up since then.

Cabra Garda Station lies at junction of Nephin Road and Navan Road. It was established in 1927 and was originally in the Phoenix Park, in the building that formerly served as the laundry for the Viceregal Lodge. The first Station Sergeant was Jack Finlay. One of the first Gardaí there was Con O'Connor, a native of Cahirciveen, County Kerry. On 22 August 1926 at an event in Abbeyleix, he cleared six foot five-and-a-half inches in the high jump. The ground and height were measured by an engineer and officials but the world record was not granted because of the absence of a steel measuring tape. He became Irish National High Jump Champion in 1926 and joint holder of the title in 1927, 1929 and 1934. In Con's time at Cabra about twenty-five Gardaí were stationed there. He retired from the force and lived out his retirement years in Villa Park, not far from the Garda Station.

In the early 1960s the demands on the Gardaí grew as the population of the surrounding districts expanded and in 1962 a new, purpose-built garda sStation was built. In the early years the local Gardaí developed a close link with the people of the area, particularly the youth, and many a Cabra person can happily recall the dances in St Finbarr's Hall and day trips to Butlins, Arklow, Bray and other seaside resorts, organized by Garda Mick Hayden and colleagues attached to the station during the 1940s and 1950s. Later generations remember the contribution of Garda Hugh Tierney and others to the local youth clubs during the 1970s.

The station still has a connection with the youth of the area and the Community Garda Unit run the TaG (Teenagers and Gardaí) programme in conjunction with Cabra for Youth; juveniles between fourteen and sixteen years, identified by the JLO (Junior Liaison Officer) Unit, are invited to join the eight-week programme. Activities include fishing, go-carting and mountain-biking. They also give talks in schools, building up a relationship with young people. The Community Garda Unit comprises five Gardaí under the direction of Sergeant Patrick 'Pat' McGilloway. In stark contrast with the early years at the station, five of the six Gardaí attached to the unit are native Dubliners. With the cutbacks in recent years, the station's public office no longer operates on a twenty-four hour basis, closing at 9 pm each evening until 7 am the following morning.

St Declan's College, Nephin Road, is located beside the Bogeys' Roundabout. Secondary education for boys came to Cabra due to the exertions of the first parish priest of Cabra West, Canon Valentine Burke, who invited the Christian

Brothers to establish a secondary college for boys. Work began in the late 1950s and in September 1960 the school opened its doors. The original building initially catered for an intake of two classes and consisted of eight classrooms, a science laboratory, staffroom and two administrative offices.

By the mid-1960s further expansion was imperative. Prefabricated class-rooms were erected as a temporary measure in 1967 to cater for an intake of three classrooms per year. Plans were drawn up in 1969 for an extension of the college and the construction of a Brothers' residence within the school complex on the instructions of Rev. Br Thomas O'Dowd, a colourful Kerryman nicknamed 'the Dude', principal of St Declan's from 1960 until his retirement in 1974. The resi-dence was duly built but the college extension was postponed. Finally, monies were made available and on 27 October 1977 the Lord Mayor of Dublin, Alderman Michael Collins, cut the first sod for the new extension and a sports complex. The work was completed in 1980, with an expanded curriculum incorporating new subjects like metalwork, woodwork and arts. The sports complex is also open to people and groups from the area and beyond.

Dominican Convent

Around the corner from St Declan's, in the direction of Finglas, lies the Dominican Convent. The Dominicans came to Ireland at the request of Strongbow, the Earl of Pembroke, and his wife Aoife, daughter of Dermot McMurragh, saying it was 'for the health of my soul and that of Eva'. By 1717 the nuns had settled in Channel Row Convent, Brunswick Street, which later became the Chapel Ward of the Richmond Hospital. The Channel Row Convent chapel became noted for its excellent standard of music and during the Christmas celebrations of 1746 the hymn '*Adeste Fidelis*' was sung for the first time. Notable Italian artists gave their services at High Masses in the convent and 'in consequence a numerous and fash-ionable congregation including many from other faiths attended choral services' during the years 1725 to 1765. Although this was during the time of the Penal Laws, and the nuns were publicly defying them, they apparently escaped prose-cution and persecution when it was found that the laws did not apply to women. From 1809 to 1819 the Dominican nuns, having failed to get a renewal of their lease on Channel Row House, temporarily moved to Vernon Avenue, Clontarf.

Aerial view of the Dominican Convent, Ratoath Road, Cabra, 1940
(Courtesy Irish Air Corps)

In May 1819 they purchased an old Segrave mansion on a twelve-acre site on Ratoath Road, beside the Royal Canal. The Cromwellian Survey of 1654 states that not only was this particular Segrave mansion built of stone and roofed with tiles, but that it had a brewery, a dairy, stables and a coalhouse connected to it. The transfer of the nuns from their temporary premises at Clontarf was made on 12 December 1819 and they set about the task of opening a school for poor children, St Catherine's Poor (or free) School, in 1820. Sister Mary Magdalen (christened Matilda Martha Butler) was the first nun to be professed at Cabra, on 28 December 1819. She became head of novices at St Catherine's. She left Cabra in October 1839 to establish a fee-paying convent school 'for upper-class girls' at Mount Street, of which she was the superior; the few novices then at Cabra followed her, which resulted in some strain between the two convents. The following year she moved the school to Sion Hill, Blackrock. She died in 1856 in Drogheda, County Louth.

In 1832 the nuns placed themselves under the jurisdiction of the Archbishop of Dublin and three years later, in 1835, opened a boarding school for boys and girls. In 1846 Fr Thomas McNamara of St Peter's, Phibsborough, obtained the agreement of the Cabra Dominican Sisters to undertake the education of deaf girls and he is acknowledged as the founder of St Mary's Deaf School. The nuns kindly offered to provide temporary accommodation for a limited number of girls. Fr McNamara made arrangements for two nuns 'accompanied by two deaf-mute girls' to go to Le Bon Sauveur, an institution for 'the education of deaf mutes' in Caen, Normandy, France, founded by the Abbé Pierre Jamet. From January to August 1846, the Cabra visitors were 'the objects of unbounded hospitality' at Caen. On their return the two nuns went about setting up a school for deaf girls at Cabra, established that same year. Additional buildings were later erected. Today the primary school section is called the Marian School and is situated in the grounds of the Dominican Convent: this modern, purpose-built school was officially opened in 1988; post-primary pupils are accommodated in Rosary School.

In 1851 construction on the chapel began and this building was extended in 1905. In 1865 a new primary school was built. Over the years various additions were made to the primary school and convent. As the surrounding area became built up in the late-1930s, the necessity for a new primary school became apparent. So in 1942 plans were drawn up and on 16 November 1943 construction began. In September 1944 the new primary school, St Catherine's Infant Schools (mixed) and Senior School (for girls) opened its doors; in 1975 there were over 500 pupils attending; in 2011 that figure was 128 with class sizes varying from ten to nineteen boys and girls. The senior school is involved in the Green Schools Initiative and has recently been awarded its third Green Flag, for conserving water.

Entrance. St. Mary's Dominican Convent, Cabra, Dublin.

Dominican Convent, Ratoath Road. The entrance was a terminus for the Number 22 bus during the 1950s and 60s (Courtesy Seamus Kearns Postcard Collection)

Convent View Cottages are located just over the wall dividing the Dominican Convent and the Bogeys, opposite Ventry Drive. These were built during the 1800s following the passing of an Act of Parliament authorizing the construction of workers' cottages on the Blind Lane, also called Cabra Lane. After the realignment of the lane and its transformation into Nephin Road during the mid-1900s, the cottages were given an exit onto Ratoath Road. In the mid-1970s Dublin Corporation built a sheltered independent living complex for elderly people on what was a large, vacant site between the cottages and the Bogeys. Similar cottages were built on Navan Road, opposite Cabra Garda Station, called Roosevelt Cottages.

Reilly's Bridge

Passing the Dominican Convent towards Finglas, the next local landmark is Reilly's Bridge, named after Henry Stevens Reilly, a Director of the Royal Canal Company. On either side of this bridge one can see the smooth grooves that have been worn into the stone by the ropes, from the time when the barges were towed by horse. Reilly's will went through the legal formalities in 1803, so he did not live to see the canal functioning as a commercial enterprise. According to the map issued by John Taylor in 1828, this bridge was for a time called Suir Road Bridge. However, the first Ordnance Survey in 1837 restored Reilly's name to the bridge; ironically one of the roads in the Finglas Industrial Estate, near Broombridge, is called Suir Road.

There was a level crossing just before Reilly's Bridge, where the Dublin to Galway railway line cut across Ratoath Road. A rather strange map, produced in 1840 for the Report of the Railway Commissioners, shows a 'ghost railway' at the level crossing, a line that was to run parallel to the Galway line as far as Dunsink, where it was to branch out and travel via Mulhuddart to Navan, County Meath. The level crossing gates were operated for many years by Hubert Plunkett, who came to Cabra in 1937. Hubert resided at that time in Clairville, which was located on Ventry Park, before moving into the redbrick railway cottage on the canal side of the railway track: it was demolished around 2008. The area around Reilly's Bridge was brought into the twenty-first century in 2015, when the new fly-over bridge with metal spans, reminiscent of the halcyon days of the railways, was opened. The old level crossing gates were then removed and the old stone bridge is now permanently closed to traffic.

Hubert's old home, Clairville, was subsequently a meeting place for the local presidium of the Legion of Mary. It also served as headquarters for Naomh Fionnbarra GAA Club, formed in 1942 to cater for the social needs of the youth of the area. Founding members included Jack Casserly, Ned Wholohan, Joe Brady and Bill Bracken Snr. Joe Brady from Dingle Road, Cabra West recalls those early years: 'We used to buy trees and cut them up outside our houses, on the footpath. We would then bag the logs and sell them locally, the proceeds going towards the running of the teams.' Club successes include Junior Football Champions 1954 and 1961, Intermediate Football Champions 1966 and Intermediate Hurling Champions 1973. Naomh Fionnbarra was once again crowned Dublin Intermediate Hurling Champions in 2009, following a 2-10 to 2-08 victory over Round Towers at Parnell Park on 25 October 2009. The club's headquarters are located in the old Dublin Corporation Playground, Fassaugh Avenue. In the early 1990s Clairville was vacated and demolished; four terraced local-authority houses were built on the site.

Broombridge Road

Broombridge Road takes its name from the bridge over the canal, called after William Broome, one of the directors of the Royal Canal Company. During the later part of the nineteenth century there were a few houses on Broombridge Road and four of these appear on the 1873 Ordnance Survey map: Broome Ville, beside Ventry Road; Broome Lodge, near the junction of Carnlough Road and Broombridge Road; Broombridge House and Tolka Park, both just over the bridge on the Finglas side, on the site of the present-day Broombridge Industrial Estate. There was a small house beside Broome Ville during the 1800s called Broomfield House. In 1870 it was occupied by one Michael Beirne, the house and land being valued at £14 per annum.

Joe Mooney lived in Tolka Park, sited on seven acres of farmland, with access past a small gate lodge on Broombridge Road. A kind man, he was better known to many thousands of Cabra folk as 'Beano'. Every summer he organized the youth of the district into clearing parties, giving them hooks attached to long pieces of wire to take out scrap metal dumped in the canal during the previous year. He paid for what was taken out, providing a useful source of pocket money for the local children. He then collected the scrap in the evening and brought it into his yard, before taking it into the city on his horse and cart to be sold to scrap merchants there. Sometimes the bigger lads would sneak into his yard, remove some scrap and sell it to him the following day, having dipped it in the canal so as to appear that it had just been removed from it. Beano was one of those great Dublin characters around the time of the housing schemes, and made his way into the folklore of Cabra.

At the bottom of Broombridge Road, where it meets Ballyboggan Road, was the entrance to an old Dublin Corporation tiphead, where many a dumped Ford Anglia had its roof sawn off so that it could be used as a raft on the Royal Canal; an orange box served as a seat and wooden planks as oars. At the end of the day the raft was sunk among the reeds, to be retrieved on the next occasion, if it had not been commandeered by another group of adventurous children in the meantime. The dump's entrance was at the present pedestrian barriers, which now separate Cabra from Finglas South. These were erected to prevent motorized traffic entering Tolka Valley Park. In a small cottage next to the entrance, on Ballyboggan Road, lived the Rices. For over thirty years, up to the early 1960s, Mr Rice worked on the railways, and was a one-time stationmaster at Liffey Junction. This was a busy station due to its proximity to the Dublin Cattle Market. Mrs Rice is remembered by many for the army of cats she kept. She probably needed them, living so close to the dump.

William Rowan Hamilton

William Rowan Hamilton has always been associated with Broombridge. He was born in Dublin on the stroke of midnight on the 3 August 1805, and showed unusual intellect as a child. Before his third birthday his parents sent him to live with his father's brother, James, who lived in Trim, County Meath. Soon after his arrival he could read English easily and was advanced in arithmetic; at the age of five he could translate Latin, Greek and Hebrew and recite Homer, Milton and Dryden. By fourteen he had sufficient mastery of Persian to compose an official welcome for the Persian ambassador on the occasion of his visit to Dublin.

In 1820 William developed a keen interest in mathematics and by sixteen he had immersed himself in the five volumes of Pierre Simon Laplace's *Traité de*

Mécanique Céleste (1798–1827; *Celestial Mechanics* 1966). His detection of a flaw in Laplace's reasoning brought him to the attention of John Brinkley, professor of astronomy at TCD. When William was seventeen he sent Brinkley, at the time President of the Royal Irish Academy, an original paper on geometrical optics. Brinkley, in forwarding the work to the Academy, is said to have remarked, 'This young man, I do not say will be, but is, the first mathematician of his age.' William remained at Trim until 1823 when he entered Trinity College, Dublin. In 1827 he was appointed Director of Dunsink Observatory, Castleknock, and in 1835 his *On a General Method in Dynamics* was published.

His investigation in algebra began around 1825 with a pioneer paper on algebraic couples of numbers in which the basic entity was not a single number but ordered pairs of numbers. He used this idea to develop a rigorous theory of complex numbers, involving the square root of minus one. This paper was remarkable as a pioneer attempt to put algebra on an axiomatic basis like geometry. The geometry of complex numbers, that is, numbers of the form (a) + (bi), in which (i) is the square root of (-1), is that of the two-dimensional vectors in a plane. In attempting to develop an analogous technique for three-dimensional space, William was delayed for many years by a fundamental difficulty that could not be resolved so long as he restricted his attention to triplets.

On 16 October 1843 the solution flashed into his mind as he was taking his customary walk from the Observatory along the banks of the Royal Canal at Cabra. Apprehensive that the solution might not remain in his mind, William picked up a stone and carved out the fundamental formula of quaternion equation on the stonework of Broome Bridge:

$$i^2 = j^2 = k^2 = ijk^2 = -1$$

He died at home in Dunsink on 2 September 1865 and his work on quaternions was published posthumously the following year as *The Elements of Quaternions*. In 1958 a simple plaque was unveiled by President Eamonn de Valera to commemorate the discovery. William Rowan Hamilton spent his whole working life at Dunsink Observatory, founded in 1785 as the astronomical and meteorological observatory of Trinity College, Dublin. Forever synonymous with Cabra West, a senior-citizens' flats complex in the grounds of the church on Fassaugh Avenue is named after him.

The discovery at Broombridge is remembered on 16 October each year by the 'Hamilton Walk', initiated by Anthony G. O'Farrell, Emeritus Professor of Mathematics at Maynooth NUI. Each year mathematicians from all over the world come to Dublin to take part in the walk, which begins at Dunsink Observatory and finishes at Broombridge, Cabra. In 2005 the walk was launched by Nobel Prize winner Steven Weinberg. Supported by Cabra Community Council, many local people join in, adding great atmosphere to the occasion; after the 2003 walk, Jack Gannon, a local, wrote a song called 'The Ballad of Rowan Hamilton', which was first performed at Broombridge following Professor O'Farrell's speech there on 16 October 2004.

Cabra Baths

Broombridge Road connects Fassaugh Avenue to Ballyboggan Road. Cabra Baths, the Broken Arch and Silver Spoon were located not far from the junction with Ballyboggan Road. They were near the ruins of Finglaswood House, on the banks of the Tolka river. These three places were a popular haunt for thousands of Cabra natives during the 1950s and 1960s. The Broken Arch overlooked the Tolka River with a six- to eight-foot-deep pool of water under it, a challenging diving board for the experienced swimmer. A ruin of one of the outhouses to Finglaswood House, it survived until the early 1970s. The Silver Spoon was just a few yards further downriver; it had a gravelly, shallow bed and served as a paddling area and a crossing point over the Tolka River. Cabra Baths, an outdoor swimming baths located on the Cabra side of the river next to the Silver Spoon, was managed by Dublin Corporation. Only boys were allowed to swim there and girls had to be content with paddling and swimming in the Tolka nearby; it was nevertheless a mixed baths, for dogs often swam in it with their owners.

Every year, gang warfare broke out between Cabra and Finglas youths for control of the baths, with over a hundred antagonists on each side. The wars were brought to an end in the late 1960s thanks to the efforts of legendary Garda and former Irish International boxer, Detective Sergeant Jim 'Lugs' Branigan. He was head of the Garda Riot Squad, formed in 1964 to deal with escalating violence then pervading the streets of Dublin. By 1967 combatants numbered fewer than fifty and by 1968 the yearly battles ceased, due in no small measure to the presence of the legendary Garda and his colleagues. The Riot Squad was disbanded the week following Lugs' retirement on 6 January 1973. In the early 1970s the baths were finally closed as indoor heated swimming pools sprang up around the city, including those at St Joseph's and St Vincent's on Navan Road and the Dublin Corporation pool on Mellowes Road, Finglas. Cabra Baths became derelict, a dump for old bikes, cider bottles and beer cans. It was filled in during 1979 and incorporated into Tolka Valley Park.

Liffey Junction and Environs

Across what were formerly open fields and now a thriving industrial estate, on the Cabra West side of the Royal Canal, is the once busy and important railway inter-section of Liffey Junction. It was also a crucial off-loading point for the livestock industry. This was a bustling railway junction until its decline in the 1960s. Liffey Junction was a busy passenger station until the early 1900s, when mainline MGWR trains stopped using it. In 1919 it was served by one early morning passenger train to the North Wall, worked by the London and North Western Railway. This train ran from Liffey Junction via Glasnevin, West Road and Church Road Junctions. In 1907 the MGWR installed a sleeper creosoting plant at the junction at a total cost of £2473, giving it some importance as a maintenance depot. A chemical manure plant was also located here, installed at the end of the nineteenth century. This plant is marked on the 1908 Ordnance Survey map. The creosoting plant fell into disuse during the early twentieth century and is now buried beneath the hills of the black 'Coke Ovens'.

An unusual incident occurred at the Junction in 1908, as the following extract from the *Railway Magazine* (Vol. XXIII, July/December 1908) describes:

> An 'extra man' in the temporary employment of the MGWR has distin-
> guished himself in an extraordinary manner. He was employed to load
> coal but his ambition seemed to soar to higher things. About nine
> o'clock one evening the signalman at Liffey Junction noted an engine
> proceeding from the Broadstone terminus at a moderate speed. The
> down signal was at danger but the locomotive overran it by about twenty
> yards, eventually stopping just safe of a junction point. At that moment
> a goods train was due from the North Wall and had the engine gone
> on there would have been a collision unless the goods train could have
> been stopped on time. The Stationmaster at Liffey Junction, in giving

evidence at subsequent police court proceedings, said the accused told him that he was 'driver Murphy from Mullingar' and that his fireman was drunk and had been left behind at Broadstone. He appeared sober. The case was sent for trial at the next City Sessions and the amateur locomotive driver liberated on bail on his recognizances.

From early in the last century up until the late 1960s, Liffey Junction offloaded cattle being brought into the city of Dublin for market, to be sold in the Dublin cattle market at Prussia Street. Many salesmasters came into Liffey Junction by train with the cattle, which were then kept overnight in local lairages. Cattle from Galway, Meath and Westmeath were brought to market via Liffey Junction, while cattle from the south and Kildare came via Heuston Railway Station and Cabra Bank Station, at the junction of Cabra Road and Carnlough Road. From the 1930s to the late 1960s, Liffey Junction gave full-time employment to about thirty men and many more were employed as drovers, driving cattle to local lairages, from there to the market for sale, and finally from the market to the Liffey docks for export.

Salesmasters were well organized and had their own representative body, the Dublin Cattle Salesmasters Association, with offices at 23 Lower Ormond Quay. The drovers were, according to auctioneer Christopher Keogh, 'a special class who thought very highly of their own worth. The pen-men were the Blue Riband of the trade and were always looked up to'. Both drovers and pen-men were very loyal to and respected by their employers. The pen-man had tremendous

Liffey Junction, Cabra, 1940 (Courtesy Irish Railway Record Society)

responsibilities placed upon him, being in charge of five or six hundred head of cattle. The driving fee in the mid-1920s was 2/6d. (16 cent) from Liffey Junction to the fields, and 1/6d. (9 cent) from Cabra Bank to the fields.

In one of many chats I had with a Jack Ennis, a well-known local drover, he recalled market day as follows: 'It was a most exciting time. Liffey Junction would be crammed with people from six o'clock in the morning. If a drover worked a 'stand', from twelve midnight to close of market, he got £1 [€1.28]; if he worked from midnight to 9 o'clock in the morning, he got 7/6d. [48 cent]. The drovers and pen-men were highly unionized and were all members of the Marine Port and General Workers Union. They even had their own Union Badge to identify their specific trade.'

James McKeon from Ventry Road, Cabra West, joined the GSWR as a cleaner in 1937: he told me about his work on the railway and his many duties, which included 'cleaning the wheels on the engines. I then worked my way up to cleaning the boiler, then the tender. Until you were fully experienced you couldn't clean the motions (mechanics), for which you got an extra one shilling a week.' He eventually became a spare fireman, then a fireman, and recalled setting out on all-night Market Specials on the 'Meath Road', that branch of railway line from Clonsilla, through Dunboyne to Navan and Kingscourt. He also worked on the 'beet specials', lodging in Tuam in County Galway for three or four months while the sugar beet was harvested and transported by rail for processing. James, who retired from CIE in 1978, recalled Liffey Junction on market day: 'It was crowded. There would be twenty men employed just washing cattle waggons. At six o'clock in the morning crowds would gather at the entrance to the station, which was on Bannow Road. This was before the houses were even built. Drovers, pen-men, casual labourers, there would be hundreds in the station at the commencement of business.'

The advent of the cattle lorry gradually brought an end to the activity at Liffey Junction, which also served as an administration point for line maintenance. Frank Neary from Drumiskin, County Louth, got temporary work on the railways in the mid-1950s before emigrating to England in 1959. He was part of the gang laying down new sleepers and installing new telegraph poles on the line and recalled riding in on his motorbike from Maynooth to Liffey Junction on Fridays to collect the wages for the gang crew. To the present-day train passenger or busy commuter there is little reminder of the halcyon days of a bustling livestock industry on the way into a modern city centre. The arrival of the new LUAS tram network to Dublin 7 has led to the opening up of the old railway line from Broadstone Station, and will transform Liffey Junction and its environs as it develops.

The entrance to Liffey Junction Station was on Bannow Road, at the point where the present laneway runs alongside Batchelors' factory. Batchelors came to Cabra West during the 1940s and since then has been one of the district's biggest employers. It is now a subsidiary of the British company Premier Foods.

Batchelors, Cabra, 1967 (Courtesy Batchelors Ltd)

Adjacent to Bannow Road is The Fassaugh House, formerly Matt Whelan's public house. Mattie Whelan sold it to Lloyds. Situated at the gateway to Cabra West, it became a well-known local landmark; it was not trading during 2016. During the 1940s, in an old shack on the banks of the railway that runs beside the pub, lived a gentleman of the road called Arthur with his army of cats. This well-educated individual rambled into town daily, returning with a parcel of meat for his much-loved charges. Arthur always talked about his cats to the new settlers of Cabra and described the spread of Dublin to local sketch-artist Michael Coogan as 'akin to the pioneers of the American Wild West are the people of the new and greater Dublin'. Always regarded as a kind and gentle person, in 1949 Arthur was found dead in the shack he called home. A contemporary of Arthur was Hally Common, who slept in ditches and 'visited places where courting couples frequented, in search of property lost during moments of high passion'. Mr Leavey, a stationmaster at Liffey Junction at the time, was very kind to Halley Common, giving him food and other basic necessities.

Perhaps one of the most popular characters in the district was Patrick Pluck, universally known as Whacker, who kept pigs in a yard at Bridgefoot Street, Dublin 8. For years Whacker was to be seen throughout the Dublin 7 district with his horse Peggy and cart, collecting swill (referred to locally as skins or slop) and giving out the customary tip on the horses to all who might ask. He retired from the business in the late 1970s and he lived in James's Street for most of his life. I myself was once one of Whacker's little helpers, on Saturdays and daily during school holidays in the late 1950s and early 1960s. Helpers all had their own bucket, and there were often arguments, sorted out immediately by the boss, over who owned which bucket: if your bucket leaked, Whacker would get a new one to replace it. At the end of the day he would pay out the wages: sometimes this would be ninepence for a full day, sixpence for a half day and thruppence for an hour or two. On other occasions he would decide to give everyone ninepence, and when those who did a full day's work protested, he would ask why he couldn't choose to part with his money in whatever way he wished. Children learned a lot about life from Whacker. On a random day each week during the summer holidays, he would buy each of his helpers a fruit slice and a bottle of minerals in Frawley's shop in one of the back lanes behind Annamoe Park.

Fassaugh Road

Fassaugh Road was formerly called Fassaugh Lane; at the turn of the last century there was a small farmhouse here, just to the west of Beggsboro House. Frank Lyons lived on the farm, kept dairy cattle and was one of the few inhabitants of the immediate locality. Following the natural expansion of the city, Frank gave up farming and resettled nearby on Cabra Road, between Quarry Road and the Seventeen Shops. Beggsboro House is built on the site of a former mansion and was the seat of the Begge family, a name that appears in Irish records from the beginning of the 1400s.

In 1533 Roger Begge of Borranstown, also called Stillcock, in County Dublin, conveyed Borranstown and sundry other lands, including those in Cabragh, to trustees for the use of himself, wife and heirs. Matthew Begge of Borranstown was found guilty of high treason in 1621 and was outlawed. In Elizabethan and Cromwellian times the Begges suffered endless persecution because of their adherence to the Roman Catholic faith. Oliver Cromwell had them transferred to Connaught. Cromwell himself was not of English, but of Welsh descent, his great-grandfather being Richard Williams, son of Morgan Williams, a Putney brewer of Glamorgan origins, who changed his name by deed poll from Williams to Cromwell as a protest against the execution of his uncle, Thomas Cromwell, Earl of Essex, by Henry VIII.

In the Ordnance Survey map of 1839 Beggsboro is shown as belonging to the townland of Grangegorman and the Barony of Coolock. In 1880 Beggsboro was set down as being on Quarry Lane under the ownership of Garrett Begge, an alderman on Dublin Corporation. Members of the family were well-known representatives on Dublin Corporation during the eighteenth and nineteenth centuries; the local authority housing schemes of Cabra East and part of Cabra West were built on part of the Beggsboro estate. Matthew Begge, uncle of Garrett Begge, built the present-day Beggsboro House at Fassaugh Road, formerly Fassaugh Lane, in 1873.

Beggsboro House, Cabra East, 1975 (Courtesy Larry Maher)

Garrett farmed over thirty acres to the back of Beggsboro House. He grew rhubarb for Williams and Woods, the jam manufacturers based on King's Inns Street. The company name is painted on the wall of the former Williams and Woods chocolate factory, on the corner of King's Inns Street and Loftus Lane. Garret also produced cabbage and broccoli for the Dublin vegetable markets. He subsequently let his land for grazing market-bound cattle. He had a huge glass-house beside Beggsboro House where he grew grapes, much to the delight of the young people around Cabra who occasionally 'boxed the fox'' (robbed the orchard) there.

Garrett Begge drew his workers from labourers' cottages in the area. Up until the mid-1980s the Begge family was still represented in the district by Charles 'Charlie' Harte of Beggsboro House, a great-grandson of Garrett. He sold the house to Eileen and Patrick Byrne, the present occupiers. Patrick first came to Cabra in 1963 and he lived over the shop next door, Fassaugh Stores, managing the business in partnership with Charlie, who died in 1989.

Liam Whelan

Part of the area of the former quarry on Fassaugh Road is now occupied by the Health Centre, called the Dispensary during the mid-1900s, and the old Dublin Corporation Play Centre (or playground), which now houses St Finbarr's GAA complex and a Gaelscoil. The playground was sometimes referred to locally as the 'Playground of the Stars', as it was here that so many young boys who later achieved soccer stardom got their first kick of a ball. Among those who played football here are Irish Internationals Joe Carolan, Terry Conroy, Jimmy Conway, Gerry Daly, Johnny Giles, Ashley Grimes and Liam Whelan. Perhaps the most famous of these is Liam Whelan, from St Attracta Road, Cabra. Born in 1935, he was educated at St Peter's School, Phibsborough, and as a boy won numerous medals and trophies for GAA football and hurling. It was no coincidence that he chose soccer, as his older brothers Christy and John played League of Ireland football for Transport United and Drumcondra respectively. He joined Home Farm and in 1951 was capped for Ireland, appearing in the schoolboy International side that defeated England 8–4.

In 1953, aged eighteen, Liam went from Home Farm to Manchester United and in that year won Youth Cup honours with his new team. He was recruited on the advice of the well-known talent spotter Billy Behan, who regarded Liam as 'my best signing ever for Manchester United'; Billy also spotted Kevin Moran and Paul McGrath, two other Manchester United signings. Billy died in December 1991. Liam made his first-team debut against Preston North End in 1955 and went on to win a League Championship Medal in 1955/56, becoming a regular first-team player. He won a second League Championship Medal in 1956/57 and was on the 1957 FA Cup Final side, when United lost to Aston Villa. Liam, cheered on by his mother Elizabeth and sister Rita, was awarded 'Man of the Match' by the sports-writers of the day and was presented with a cigarette lighter for his achievement.

Liam shared a room in Manchester with friend and team-mate Bobby Charlton, who recalls seeing him reciting the Rosary each night, not unusual for a young Roman Catholic from 1950s Ireland. When Bobby got his first cap for England, he had a photograph taken sitting on a table beside the treasured cap, signed the photo and presented it to Liam, whom he remembered as a kind and generous individual who answered every letter from fans all over Great Britain and Ireland.

On 6 February 1958, in what has become known as the Munich Air Disaster, Liam lost his life along with seven other United players. The plane taking the team home from a European Cup tie in Belgrade crashed when it failed to take off from Munich airport in snow. One of the survivors, Harry Gregg, recalled Liam's last words, spoken to goalkeeper Ray Wood: 'I think we are going to crash. If anything bad is going to happen, I'm ready for it. I hope we all are.' Liam was just twenty-three. He was engaged and was due to marry in June that year. In a short but spectacular career, which saw him score forty-three goals in seventy-nine League matches for United, he was capped by his country four times, and represented Ireland in Internationals against Holland, Denmark and England (twice).

Liam is buried in Glasnevin, where his grave was for many years tended regularly by his sister Rita; even today there is rarely an absence of fresh flowers there. Neither is Liam forgotten by Manchester United – every Christmas the club sent a card to his mother Elizabeth and they brought her family over to see the 1958 FA Cup Final, which United lost to Bolton Wanderers 2–0, and again to the 1963 Final against Leicester. In February 1983, on the twenty-fifth anniversary of the Munich Air Disaster, they flew Elizabeth and sixteen other family members to Manchester for a commemoration ceremony at Old Trafford. And for many years, every February, three ordinary Manchester women sent a card and money to Elizabeth for fresh flowers for the grave. Liam Whelan, a football legend, still lives on in the hearts of many. In December 2006 he was honoured by his own city with the naming of the railway bridge on Connaught Street. A simple bronze plaque, erected by Dublin City Council on the bridge, reads as follows:

To honour the memory of Liam Whelan
A Cabra boy who played for Ireland and Manchester United
A Busby Babe who died in the Munich Air Disaster in 1958 aged 22 years
Unveiled by the Lord Mayor of Dublin Councillor Vincent Jackson
December 2006

Quarry Road and Environs

Quarry Road, formerly Quarry Lane, was called after a quarry near the present-day Marian shrine at the roundabout with Fassaugh Road; it was filled in at the beginning of the twentieth century. Both Quarry Lane and Fassaugh Lane are marked on the Ordnance Survey map of 1838. Homestead was the only house on the old Quarry Lane and for many years it was the Snow family home. A fine residence with a spectacular fireplace in the sitting room, it was a well-known local landmark and one of many country mansions adjacent to the city. In the early 1920s the Snow family sold land to the Sailors and Soldiers Trust, which then built houses on Fassaugh Lane for disabled servicemen of the Great War, 1914–1918. A prominent Cabra family, the last of the Snows to reside at Homestead was one Edward Sinclair Snow and his wife Frances (*née* Crolly). Their granddaughter, Bobby Hudson (daughter of Colonel Andrew Kirkwood and his wife Mabel (*née* Snow)), who was born in Lahore, India, told me about the views, across fields and hedgerows, towards St Peter's Church in Phibsborough, which she enjoyed from her upstairs bedroom during visits to her grandmother on Quarry Lane.

In 1923 the Snow family sold Homestead to Liam Kavanagh, one of the biggest dairy farmers in the area, who grew cabbages on nearby reclaimed land. He continued farming until 1937. The house still survives as the Homestead Bar, a popular local pub. The farm buildings attached to the property were on the site of the present-day Cabra Grand. 'The Grand' was a once-popular cinema and a regular haunt for thousands of Cabra boys and girls during the 1950s, 1960s and early 1970s. It first opened its doors on 16 April 1949, a Saturday night of course, with a screening of *Sitting Pretty* starring Maureen O'Hara, about a suburban couple, Tracy and Harry, who have three tearaway young boys. Its last screening was on 31 January 1970, featuring *The Big Gundown* starring Lee Van Cliffe. It became a Gael Linn Bingo Hall, and still operates as such today.

Homestead, Quarry Road, Cabra, early 1900s (Courtesy Bobby Hudson)

The well-known journalist and author Gene Kerrigan, from Ventry Park, Cabra West, was born in October 1949 and started his working life as an assistant projectionist at the Cabra Grand, where his uncle Larry McDonagh was for many years the chief projectionist. He left the Grand after five years, and spent another ten years in the trade, five at the Capital Cinema and five in the Ambassador Cinema, Parnell Street, both of which closed down.

In the late 1970s he found himself among the unemployed. He had previously tried his hand at writing and had articles received by numerous publications, including *Hot Press* magazine. In 1977 he became a full-time journalist with *Magill* magazine. Covering the Dunne case for the *Sunday Tribune*, he later wrote a book on the subject. *Nothing but the Truth* covered the case of William

Dunne, who was brain-damaged on birth and whose twin was stillborn, and the struggle of his parents Kay and Willie in their medical negligence claim against Holles Street Hospital. Following the demise of the *Sunday Tribune* he moved to the Independent group and his *Soapbox* column has been a fixture in the *Sunday Independent* for many years.

Now living in Raheny, Dublin 5, Gene Kerrigan has written many books over the years, including *This Great Little Nation*, covering the corrupt landscape of Irish public and business life. Since 1990, when he achieved the AT Cross Journalist of the Year prize, he has won many prestigious awards. He has successfully entered the genre of crime writing and in October 2012 his book *The Rage* won the Gold Dagger best crime novel of the year in the Specsavers Crime Thriller Awards. His book about the 1916 Rising, entitled *The Scrap*, was published by Doubleday in October 2015 to widespread critical acclaim. In a review of the books of 2015 in the *Irish Times*, Colm Tóibín described it as 'the best history book I read … as brilliantly paced as one of his thrillers'.

At the back of the Homestead, across the inter-connector (the railway line laid in 1867 to connect Kingsbridge and Amiens Street stations), is Cabra Bank Station. Like Liffey Junction, it was a busy cattle station from the 1920s through to the 1960s, but with the ending of the cattle trade the station declined. In the early 1970s it became busy again following the construction of a bulk-cement terminal, which operated for almost twenty years; after this the terminal fell into a state of dereliction. With the overall upgrading of the city's transportation infrastructure, redevelopment works began on the line in 2015.

Just off Quarry Road, on Leix Road, is where Patrick 'Paddy' Carroll lived for most of his married life. Born in 1898, he served with the Irish Citizen Army in the GPO during the Easter Rising. Following the surrender he was released from detention due to his young age. He continued to serve with the Irish Citizen Army during the War of Independence. Taking the republican side during the Civil War, he was posted to North Great Georges Street when fighting broke out; when his position there came under fire from a Free State armoured car his unit retired to Healy's pub in Marlborough Street, holding out there for a week. Arrested in April 1923 and interned until October of that year, he worked in W.D. & H.O. Wills, the cigarette company, and later in the Department of Social Welfare. He died on 5 April 1971 and is buried in Glasnevin Cemetery.

Kilmartin's of Quarry Road, Cabra, early 1970s (Courtesy Lar Boland)

Quarry Road leads on to the New Cabra Road, where the aforementioned Seventeen Shops (the number varies but has totalled more than twenty since the early 1960s) are located. One of the Seventeen Shops was Reid's newsagency and grocers, which also served as a sort of social centre; locals called in for a chat as much as for their messages. It was established in 1934 and the original proprietors were George Reid and his wife Harriet (*née* Dunne), who came to Cabra to view houses on Cabra Drive with the intention of buying one as their new home. Passing by the newly-constructed shops on Cabra Road, they decided to buy one of them instead, living overhead. Their son Archie started to work in the shop as an assistant; he met Dorothy (born on 21 January 1930) and they married in Trinity Church, Limerick in 1954. Archie and Dorothy ran the shop for many years, handing over the business to their son and daughter, George and Yvonne, who in turn ran the premises until it finally closed its doors in 2013.

Near the Cabra Grand, at 19 Offaly Road, was the home of Matt Kiernan: born on 17 June 1898, as a young man he left his home town of Ballivor, County Meath, and joined An Garda Síochána. He became famous in the world of the uilleann pipes through his love of music and of that particular instrument. A founding member of Na Píobairí Uilleann, he worked in conjunction with great pipers and theorists for the advancement of the uilleann piping tradition. He also manufactured pipes in a workshop at the rear of his back garden, first in his spare time as a serving Garda and then, in retirement. Known for the quality of his pipes, a lack of ability to pay never stopped anyone from securing a set. He made pipes for and taught pipes to both young and old in an open house on Offaly Road, where 'the teapot never got cold'. Matt once described the pipes as being 'a notoriously fickle instrument, hard to keep in full working order' and compared them to being 'like a contrary woman, you've got to humour them'. He must now be rejoicing at the fact that there are many fine female pipers today.

Matt Kiernan, uilleann piper
(Courtesy Seamus Meehan)

Matt Kiernan is regarded as the first pipe-maker to remove the shroud of secrecy historically attached to the tradition of making and tuning uilleann pipes; he shared his pipe-making skills widely, and his neighbour Tom Meehan made practice sets at Matt's house, having learnt the skills from him. Leo Rickard, a noted contemporary piper and a member of the Rowsome Uilleann Piping Quartet, obtained his first practice set of pipes from Matt in 1976. Matt died in 1986 and following his funeral Mass, in Christ the King church on 21 July 1986, he was taken to his native Ballivor for burial. At the graveside oration Peter Maguire, piper and a retired Garda, stated that '80 per cent of pipers first learned their craft through him'.

Cabra Grove and the Geblers

Cabra Grove is on the opposite side of Cabra Road, just up from the crossroads at Immal Road and Annamoe Terrace, in the direction of the Topaz garage. When constructed in the mid-1930s it consisted of a terrace of six houses; it now has seven. The Gébler family lived here from the mid-1930s. Adolf Gébler, a Czech national who originally came to Ireland in 1908, ran a shop in Dublin and played the clarinet at the Gaiety Theatre. He met Margaret Rita Wall, an usherette; they married in 1910 and had five children. Their first child Ernest was born in 1915, but Adolf was interned as an enemy alien in 1914 following the outbreak of the First World War and did not get to see his son for nearly four years. In the 1920s he left Dublin and moved his family to Wolverhampton, returning in 1930 to take up a position playing with the Studio Players, which was the forerunner to the RTÉ Orchestra. Ernest, who had stayed on in Wolverhampton, left England in 1939 and moved in with his parents at Cabra Grove, determined to become a writer. He immediately bought a Remington typewriter and a number of novels ensued, including *Plymouth Adventure*, which was published in 1947. It sold four million copies and was made into a Hollywood film featuring Spencer Tracy. By this time Ernest was living in County Wicklow.

Daly's Pharmacy (formerly Magnier's), Cabra Road, 2016 (Courtesy Lar Boland)

In 1950 Edna O'Brien, then a twenty-year-old from Tuamgraney, County Clare, secured her licence as a pharmacist and started working in Magnier's Chemist at the Seventeen Shops, Cabra Road, now Daly's Chemist. According to Dorothy Reid, Edna found lodgings on Cabra Grove and while working in Magnier's Chemist shop met Ernest Gébler: 'She met him in 1952, the same year that he got divorced. Ernest did not meet with her parents' approval and they moved to London, where they married in 1954, and had two children.' They separated in 1964. Edna O'Brien became an acclaimed writer; her first book *The Country Girls* (1960) was a sensational success and was later made into a film. Over the years she has written countless novels and short stories. Their son Carlos Gébler is also a writer and his novel *The Eleventh Summer* became a bestseller. The Gébler family featured in an RTÉ documentary, *Flesh And Blood*, aired on 21 July 2009. Successive *Thom's Directory* editions from the late 1930s list the householder of 3 Cabra Grove as Adolphus Gelber, although the 1958 edition lists him as A. Gabler. The house was sold in 1960. Ernest Gébler returned to Ireland around 1970, after spending a number of years in the USA, and lived in Dalkey, where he died in February 1998, aged eighty-three.

From Old Cabra to Cabra West

In the early 1930s the landscape of Cabra changed dramatically with the extension of the city suburbs into the rural tranquility of the surrounding area. In 1930 work began on the Corporation housing scheme at Old Cabra, on both sides of New Cabra Road. In September 1932, the year of the Eucharistic Congress, the foundation stone for Christ the King Roman Catholic Church was laid. It was officially opened on the last Sunday of October 1933, feast day of Christ the King in the Roman Catholic calendar.

Christ the King was attached to Arran Quay parish and it was not until eight years later, in 1941, that it was formally established as a parish in its own right. The first parish priest was Canon Ó Ceallagháin, one of Dublin's well-known characters of the time. He drove around in his distinctive black car. In 1965 his team included Fathers John Cleary, Brendan Supple, Christopher Kenny and Sean Quigley. He served the community of Cabra from his appointment until his death in 1973. He was succeeded by Fr McDowell, who served until 1979. The church has a historic aspect: it is adorned with artifacts used during the 1932 Eucharistic

Congress and presented to the parish; these include some fine brass candlesticks and a thurible. The community experienced the evil of clerical child sex abuse during the tenure of Fr Ivan Payne at Christ the King. Andrew Madden, who lived near the church, was sexually abused as a young altar boy by Fr Payne; the abuse started in 1976 when Andrew was just twelve years old and lasted for three years. He has written a book on his experiences, and the damage wrought on his young life entitled *Altar Boy: A Story of Life after Abuse*.

In 1939 the agricultural and market-garden lands bordering Old Cabra were transformed when work began on the most ambitious public housing project in Europe at that time. The new suburb of Cabra West came to life prematurely following the bombing of the North Strand in Dublin by the Luftwaffe, the German Air Force, on 31 May 1941. This resulted in the loss of forty-one lives and many injuries; in addition hundreds of people were made homeless. The German bombers were believed to have lost course and, thinking that they were flying over Belfast, dropped their deadly cargo. Damage was considerable. The authorities acted swiftly; the day after the bombing, some of those made homeless became the first tenants in the new housing scheme of Cabra West, moving into their homes as builders were quickly plastering walls, hanging doors and laying pathways to non-existent footpaths.

In 1944 a temporary tin church was erected on a site at Dunmanus Road, Cabra West. In July 1951 the first sod for a new church was turned and on 6 December 1953 the Church of the Most Precious Blood, costing approximately £96,000, was officially opened and blessed by John Charles McQuaid, Roman Catholic Archbishop of Dublin. The distinctive, carved Stations of the Cross were especially imported from Switzerland. In 1965 the five-member parish team comprised the parish priest Fr Sean Byrne and Fathers Stephen Greene, Michael Ward, Cecil Johnston and Paul McGennis. The phone number was then a five-digit one, 46330. A magnificent organ, installed by Messrs Pells of Holland, has over the years attracted foreign organists of repute. John McElroy was the organist from 1954 until his death on 5 April 1971. This visually impaired man also played the piano and accordion and is best remembered for the small shop he ran on Carnlough Road. It was called locally 'the blind man's shop', beside the bus stop near the junction with Cabra Road. Long since demolished, containers for recycling glass now occupy the site.

St Finbarr's Boys' National School, Kilkiernan Road, was founded in 1943 and is presently a DEIS school with a maximum of twenty two pupils per class.

The school's first teacher was Paddy Bawn Ó Broin, a well-respected and much-liked figure in the Cabra West community. A talented musician, he arranged extra-curricular school activities such as tin-whistle lessons, bringing in people like Seán Potts (senior and junior) to join in the classes. From time to time he ran sell-out concerts in St Finbarr's Hall, featuring Dickie Rock, who hails from Dingle Road, Cabra West, and the Miami Showband and the Chieftains. A life member of An Óige, he had a love of the countryside and enjoyed cycling too. His first visit to see the school where he would soon work, while it was under construction, was by bicycle, accompanied by his father. Shortly afterwards he moved into Martin's Grove, Blackhorse Avenue, and spent the rest of his life there. Finbarr's School is progressive and has recently forged a number of links with industry, such as Intel and IBM; it has benefited greatly from these links and has been awarded high-specification computers for the children.

Cabra Community College, also on Kilkieran Road, was constructed in the early 1940s. It first opened its doors in 1945 under the auspices of the City of Dublin Vocational Education Committee and was the first co-educational school of its kind in Ireland. Originally called Coláiste Éanna, and referred to locally as 'the Tech', in recent years it has expanded its range of courses and caters for second-level and mature adult students. On 1 July 2013 with the passing of the Education and Training Boards Act, the City of Dublin Vocational Education Committee was rebranded as the City of Dublin Education and Training Board, incorporating some of the functions of FÁS, the former State training agency. The school's mission is to provide quality education, anchored in a stimulating and inclusive learning environment. The school grounds are shared with Beggsboro United, founded in 1939, which takes its name from the Begge family of Cabra.

Most of the street names in Cabra West are called after picturesque bays around the Irish coast, such as Drumcliffe Road, Dingle Road, Carnlough Road, Kilkieran Road and Killala Road. Many of those who grew up in the new suburb have made their mark in different spheres, such as Dickie Rock (entertainment), Gerry Daly (sport) and Joan Bergin. Growing up on Killala Road, Joan Bergin became a designer and her assignments include the film productions of *My Left Foot* (1989), *In the Name of the Father* (1993) and *The Prestige* (2006), and the TV productions of *The Tudors* and *The Vikings*.

Aerial view of Cabra West, 1950 (Courtesy Fr Cecil Johnson PP) with St Joseph's School for the Deaf on the left and Cabra Bank Station on the right

Public Transport

The first bus to serve Cabra was the number 12 in 1930; this single-decker ran from Eden Quay to Cabra Road. It replaced the former Number 12 tram, which ran as far as the old tram terminus at Doyle's Corner in Phibsboro; this now serves as a car park. As the housing stock in the area continued to grow, it became obvious that extra bus services were required. On 9 October 1944 the first Number 22 bus went on the road, running between Cabra West and O'Connell Street. In 1946 the route was extended to serve the south side of the city and began operating between the terminus at the Dominican Convent, Ratoath Road and Mourne Road, Drimnagh.

For many years all buses running along the New Cabra Road into town stopped at the bus shelter at the Seventeen Shops, where the conductor 'clocked in'; there could be a few minutes' pause before the conductor pulled the arm at the side of the clock and the distinctive bell-ring signalled the successful completion of the process. This practice was discontinued in the early 1970s. The locality's bus services were further expanded in 1950 with the addition of the 22A route, which ran from its terminus at the cul-de-sac on Bannow Road out to Drimnagh. The waste-recycling company, Hanney, was located there until recent years and the buildings are now vacant. The site was acquired by the Dublin Institute of Technology for a proposed sports complex; by September 2015 the floodlit training pitches were in operation.

In 1987 the Number 12 bus ran for the last time. Many elderly people in the district had their independence curtailed, as the altering of the 22A did not cover the entire route of the 12. John 'Spud' Murphy of St Attracta Road was one of many whose travel was restricted. Spud was well known to the busmen on the 12 and when he became physically unable to walk long distances, the crew would pick him up at the entrance to the 'backers' (back lanes) on Fassaugh Road and drop him off for his weekend pint at the door of the Homestead on Quarry Road or at Downey's on Cabra Road. He would then be collected from the door of the pub and dropped off at the backer on his way home. If walking along the road and a bus came, he just put out his stick and it stopped for him. This bit of unique Dublin city life ended with the demise of the 12.

Cabra Today

Cabra, comprising East Cabra (or Old Cabra) and Cabra West, is now a settled and mature district. It is convenient to all amenities and is a very desirable place to live; former local-authority houses are sought after by people wishing to live close to the city centre. During the boom years houses were fetching €300,000 to €400,000. In 2015 this fell to €220,000. Cabra boasts many sports, social clubs and specialist activity groups, primary schools and second-level colleges, financial services and a modern, thriving Credit Union. A commuter-rail service opened in 1989. Transport services will be augmented over the next two years by the extension of the LUAS light rail network. The amenities provided by the Phoenix Park, the Bogeys, the Tolka Valley Park and the Royal Canal are on its doorstep.

A visit into any shop or café, pub or club will instantly reveal that the people of the area have retained their friendliness and sense of community, social traits so distinguishable during the formative years of the new estates and the hardworking original pioneers who populated them.

5 | Cardiffsbridge

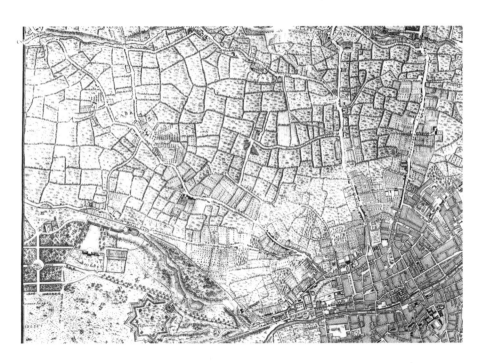

Up until the early 1960s the village of Cardiffsbridge, midway between Cabra West and Finglas on the road to Ratoath, County Meath, was a sleepy little hamlet. Villagers socialized in the village pub, The Jolly Toper, and in summertime enjoyed outdoor *ceilidhes* at the crossroads by the bridge. Cottage industries like dairying and breeding Angora rabbits thrived and locals were expert rod-fishermen on the renowned trout waters of the Tolka River, which flowed through the heart of the community. The old bridge is all that survives of the once picturesque little village.

Cardiffsbridge was once in the possession of the Kerdiff family, who settled both here and at Dunsink during the sixteenth century. The Kerdiffs purchased a mill works that in 1577 had been the property of the Dillons of Cappock. The mill was locally referred to as Kerdiff's Mill and over time the area became known as Cardiffsbridge, a corruption of Kerdiff. The mill was on the left-hand side of the old bridge and during the 1800s it was operating as an iron mill, manufacturing shovels. According to Cosy Finnegan, the last resident of the village, the works had a familiar redbricked chimney, 'as high as Nelson's Pillar in O'Connell Street in Dublin city'. Production continued until the closure of the mill in 1870. During the 1830s it gave employment to sixteen people in winter and ten in summer.

Adjacent to the mill, on the back road to Blanchardstown, were three houses, known locally as 'the mill race'.

The water used to generate the power for the mill was taken from the Tolka River, about a half-mile upstream from the production plant. The course of the race can clearly be seen on the 1838 Ordnance Survey map. With the change-over to steam power the chimney was constructed. Ash and cinders from the boiler-room were deposited on the Finglas side of the river, just downstream from the bridge and in time this bank became known locally as 'the Cinders'.

Cardiffsbridge is now the location of a nature park, developed by Dublin Corporation Parks Department. The plans for the creation of the park included the restoration of the old bridge using stones found lying in the Tolka River. During the restoration works a fourth arch was discovered, excavated and opened so as to allow the river to be diverted through it. It was this arch that linked the former mill race from the old iron mill. In order to create a living park, the Parks Department consulted the former Eastern Regional Fisheries Board, following which they renovated the river bed to facilitate the territorial habits of the trout, once teeming in this stretch of water. The exotic and colourful kingfisher is often sighted here along the river banks. The old bridge is just a short distance upstream of the new one that leads the Ratoath Road through Finglas.

Campbell's Garage

This is a familiar local landmark to most people who travelled along Ratoath Road. Situated at Reilly's Bridge, it was a former forge where carriages were repaired and horseshoes fitted. The proprietor during the 1980s and 1990s was Jimmy Campbell, who took over the business from his father, Paddy, continuing in a tradition of assisting the traveller on the site of the old forge, though now with mechanized, not horse-drawn, vehicles. The Campbells were a well-known family in the district; during the 1950s and 1960s Mrs Campbell used to sell lolli-pops and sweets from the house at weekends, much to the joy of children out for the day. Paddy Campbell is believed to have been the first person to present the mechanical hare outside Shelbourne Park, the Mecca of greyhound racing. He organized dog-racing events all over the district, at Ashtown Cross, behind Kelly's Inn, behind the Anglican church in Finglas, at Dubber Cross and St Brigid's Well.

A dog-racing fanatic, it was following a visit to Shelbourne Park that he started a countrywide outdoor greyhound racing craze in the late 1920s and early 1930s. He came home from Shelbourne Park one day and rigged a drum contraption to his Ford Model T motor car, adapting it so that it could be used to and to great interest power a mechanical hare for greyhound racing. His races brought in the crowds and a craze swept the country.

An article in the Dublin *Evening Mail* of Monday 6 June 1932 under the banner headline 'New Pastime: Greyhound Racing on Garden Lawn. County Dublin Novelty', refers to the new craze, describing the operation of the mechanical hare:

> You jack up the back wheels of your motor car and take off one of the tyres. To the wheel you fix one end of the wire. To the other end of the wire you fix the stuffed hare. The second length of wire is stretched across the lawn and pegged, so that it is two or three inches above the ground. It forms a track on which the hare runs. When everything is ready, you start your car. The back wheels revolve, forming a windlass that winds up the wire and pulls the hare across the lawn at a breathless speed, with the hounds in full career behind.

Living beside the Royal Canal, the family used the towpath for travelling into and out of the city and to attend half-eight Mass every Sunday morning in the small church in Glasnevin Cemetery. The inauguration of the new bridge over the railway line and canal in 2015 has resulted in the garage now being located in a cul-de-sac.

Opposite Campbell's Garage, in the grounds of the now-defunct factory premises of the Ormond Printing Company, formerly occupied by the Sellotape factory, is a wayside pump that was once a popular local landmark. This pump was originally surrounded by a small shelter wall and had a beak to hold the handle of a bucket. The initials 'T&T' on the pump refer to the old Dublin firm of Tonge and Taggart, ironfounders, run by four generations of the Tonge family. During the early 1970s it was taken over by the Smurfit Group after 200 years in business. The pump is situated behind the wire perimeter fence surrounding the factory, its silent handle never to be swung again. The pump provided the domestic water needs of the small community nearby.

The Dalys lived beside the spot where the pump is located and the Fanning family lived opposite. The entrance to the Fannings was visible until 2002 and up until 1995 the passer-by could just about see the foundations of the old cottage, inside the gate. There was an animal water-trough in the field, visible from the road until 1995. There was a well beside the Dalys' house, which was still flowing in 2002. The road then curved downhill to the village of Cardiffsbridge. Unbelievably, open fields stretched from this spot on Ratoath Road right out to Blanchardstown until the last years of the twentieth century. Following the approval of rezoning proposals for Pellettstown, the lands were developed and became the high-density housing complex existing today, from Ratoath Road to Ashtown Railway Station.

Water Pump, Ratoath Road, 1976
(Courtesy Larry Maher)

Village Life

Cardiffsbridge had all the trappings of a country village. The Jolly Toper is marked on the 1936 Ordnance Survey map. There was a skittle alley at the back of the pub and a century ago the O'Keeffe family called 'time' here. In the early 1900s the licence passed to the Finnegan family and during the Second World War Miss Rose 'Cosy' Finnegan inherited the premises from her mother and ran it as a grocery shop during the 1940s, as the licensing business dwindled during the shortages resulting from the war. Unfortunately, Cosy let the licence lapse during this time and with the rationing that followed was forced to shut up shop and take a job in the city. As an inn sign The Jolly Toper was, according to Larwood's *History of Signboards*, well known across the Irish Sea. It later gave its name to a popular hostelry in Church Street in Finglas Village, now called the Village Inn.

Cosy and her brother were the last inhabitants to leave the village of Cardiffs-bridge. Their small, homely cottage was demolished in 1976 and they were rehoused on Clune Road in Finglas. Of her new home, Cosy remarked: 'Gosh, I'll never get used to having stairs.' I frequently visited Cosy in her old house in Cardiffsbridge and there met some former villagers, who regularly dropped in on her. It was like visiting a cottage in the heart of the country. They all fondly recalled that there was always music, song and dance on the premises of The Jolly Toper. In summertime they sat outside the pub, drinking in the sunshine and enjoying the impromptu *ceilidhes* that took place by the bridge.

A flat square stone on the bridge wall was where local men played cards, often until the early hours of the morning. There was 'terrific fishing' on the stretch of the Tolka river running through the village and trout were always in abundance. 'Ally' Lyons, who settled in Cabra West when the village of Cardiffsbridge was rezoned, was one of the best fishermen around and he gave advice to many young men entering the sport for the first time. His entertaining and informative angling column appeared for many years in the *Evening Press*.

Another local, 'Lumpy' Brown, laid nets in the Tolka river from Glasnevin down to the village, then walked along the river, hiding the trout as he caught them, collecting his full catch on his way home to Cardiffsbridge. Fintan Brennan, Ratoath Road, remembered 'often catching thirty or more trout of an evening'. The former Central Fisheries Board, keenly aware of the resource of the Tolka River, took various measures to restock and foster the trout fishery over the years.

A small thatched cottage was located beside The Jolly Toper and this was converted to a slate roof during the first decade of the twentieth century. On the left-hand side, coming towards the bridge from Cabra West, there was a small dairy and shop belonging to the Callaghans. This did a lively trade with day trip-pers. The shop was later taken over by an uncle of Cosy Finnegan. There was a well and water pump at this spot; the pump is long gone but the well can still be seen among barely noticeable ruins of the shop and adjoining wall.

Just beyond The Jolly Toper was an area covered by flowers and dotted with garden seats where in summertime locals and visitors would sit and rest. This area belonged to the Newmans, who carried on a small cottage industry, rearing Angora rabbits down by the sandpits beside Moffets' land. According to the *Encyclopedia Britannica* Angora is a domesticated breed that includes English and

French Angora varieties and appeared as early as 1723 in France and was imported to the USA and canada in the late 1920s. Angora rabbits produce high-quality meat and excellent white, black, blue or fawn wool, with white being the preferred colour. Annual yield is about twelve ounces (340 grammes) of wool, harvested by shearing every three months. Because of their high cost Angora rabbit fibres are used only in luxury fabrics and garments, sometimes in blends with other fibres. According to Cosy the Newmans produced two colours of wool, white and black, and Jim Callaghan looked after the rabbits and tended the flowered areas and the Newmans' garden.

Gerry Moffet (listed as Maffet in editions of *Thom's Directory*) lived in a big house on the right-hand side, over the bridge heading towards Finglas. Before coming to settle in Cardiffsbridge, he lived for a spell in the former Craigie home of St Helena's, Finglas; a retired Post Office official, he often frequented the La Scala in the city. He would travel into town on horseback, placing his horse in a livery stable for the day. While riding home from town along the canal towpath one day, a newspaper struck his horse as he was approaching Cross Guns Bridge. The horse bolted, throwing him into the canal. From then on he walked every-where, a well-known sight.

Village of Cardiffsbridge, 1938 (Courtesy *Evening Press*). The two-storey house in the background is The Jolly Toper

There were twenty-two acres attached to his home where he kept thorough-bred horses. He lived on the top floor of this fine, big house, with its beautifully carved mahogany staircase. He had a reputation for being 'spotless'; however, due to illness, he found it increasingly difficult to tend to his household and other affairs and in time his thoroughbred horses interbred and became wild. The wild horses and the reclusive lifestyle of Gerry resulted in them both becoming part of the local folklore. One winter's night in 1936 when he went out to feed his horses he had a heart attack and died. He collapsed on the spot known locally as Moffet's Hill. A big orchard was located around the hill and it was here that the local village children 'boxed the fox' during the summer months.

Not far from the village was the mansion and lands of Lady Eva Forbes, sister of the Earl of Granard. According to the locals, she 'kept to herself, and was chauffeur-driven to eleven o'clock Mass every Sunday in St Peter's, Phibsborough, in a black 1927 Ford 14.9 motor car'. The car was said to be always gleaming and in immaculate condition.

Cardiffsbridge was a regular stage point for calculating horse-drawn coach and outside car fares in all the almanacs and directories. In 1824 it cost 2/8d. (17 cent) to come to the village by coach, or 1/4d. (8 cent) by outsider, from the GPO in Dublin. By 1838 these fares had risen to 2/10d. (18 cent) and 1/6d. (9 cent). However, in 1869 the fare had settled at two shillings (12 cent), whether or not a covered coach was engaged.

King James's Castle

Finglaswood House overlooked the Tolka on the Finglas side of the river, not far from the little pedestrian bridge inside the Tolka Valley Park entrance at the end of Broombridge Road. The excellent Dublin City Council par-three pitch-and-putt course covers part of the lands once attached to the property. Like so many old houses in the neighbourhood of Dublin, local folklore has it that James II slept here following his defeat at the battle of the Boyne in July 1690. It was a Segrave property at that time and they were supporters of his cause. Given the cautious nature of James's character, though, he probably sheltered in Dublin Castle, inside the safe confines of the city walls. The following is a description taken from *The Neighbourhood of Dublin* of 1912 by Weston St John Joyce:

Due south of Finglas, and situated on the banks of the Tolka, is the conspicuous ruin of Finglaswood House (King James's Castle), an ancient structure which during the Commonwealth was the residence of Henry Segrave, whose possessions were forfeited to the Government. Adjoining the house, and leading up to Finglas, is a narrow, shady path known as 'Savages Lane', from a family who occupied the house about eighty years ago.

The most notable feature in the building is a lofty square turret, the lower part of which appears to be very ancient, probably dating from the time of Queen Elizabeth, while the upper portion, constructed of brickwork, seems to be of most recent date and is covered by a modern, slated roof. The defensive character of the original structure is indicated by a massively built turret with its inconspicuous loopholes commanding the approach to the entrance door and by the arched entrance at the back to an underground passage, now fallen in, which probably led to some secret exit, while inside the front wall a large well furnished the place with water.

Attached to the establishment was numerous out-offices, bake-houses and stables, with extensive walled gardens which still contain a few of the old fruit trees and in the western side of the house may still be seen the remains of the great kitchen fireplace. About 100 years ago this house was used as a tannery, and since that time has been falling gradually into decay. Over the halldoor there formerly was a stone tablet bearing the arms of the Segrave family, the ancient terri-torial proprietors. The whole structure presented the appearance of a dwellinghouse built on the nucleus of an old castle, which, however, has suffered destructive alterations in the process as to leave but little by which to judge its original design or character.

Built on lands that had been rented in 1552 by Archbishop Hugh Curwen to James Segrave and Patrick Sarsfield, in its original design it marked the transition from defence to comfort and is described in the Commonwealth surveys as a stone house with offices, 'surrounded by a garden, orchard and ornamental plantation'. A stone over the door bore the Segrave arms and the residence was in the posses-sion of the Segraves for many generations. When Henry Segrave died here in 1641 his widow, Alice Noble, made her will in which she gave to her unmarried daugh-ters, Alice and Elinor, houses called The Saracen's Head and The Horse-shoe, with a horse each 'to carry them on their journey up and down'. The house later passed into the hands of the Savage family, who lived there for many generations and in 1839 used the house as a tannery. They gave their name to a right-of-way by St Helena's and into Finglas village, called Savage's Lane, clearly marked on the Ordnance Survey map of 1936.

The ruins were a pleasant sight across the rolling countryside from the vantage point of Reilly's Bridge, Ratoath Road. Dillon Cosgrave, in *North Dublin City & County*, describes them as seen from Reilly's Bridge. As an adventureland for the young boys and girls of the new and throbbing suburbs of Cabra and Finglas, it was the scene of many an exciting re-enactment of the *Gunfight at the OK Corral*. Until the mid-1960s thousands would visit the site each year.

Ballyboggan Road

Ballyboggan Road is at the end of Broombridge Road and connects Ratoath Road and Finglas Road. Formerly called King's Lane, a number of fine residences on this thoroughfare are listed on the Ordnance Survey map of 1870: these included Rivermount House and Tolka Lodge, both clearly marked on the Ordnance Survey map of 1948, and Riversdale House, home of the Duffy family. Fred Duffy was the last member of the family to reside here, vacating it in 1973. Unfortunately the house was burnt down while vacant. Shortly after the fire I took photographs of the entrance pillar and the demolished ruins of the homestead. Rivermount House, situated on three-and-a-half acres, fell victim to vandalism in the 1980s. Its ruins were visible until 1990, when the whole area was cleared to allow for the residential development of redbrick houses called Glasnevin Woods. A two-storey apartment block within the complex is called Rivermount House; Rivermount in Finglas South also gets its name from the old house.

All the land in this area, including that of the vast industrial estate, was used as lairage for cattle prior to market day. The Duffy family was deeply involved in the livestock trade and their firm, Duffy, Mangan and Butler, employed many people from the Dublin 7 area; indeed, during the 1950s and 1960s, all the firm's drovers came from the district. Riversdale had a great orchard and children loved 'doing it' every summer. Some years the orchard was 'skint' as early as July. Duffy, Mangan and Butler had lairage parks on the right of Nephin Road; they were one of the oldest institutions serving the industry, having originally sold cattle in Smithfield prior to the transfer of the market to Prussia Street.

Next door to the Duffy household, in Tolka Lodge, lived the Bailey family, who were later succeeded by Willie Clarke. Beginning his working life as a policeman, Willie later became a doctor. He tragically died in an air crash a few years after taking up residence in Tolka Lodge. The house was built around 1780, and it has a fine entrance and two large bay windows. The present owner is Donald Macaulay, who moved here in 1964 and who has painstakingly taken care of its preservation since then. The only other old houses remaining on the Ballyboggan Road are the cottages by the industrial estate and facing Glasnevin Woods. In the early 1990s the little cottage of the Finnegans, on the Finglas side of the road next to Ratoath Road, was vacated and the site incorporated into Tolka Valley Park. Just beside Finglas Bridge, built originally in 1765 and widened in 1815, at the back of Tolka Lodge, stood the Merville Dairy.

Merville Dairy

The ice-cream production element of the Merville Dairy, later subsumed into Premier Dairies, was located at Finglas Bridge. Called Merville Cream Ices, they established themselves on the site in 1940. The factory belonged to the Craigie family, who originally manufactured electric fires and elements for electric kettles there; it was later leased to a polish manufacturing firm until 1939. Victor Craigie, a Director of Premier Dairies, informed me that the building was constructed as a pin factory, and described as such on the 1870 Ordnance Survey map. The factory used the Tolka River as a source of energy and a massive waterwheel was located on the banks of the river, complete with an incoming and tail race. The tail race came into the factory at the rear of the premises and then across the yard outside. In 1952, following severe flooding, a retaining wall was built and the mill race diverted away from the factory premises. The Merville Dairy was on the summer agenda of many a local schoolboy; they scaled the boundary wall from the Tolka river and headed for the corner where the reject chocolate from the choc-ices was dumped. I remember climbing the factory wall with friends and filling brown paper bags (in the days before the first plastic bag, a Roche's Stores Bag, appeared on the scene) with the discarded chocolate, then legging it before being detected.

Ardgillan Estate, now a public amenity run by Fingal County Council, supplied the Merville Dairy with milk.

At the turn of the nineteenth century Victor's father started a cattle-dealing business, with one hundred head of cattle, opposite the present-day ESRI headquarters in Glasnevin, formerly the IIRS. In 1902 the family established a golf-links, which stretched from the site of the old Premier Dairy factory, now a large apartment complex, up to Beneavin. Known as Finglas Golf Club the links was a popular social entertainment spot until the Craigies were forced to close it down due to the loss of the patronage of British military officers, who left to serve on the battlefronts of France and Belgium during the First World War. The Craigies distributed the milk themselves, straight from their farm, up to 1926. In that year they started the processing of milk at their dairy on Finglas Road. In 1969 Merville Dairy merged with Dublin Dairies and Sutton Tel-El Keiber Dairy and production was concentrated in the Premier Dairies complex on the Finglas dual carriageway. The old Merville Dairy premises were demolished, but the boundary wall remained in place until the end of 1995. In the late 1990s an apartment complex was constructed on the site of the former Merville Dairy.

Merville Dairy (Courtesy Old Dublin Society)

At the Finglasbridge end of the Ballyboggan Road, between the road and the river, a pitch-and-putt course operated for over twenty years from the mid-1960s. The land was sold and a small private housing scheme began during the summer of 1992. Part of the bank of the Tolka river at the end of the course has remained in its natural state to this day. A small river ran openly from the back of old Finglas village, behind Farnham House (which once belonged to Lord Farnham and served as an asylum for over four generations). It ran through the golf-links, behind the Royal Oak and into the Tolka River. This stream was used as a cooling water source by the dairy. There were two quarries at the back of Premier Dairies and these were also used as another source of cooling water. As houses continued to be built in the Finglas area they stemmed the flow of water in the general area and the quarries eventually dried up and were filled in. The stonework for the Ashbourne Road came from these same quarries.

Premier Dairies moved production from Finglas Road to Rathfarnham on Dublin's southside in the late-1900s and its former plant on the Finglas Road now incorporates a high-density apartment complex, although industries related to agricultural activity continued to operate in the Cardiffsbridge area. In a factory just inside the entrance to Bellevue Industrial Park, which includes Finglas Business Park, The Irish Yeast Company operated for many years until its recent closure; the factory lay idle in 2016. Henshaw Meats, founded by Peter Henshaw of Broombridge Road, Cabra West, originally operated from the city abattoir on North Circular Road. With its closure in 1977 he moved into a small factory in Bellevue and from modest beginnings and a small workforce of twenty-two, by 1993 it employed over a hundred, all from the surrounding Cabra, Cardiffsbridge and Finglas areas. The factory closed down at the beginning of the century. In 2015 Ryan Meats, established in 2005, moved into the premises; it presently employs fourteen people.

Walter Meleady was born in Bellevue in the early 1950s and grew up here with his siblings and the children of three other families. He later settled in Ashbourne, County Meath and in 1993 he recollected what life was like growing up there:

> During the 1950s and 1960s there were six Meleady children, five Mulhall children, three Gleeson children and two Fitzpatrick children reared on this farm, which was used for lairage for the Dublin Cattle Market. We all enjoyed a beautiful childhood among the fields and the beech and chestnut trees. Attached to the outbuildings at the back was a small slaughterhouse, which catered for local butchers, including Heron Bros of North Circular Road. Over the years this slaughterhouse expanded and became Gleeson's Meat Wholesalers, which was eventually taken over by Peter Henshaw. James Gleeson knocked all these houses and outhouses down in 1976, just two days after we all vacated the property, and sold the surrounding fields to make way for an industrial estate. In the last century I believe that Bellevue and the adjoining properties were used as a mental hospital by a Dr Parkinson.

6| Grangegorman

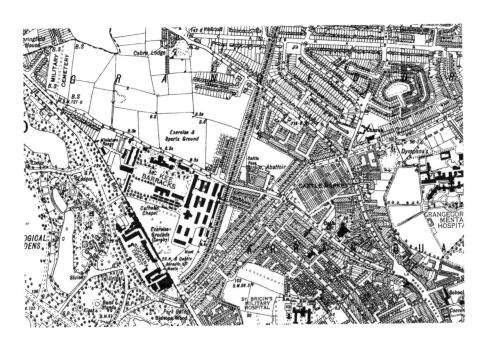

Grangegorman, or Gurmund's Grange (territory of the celebrated Irish king who was the father of the beautiful Isolde, whose romantic story in turn has inspired musician and poet), borders on the districts of Cabra and Phibsborough. Its history is intertwined with that of the surrounding neighbourhoods. In past times it embraced four townlands, Grangegorman Middle (Cabragh), Grangegorman South, East and West. After the Norman invasion of 1170 the area was in the possession of the Priory of the Holy Trinity, Christchurch Cathedral. The priory later acquired the remaining lands in the district by deed of gift from Hugh Hussey, Lord of Galtrim, who had himself obtained them as a grant from the crown. Despite their proximity to the Canon's house at Christchurch, the Grangegorman lands were provided with a manorial residence comprising a hall and several rooms. The original site is near the present-day junction of Prussia Street and Manor Street. In the fourteenth century there was a village at the northern end of Manor Street consisting of sixteen cottages. Inhabitants included three ploughmen, a plough-driver, two carters, a lime-burner and a thrasher.

The manor house at Grangegorman was maintained independently of the Priory House and whenever the Prior visited it, provision was made by the servants 'for his entertainment'. Thus, in the summer of 1346, when the Prior was conferring there, wine, ale and bread were brought for him. In the autumn of that same year, on two nightly occasions, similar purchases were made on his account, with the addition of larks. As a cellarer was included among the Grangegorman residents and brewing was carried on there, it is remarkable that the purchase of wine and ale should have been necessary: it is possible that the cellarer's duties lay at the Priory and the Grangegorman ale was not of a sufficiently high quality for the refined taste buds of the Prior. Besides the cellarer, the staff at Grangegorman included an overseer and ten servants, in addition to the farm workers who included a bailiff, two foremen, two carters and six ploughmen.

In medieval times Salcock's Wood was located where New Cabra Road now runs. It is clearly identified on John Taylor's 1816 map of Dublin as Sallcock's Wood, though by that time it covered just a very small area. The dense wood provided a feeding ground for wild swine as well as valuable timber and was carefully guarded by its managers. It is recorded that in 1493, on the Feast of the Ascension, the ditch was broken down and eight cows put into the wood by an inhabitant of Little Cabragh without permission. Around the same time the wife of Donald Swinard cut down two ash trees. In 1550 the Priory covenanted to give one of its tenants eight oak and four ash trees for building purposes. During the late 1500s Salcock's Wood was subdivided and plots were leased. In 1574, on account of his generosity to Christ Church Cathedral the Bishop of Meath was given one of these plots and in 1594 no less than seven of them were let; the tenants included an alderman, an organist, a servant of the Solicitor-General and three clergymen. In the 1640s a large farm at Salcock's Wood was owned by one Richard Mason, whose livestock included thirty-nine cows and nine horses. His livestock was stolen in 1641 and in a deposition made four years later he tried to implicate Henry Segrave of Little Cabragh and one 'Clarke of the Bay' from Mulhuddart in the theft.

In a lease of lands at Much Cabragh to John Parker in the 1500s it was provided that he should be allowed to 'carry away annually six cart-loads of timber from the wood and to keep forty swine in it', as well as to 'hunt, hawk and fish there and elsewhere in the lordship of Grangegorman'. He was also permitted to have six cartloads of furze, which appears to have grown in large quantities between the villages of Grangegorman and Glasnevin. During the 1600s the chief thoroughfares in the Grangegorman district were the road to Cabragh (Manor Street, Prussia Street and Old Cabra Road) and the road to Ashtown (Aughrim Street and Blackhorse Avenue). On the road to Cabragh, near a place called Rotten Row, a headless cross could be seen and on the road to Ashtown a place known as the Long Mile's End marked the traveller's progress.

A reader might wonder where the aforementioned John Parker would use his right to fish on foot of the lease of Much Cabragh granted all those centuries ago. In fact, fish were plentiful in the district, in the clean waters of the river that flowed through the area, the Bradoge Water. Marie Kenny of Dalymount, Phibsborough, showed me the deeds to her house, which includes a clause 'to hunt, hawk, fish' at 'all convenient times and seasons'. Dalymount was just a short walk from the Bradoge.

Rising in Cabra, next to the Royal Canal and Liffey Junction where the waste ground in the vicinity of the river's source is sometimes swampy and always damp, the Bradoge is now covered over from its source to its entry into the Liffey near the Ormond Hotel. As a flowing river it meandered past the junction of present-day Fassaugh Road and Quarry Road, crossing Cabra Road, passing the back of Charleville Road, along Grangegorman Lane, under the present day Health Services Executive offices, past the front of Broadstone Station, across Constitution Hill and through the grounds of King's Inns, along the middle of Henrietta Street and Bolton Street, under Green Street Courthouse and Halston Street and finally under the Corporation Fruit and Vegetable Market, to enter the Liffey at the east end of East Arran Street, formerly called Boot Lane. In 1909 it became a sewer from the spot where it entered the city proper at Grangegorman.

Now hidden away from us for all time, the Bradoge Water was once an important little river judging by the many local place names. Broadstone, at first sight an ordinary English name, is really derived from our form of the Norse 'Bradoge-Steyn', the stone of the Bradoge. Halston Street was in earlier times known as Bradoge Lane and Chancery Street as Pill Lane, so named from the estuary of the Bradoge; the word 'pill' means a creek or pool and John Speed's 1610 plan of Dublin shows the estuary of the Bradoge and some other inlets. It appears on William Duncan's 1821 map of Dublin as Bradoge River, where its course is very clearly delineated; it also appears on the 1876 Ordnance Survey map as Bradoge Water.

The district was the property of the ancient Abbey of St Mary, whose abbots had a pier on the Bradoge and a fleet of vessels with which they traded with English and mainland European ports. The Abbey Green was at Green Street and here the Bradoge Water was crossed by a little bridge near the quiet retreat of the monks, known as the Park of the Anchorites. The area around Aughrim Street was densely wooded up to 1769, and here the Bradoge Water was, no doubt, a welcome guide to travellers coming into the city. An RTÉ Radio documentary, *The Hidden River*, produced in 1984 by Peter Mooney, who lived in the district until his untimely death in May 2015, gave a lively account of the Bradoge river. It may be of interest to know that there is a Bradoge river in County Donegal, entering the sea at the popular holiday resort of Bundoran.

In the mid-1500s Grangegorman Manor was the residence of the Right Honorable Francis Agard, who at the time of his death was the virtual ruler of Ireland. Besides the manor and farm the cathedral also leased to him 'a kiln and a sheepfold, a moiety of an orchard, the meadow of Garget's Mead' in which the lessee reserved a right to graze four horses. Like most prominent men in the Elizabethan age, Agard rendered State service in both a military and civil capacity. He appears in 1548 as serving in Scotland under Lord Seymour de Sudeley as captain of a troop of horse; in 1556 rendering 'good service' against Shane O'Neill; in 1569 as 'venturing his life as governor of the Wicklow tribes'; in 1574 acting as head of a commission in Munster and in 1576 allaying unrest in the eastern part of Leinster. He was highly thought of by the English court, and Queen Elizabeth I relied on his experience and judgment even to the exclusion of her Irish officials. A frequent visitor at her court, he died in the autumn of 1577. Her Lord Deputy, Sir Henry Sidney, spoke of him as his 'fidus Achates' and said after Agard's death that a greater loss could not 'in any sort have chanced him'.

Agard was succeeded at Grangegorman by a son-in-law, Sir Henry Harrington, a cousin of the famous Elizabethan writer Sir John Harrington. In governing the O'Byrnes and O'Tooles of Wicklow, Sir Henry was frequently in the public eye. His policy of civil administration varied between outright coercion, gentle persuasion and bribery; the bribery earned him the censure of Sir John Davies, for 'permitting the barbarous custom of the people'. In battle he proved himself a brave, though somewhat foolhardy, commander. Following the death of Harrington in 1613 Grangegorman appears to have passed to the representatives of Agard's eldest daughter. Around 1630 Lord Ranelagh was negotiating for its purchase but at the time of the 1641 Rising it was still in the possession of the Agard family. In the *Commonwealth Survey* it is returned as containing 500 acres under crops and 300 under grass, with an old stone house valued at no more than forty pounds.

During the early part of the eighteenth century Grangegorman became the residence of Sir John Stanley's nephew, Charles Monck. Charles Monck married a granddaughter of Sir John Stephens of Finglas, and through her acquired the residence of 'Charleville', Enniskerry, County Wicklow; Charles died in 1751. The Monck family's long association with the general district is commemorated today in such place names as Royce Road (from the name of a family intermarried with the Moncks), Rathdown Road (from the family title of Earl of Rathdowne) and Monck Place; and by Charleville Road and Enniskerry Road (from the family's Charleville residence in County Wicklow). The first Earl of Rathdowne was Henry Stanley Monck; the fourth Viscount Monck, Charles Stanley, who was born in 1819, became the first Canadian Governor General. He died at his home in Enniskerry on 29 November 1894.

In the mid-1700s the northern part of the parish of Grangegorman contained few houses and probably one of the earliest buildings to be constructed was that of the female orphan house and church, beside the present junction of North Circular Road, Old Cabra Road and Annamoe Road. Founded in December 1790 and incorporated by an Act of Parliament in 1800, in 1807 it catered for 140 children and its treasurers were Messrs La Touche; its postal address was 191, 193 and 195 North Circular Road. In 1912 it catered for eighty-four children and the Matron was a Miss Large; the chaplain was Rev. Henry Taylor and the chemist a W.D. Porter, who then had an apothecary located at 59 Madras Place, Phibsborough. It is clearly marked on the Ordnance Survey maps of 1875 and 1938. In 1964 the property was acquired by Park Developments Ltd, the following year the buildings were demolished and the present office block, Park House, was constructed on the site. Part of the original boundary wall still survives.

Michael Collins was living at 16 Rathdown Road at the time of the 1916 Rising, and furnished that address to the British authorities following his arrest. This was the home of Patrick Belton; the pair had met while working in London. Patrick Belton was born in 1884 and he joined the Civil Service in London. Assigned to the Land Commission in Dublin in 1910, he took part in the Easter Rising, resulting in his suspension from the Civil Service. Upon his release he established a dairy farm and market garden and later purchased Belfield Park in Drumcondra, adjacent to Puckstown Lane. He later became a developer and built many houses in Drumcondra, Santry and Donnycarney. It was he who named the present-day thoroughfares of Collins Avenue and Griffith Avenue.

Grangegorman Road

At the junction of Grangegorman Road and North Circular Road stood Sheridan's Garage, well known to many in the district during the 1950s and 1960s. William Sheridan owned the house on the corner, Phoenix House, which had a distinctive carving of a phoenix above the entrance. There were three children in the family, two sons and a daughter, and a live-in housekeeper called Sally. A sweet shop and an off-licence adjoined the house. Although listed, the building was demolished in recent years after concerns about subsidence. Sheridans owned the whole block, as far down as the new 'upside down' houses at the wall of St Brendan's; these houses have the bedrooms at ground-floor level and the living area on the first floor. The garage was later sold to Dan Diffley Motors. A larger-than-life employee at Sheridan's Garage was Stan Daly, foreman and mechanic; he spent over thirty years working there. The garage is now occupied by Derek Delaney Motors. Dave Stewart and Sons, a car repair and servicing centre, is directly across from Sheridans. Dave first started working here in 1965, when he was thirteen, as an apprentice to Art McAssey. He served his time as a mechanic and took over the business when Art retired.

St Brendan's Hospital, called 'Brendan's' locally, was situated on approximately seventy acres and was accessed from Grangegorman Road, which runs from Brunswick Street to North Circular Road. Opened in 1815 as the Richmond Lunatic Asylum, and later called Grangegorman Mental Hospital, it was the first public mental hospital in Ireland. The complex contained a number of buildings, some designed by the noted architect Francis Johnston. The Mental Treatment Act 1945, implemented in 1947, brought the treatment of mental health into the twentieth century and at this time there were approximately 2000 patients within its walls. In April 1959 the name was changed to St Brendan's Hospital and in that year the number of patients totalled 1800.

The noted trade unionist Mary 'Maura' Breslin (1914–84) began her working life as a staff nurse at Brendan's. A member of the Irish Women Workers' Union, she became its President in 1958. In 1971 she became General Secretary and was the first woman to be elected onto the executive of the Irish Congress of Trade Unions, in 1973. In the late 1970s she targeted large corporate employers, including the Bank of Ireland, in a high-profile and successful campaign on behalf of women contract cleaners on low pay.

With the appointment of the far-sighted Dr Ivor Browne as the country's Chief Psychiatrist in January 1966 the treatment of patients changed dramatically, and one of his first proposals was the immediate reduction in the height of the entrance boundary wall to three feet. This was followed by the appointment of a well-known Dublin variety artist, Ben Bono, as Recreation Officer and the adoption of a policy leading to the gradual placement of people with mental health issues in the wider community. Later, a greater tolerance to mental health developed, with attitudes influenced by organizations such as the Mental Health Association and the Schizophrenia Association of Ireland.

In addition, the emergence in Ireland of groups such as Camphill Community and the L'Arche Community, each with their own unique way of caring for those with special needs, provided an alternative model to the institutional one. Yet another change came with homeless services by voluntary organizations like the Simon Community. All these organizations rely heavily on volunteers, giving young people a platform to share their lives with those whom they serve and in this way developing a broader understanding of mental health issues. All these changes, over a period of time, led to the vacating of St Brendan's; however, the well-documented lack of provision of outside supports resulted in discharged patients becoming homeless, and with the substitution of prison accommodation for that formerly provided within the grounds of the hospital.

During the early part of the present century proposals were made for the redevelopment of the site as a new university campus for the Dublin Institute of Technology (DIT). The first development was the construction of the Phoenix mental health care centre to replace Brendan's, accessed from an entrance on North Circular Road. A number of DIT faculties opened on the campus during 2015, including fine arts. This first phase saw the refurbishment of seven historic listed buildings, now used by one thousand DIT students. The hospitality faculty, presently located in Cathal Brugha Street, is scheduled to locate in Grangegorman in 2018. A new six-storey block to house the Research Centre was completed in late 2015 on a site next to the Grangegorman Road entrance. St Laurence's Roman Catholic church has been renovated for use as a multipurpose building and serves as a lecture room, a quiet room and for religious purposes. In a spirit of inclusiveness, the grounds of the new campus, landscaped and containing a children's playground, are open to the public, providing an excellent outdoor amenity. New entrances into the campus have been created at Park Shopping Centre, Prussia Street (Tesco) and at the bottom of the little cul-de-sac (called 'curley sack' locally) of Fingal Place, off Prussia Street.

Opposite the entrance to Brendan's is the former Richmond General Penitentiary, currently used by the Health Services Executive as an administrative centre: this imposing building was constructed in 1812 and completed in 1816, a date confirmed by the distinctive weathercock on the cupola. Designed by Francis Johnston, the name Richmond derived from Charles, 4th Duke of Richmond. Through the years the building has functioned as a debtors' prison, a female jail and a holding place for women awaiting forced deportation to Tasmania, then called Van Diemen's Land. It also served as a cholera hospital. A nurses' home, of redbrick construction and similar to one at the Mater Hospital, North Circular Road, was built in the early 1950s on a site beside the old penitentiary; it was demolished in 2014 as part of the DIT development plan.

Off Grangegorman Road is tiny Stanhope Street, dating from 1792 and named after Philip Dormer Stanhope. The naming occurred forty-five years after the Viceroyalty of Philip, 1st Earl of Chesterfield, and that of his kinsman and immediate successor to the Viceroyalty, William Stanhope, 1st Earl of Harrington. On 8 January 1745, as Lord Lieutenant, Philip warned that 'poverty' was a far greater threat in Ireland than 'popery' and ran a benign administration. He made many improvements to the Phoenix Park, including the erection of the Phoenix monument, for many years called 'Chesterfield's Column'; it is known universally as 'the Eagle monument'. The main road in the Phoenix Park is called after him. A 'house of refuge for industrious females' was opened here in 1811. Stanhope Street Convent and secondary school is situated on a large site extending along Kirwan Street and has another entrance on Manor Street. It was established on 2 February 1819. Kirwan Street, joining Grangegorman Lane to Manor Street, and Kirwan

Cottages are called after Dr James Kirwan, Coroner of Dublin, member of one of the tribes of Galway and a former owner of property in the district.

Stanley Street

After the Restoration of King Charles II to the throne of England in 1660, the village of Grangegorman was recorded as containing over forty houses, including two rated for four hearths and four rated for three hearths. The Manor House, rebuilt at this time, became the residence of Sir Thomas Stanley, one of Henry Cromwell's knights and after whom Stanley Street is called. Like many of Henry Cromwell's friends, Sir Thomas proved to be a good royalist and was the representative for County Louth in the Restoration Parliament. He was greatly identified with Tipperary and Waterford and appears to have been a close friend of Valentine Greatrakes. Valentine was famous in his time for curing various ills by simply stroking the part affected. On his death in 1674 Sir Thomas left more than one son and a daughter Sarah, who married Henry Monck, an ancestor of Viscount Monck, in 1663. Sir Thomas's Grangegorman possessions passed to his youngest son, John Stanley (remembered as Mrs Delany's uncle). When John was made a baronet by William III, he was described as being from Grangegorman; he lived in England for most of his life, where through the influence of the Granvilles he obtained various offices. His principal connection with Ireland was through his tenure of Chief Secretary, a post he held during the viceroyalty of the Duke of Shrewsbury. In a letter to Dean Jonathan Swift, author of *Gulliver's Travels*, who regarded him with great esteem, he writes as 'one who was an utter stranger to the country' and says that it is 'the most eating, drinking, wrangling and quarrelsome place that I ever saw'.

A Dublin City Council depot is located in Stanley Street, which is the last remaining street in Dublin containing its original tram tracks; the section of tram tracks that were once within the confines of the depot were removed in 1992 and used as track for the outdoor tram display in the grounds of Howth Castle demesne. There was a rubbish destructor in the depot and the tracks were used to facilitate the removal of street sweepings and crushed waste in freight carts to Fairview during land reclamation works there in the early 1900s. Three electric tram locomotives, from R.W. Blackwell and Company of London, transported the waste. As late as 1991 there were two blacksmiths based in the depot, engaged in what was then a dying trade. The depot is now used by the fire brigade service, for repair and maintenance of the fleet: according to the gatekeeper, Martin Cannon, it's a busy place, as vehicles attached to the fire brigade service are in operation twenty-four hours a day all year around and have to be quickly repaired and maintained.

Brunswick Street

Before 1766 Brunswick Street was called Channel Row, deriving this name, still heard in the area in the early 1900s, from a channel connecting the little river of the Bradoge. The street takes its name from Charles, Duke of Brunswick, who married Princess Augusta, a sister of George III, in 1764. He was killed in battle during the Napoleonic wars, as was his son and successor: Charles died at Jena in 1806, his son at Quatre Bras on 16 June 1815. Brunswick Street National School opened on 2 February 1869, with classes starting the following week. The site was purchased by the parish priest of Arran Quay, Canon Brock, for £1000 and the building, designed by Thomas Ashlin and constructed by Comerfords, 'builders of distinction' of North King Street, cost £4000. The structure consisted of four large and two small rooms, with a facing of cut granite. Over 300 boys attended on the first day but within a few short months this swelled to 500. Locally known as 'the Brunner', one of its noted past pupils is Sean P. Cromien, a Secretary of the Department of Finance. Paddy Crosbie, famous for his *School Around the Corner* television programme during the early days of Telefís Éireann, was also a pupil and in later life returned as a teacher, spending almost all his later career at the school.

Brunswick Street was the residence of Frances (Fanny) Jennings, the wife of Richard Talbot, the 'Great Tyrconnel'. During the short-lived reign of James II, Richard Talbot was the most powerful person in Ireland. He married Fanny in 1681, who then became Duchess of Tyrconnel. She was at Saint-Germain when Richard died, in the Williamite wars during the siege of Limerick, in early August 1691. She returned to Ireland shortly thereafter, settling in Carmichael House which still stands on the corner of North Brunswick Street and Morning Star Avenue. Called the Carmichael School of Medicine, it was originally a school of medicine, later serving as a residence for medical students. It was designed by

Rogers in the Victorian Venetian style and is strongly reminiscent of Woodward's Kildare Street Club. Accounts vary as to the financial means of Frances following the death of her husband and the change in the Irish political landscape, but she apparently had some money, as she founded a nunnery in North King Street for the Order of the Poor Clares. During a March night in 1731 she fell out of bed and, being too feeble to rise or call for aid, she was found on the floor the next morning, so perished from the cold that she died within a few hours. She was buried in the vaults of St Patrick's Cathedral.

Dillon Cosgrave in *North Dublin City & County* places her residence at 63 North King Street – now occupied by Brunswick Street schools. In the late 1980s I discussed this matter with a teacher there, Brother Con Foran, who was considered a mine of information on the local area: he believed that Frances lived in the house just beside the Morning Star Hostel next to the old Richmond Hospital complex, and that he was told this many years previously by the grandfathers of boys attending the school. According to Sir Charles Petrie in his book *The Great Tyrconnel*, Paradise Row, Arbour Hill was where Fanny lived. The location given by Brother Foran, however, is quite plausible, as some elderly people in the district maintain that the information had been orally handed down through the generations.

Frances Talbot was a sister of Sarah, Duchess of Marlborough, who married John Churchill on 1 October 1678: he was the famous English general who first experienced military success at Kinsale and Cork during the Williamite wars; according to Sir Charles Petrie he then relinquished his command and returned to England, as he did not want to face his brother-in-law Richard Talbot in battle. He subsequently entered the pages of history on many continental European battlefields, including Ramillies and Landen. In his early military years John Churchill lived in Lower Bridge Street, facing Church Street on the opposite side of the River Liffey, then one of Dublin's 'most fashionable streets'.

Richmond Hospital

The former Richmond Hospital on Brunswick Street occupied the site of a convent, Channel Row Nunnery, sacked by Williamite forces following their victory at the battle of the Boyne in 1690; the convent was vacated by the Dominican nuns in 1809. The hospital complex comprised a group of three hospitals known as the

St Laurence Hospitals, comprising the Richmond, Whitworth and Hardwicke. The Hardwicke Fever Hospital was built in 1803, the Richmond Surgical Hospital in 1811 and the Whitworth Medical Hospital in 1817. All three buildings were designed by Francis Johnston and named after British viceroys in office at the time of construction. The part of the former hospital complex today facing Brunswick Street schools is a splendid redbrick palace complete with copper domes and verandahs facing onto a courtyard. It dates from 1900, and its unique architecture gives an Elizabethan or Jacobean impression to passers-by. It replaced the original Richmond Surgical Hospital, behind a dairy farm. Upon the hospital relocation to Beaumont, Dublin 9 in the 1980s, the Hardwicke and Whitworth were converted into apartments. The redbrick building was occupied from the mid-1990s by the Road Traffic Courts of the Dublin Metropolitan District Court, now located at Parkgate Street. The building was undergoing restoration work in 2016.

Richmond Hospital (Courtesy Dublin Ghost Signs)

The Morning Star Hostel for men and Regina Ceoli Hostel for women are located just up the avenue; they are run by the Legion of Mary, a Roman Catholic lay organization, and provide sheltered accommodation for homeless adults. Built in 1772 as a workhouse, the House of Industry, as it was then called, was set up to 'rid the streets of sturdy beggars and idle, strolling and disorderly women'. The Morning Star Hostel building once held the notorious 'Billy in the Bowl', a beggar born without legs who got about in a large bowl reinforced with iron bands, made for him by a kindly blacksmith. His powerful arms and hands compensated for his lack of mobility. He progressed from begging to robbery, and then to murder, through overpowering his unfortunate victims by the strength of his arms, hands and chest. Due to his deformity he was overlooked as a suspect in a string of murders in the Smithfield area. However, he was finally detected in 1786. His legend lived on in the district, and he even gained a mention in James Joyce's *Finnegans Wake*.

The building later became a part of the North Dublin Union and in 1926 it was vested in the Legion of Mary following an approach to them from the Department of Local Government. With the help of many volunteers it was repaired and cleaned up and on 25 March 1927 they had it ready to receive the first two homeless residents, Seán Casey and John Moloney. By 1930 there were 130 men resident in the hostel and work was provided in the yard, making concrete blocks for sale to the building trade and collecting old newspapers for sale to used-paper merchants. This activity ended with universal social welfare payments. The hostel is still in operation and in recent years underwent a multi-million euro renovation to bring it up to present-day requirements. The Regina Coeli Hostel next door provides accommodation to forty homeless women, aged eighteen to sixty years, in individual rooms.

All Saints Church, Grangegorman

All Saints Church is situated on Phibsborough Road, in a quiet spot not far from Monck Place. Built in 1825 following the division of St Paul's parish, North King Street, improvements were carried out and the church extended in 1867. In 1966 the greater part of the North Aisle was destroyed by fire. However, the Church of Ireland congregation rallied and the building was restored and reopened in May 1968. The distinctive church organ, lost in the fire, was irreplaceable. A piano served as substitute for nearly twenty years until a new organ was installed in

1986; it was dedicated to the memory of Victor Leeson, organist and choirmaster from 1943 until 1986. A new rectory was built in 1979, on the site of the former stables at the back of the church. Dublin Corporation acquired the old vicarage, including almost all of the locally famous orchard, and in 1985 constructed a new fire brigade station on the site.

Some interesting clergymen have been attached to All Saints down the years, the most notable of these being the second vicar, William Maturin, of Huguenot ancestry. He was born in 1806, the eldest son of Charles Robert Maturin, a Church of Ireland clergyman and noted novelist, who was curate at St Peter's, Dublin. William was related to Henry Maturin, Rector of Gartan, Donegal (1805–80) who chartered a boat from his own funds to import food for the starving in his district during the famine years (1845–48). William too became a novelist and also wrote plays. He graduated from TCD in 1831 and was ordained a priest; he was appointed Rector to All Saints in May 1843, a post he held until his death in 1887; he was also Keeper or Librarian to Marsh's Library, a post he held from 1872. William Maturin married Jane Cooke, daughter of Captain Robert Bentley, on 17 August 1843, the same year he moved into All Saints'. The couple raised their ten children, five sons and five daughters, in the Grangegorman vicarage. Two of their daughters became nuns and three of their sons entered Church ministry.

Maturin was a gifted orator with extreme tractarian views. Although he drew large crowds, he was not so popular with his Church superiors, who regarded him as a maverick. He was described by Provost Mahaffy of Trinity College as 'the best preacher in all Ireland' and George Tyrrell spoke of him as 'one of the few preachers to whom my own father could listen without blaspheming afterwards'. William died on 30 June 1887 at Monkstown, County Dublin.

The aforementioned George Tyrrell was born on 6 February 1861 at 91 Dorset Street, son of William Henry Tyrrell, sub-editor of the *Dublin Evening Mail*. From 1876 he was drawn to the High-Church circle of William Maturin at All Saints and was a constant presence there for over three years. He became influenced by Robert Dolling, a friend of William Maturin, and his spiritual journey later led him to attend Gardiner Street Roman Catholic church; his conversion to Roman Catholicism followed on 18 May 1879. He entered the Society of Jesus in 1882, and was ordained a Jesuit priest on 20 September 1891. Noted for his deep spirituality, he was a prolific author and wrote for the Jesuit journal *The Month*;

his first book was entitled *Nova et vetera*. He fell foul of Church authorities and was excommunicated; shortly after that, in February 1906, he was expelled from the Jesuits at the behest of the Pope. He died on 15 July 1909 at Mulberry House, Storrington, Sussex, of Bight's Disease. He was refused a Roman Catholic burial and was interred in the churchyard of the Anglican parish of Storrington: Basil William Maturin and the Abbé Bremond were the only Roman Catholic priests to attend the funeral.

Basil William Maturin was born in the Grangegorman vicarage on 15 February 1847, the third eldest of the ten Maturin children. He entered religious life in 1870 as a Church of Ireland deacon, but converted to Roman Catholicism on 5 March 1897 and was ordained in Rome the following year. Huge crowds came to hear him preach at St Margaret's Chapel on St Leonard's Street in Westminister, London. He became a compelling speaker and went on a preaching tour of the United States in the spring of 1915. He was returning home on the *Lusitania* when it was torpedoed on 7 May 1915; his body was washed ashore sometime after the sinking.

Cecil Frances 'Fanny' Alexander (1818–95) was a famous hymn-writer who has connections with All Saints. Her husband, who later became Bishop of Derry, was an assistant curate at Grangegorman. Fanny loved the gardens at All Saints and the company of the Maturin family. At the time the gardens, on a hill overlooking the city, offered panoramic views of the Dublin mountains; they are vividly described in one of her well-known creations, 'All Things Bright and Beautiful':

> The purple-headed mountains
> the river running by
> the sunset, and the morning
> that brightens up the sky.
> The cold wind in the winter,
> the pleasant summer sun
> the ripe fruits in the garden
> he made them every one.

Rev. J.W. Armstrong, Archbishop of Armagh, was assistant curate at Grangegorman from 1938 to 1944; Rev. R. St Laurence Broadberry, Canon of Canterbury, assisted from 1956 to 1958. From 1966 to 1976 a much-loved and well-known curate assisted at All Saints. Frederick Robert Willis, born on 16 June 1900, who served with the Indian Mission and was Bishop of Delhi from 1951 to 1966, settled in the church grounds on his return to the West. Everyone in the area knew him and throughout the district he was affectionately referred to as 'the Bishop on the Bicycle'. He died on 13 November 1976 and was succeeded by Canon Norman Commiskey, who died in 1984.

A well-known figure at All Saints was Archdeacon Raymond Jenkins, resident curate from 1939 until 1976. Archdeacon Jenkins was familiar with the personalities of the district and on the lives of the various clergymen who served in the area down the years, and has written a book on the life of William Maturin. He spent a number of years of his retirement living within the Church complex, moving to Damer Court in Upper Wellington Street, just off Mountjoy Street, in 1990. He died in 1998, in his hundredth year. A national school was once attached to the church but closed down in the mid-1950s following the drift of the parish population to the outlying suburbs. The former school building now serves the community as a parish hall.

The present rector and resident of the vicarage is Archdeacon David Pierpoint; he also serves as Church of Ireland chaplain to An Garda Síochána. Ordained in 1985, he celebrated twenty years of ministry at All Saints in 2015; he oversaw the renovations of the church in 2001. David is related to Folliott Sandford Pierpoint (1835–1917), the hymn writer who composed the famous Christmas song 'Jingle Bells'.

Fire Station

The Dublin Fire Brigade was the first unionized fire service in the world. In the beginning there were four fire stations: the area covered by Dublin 7 was served by Number 3 Station, originally located on Buckingham Street. In 1891 it relocated to a new, purpose-built fire station on Dorset Street, adjacent to Dominick Street. Joe Connolly from the Number 3 Station fought in the 1916 Easter Rising with the Irish Citizen Army and he later became Chief of the Dublin Fire Brigade. A total of five members of the Dublin fire service took part in the rebellion.

From its base in Dorset Street the Dublin Fire Brigade served the district for many years; however, with a capacity for just two vehicles, the premises became inadequate for the needs of a growing and expanding city: in 1985 it transferred to a new, modern fire station at Grangegorman, on Phibsborough Road, next door to All Saints Church, on a site formerly occupied by the old vicarage. The foyer of the station is like a mini museum and showcases its past in photographs and exhibits. At the rear of the station there is a Garden of Reflection, which commemorates deceased members of the service; this was paid for by the fire crew, who also voluntarily upkeep and maintain it. The present-day complement is ninety-eight, headed by a District Officer. Two fire tenders, a rescue tender and an ambulance are based at the station. The ambulance service began in the 1880s; the Dublin Fire Brigade crest contains the City Arms and it forms the official Guard of Honour for the Lord Mayor of Dublin. Interestingly, the Grangegorman Fire Station is one of the few still using the iconic fireman's pole. The former station still exists; it has been used for various community activities over the years and was undergoing remedial works during 2016.

The following descriptions of some of the fires tackled in the district during the early years of the service come from Fire Brigade annual reports:

Connaught Street: On 30 October 1884, following receipt of Police telegraph, the brigade rushed to the premises of William Murray, Dairy Proprietor, Connaught Street, off Phibsborough Road, where a fire, originating in a small hayrick containing eight tons of hay valued at £33 6s. 8d., was raging. The hayrick was situated near the dwelling house, a building of one storey high, with a thatched roof and consisting of four apartments. The brigade had to extend 1700 feet of hose from standpipes in order to fight the fire, which was then brought under control. The house and outoffices were undamaged. The cause of the fire was unknown.

Thomond Terrace: Police telegraph informed the brigade of a fire at Briget Franey's Drapery store at 4, Thomond Terrace, Blacquire Bridge, on 29 January 1887. The No. 15 brigade arrived on the scene, with four supernumeries, two turncocks, one brigade engine and three hose carriages. There was a good water supply. The brigade worked two lines of hose from stand-pipes; water pressure was 50 lbs. The fire originated in the shop of a two-storey back building consisting of seven apartments; three were destroyed and four with contents, were saved. The fire was brought under control and the brigade departed the scene, but left two men with one line of hose as a watch-line, until 7.15am on 30 January. Councillor Edward McMahon was present. Damage was estimated at £270. The premises were insured with Scottish Provincial for £300. The expenses of the fire brigade totalled £1.5s 0d. (€1.60).

Church Street: On 2 July 1893 the brigade was called to 26, Church Street, owned by Mrs Mary Halligan. The fire originated in a loft near stables containing a load of straw and twelve hundredweight of new mown hay, which overheated. The brigade worked two lines of hose from hydrants, with a water pressure of 90 lbs. Stables, straw and adjacent tenement houses were saved. The hay was destroyed and portion of the roof damaged. The cause of the fire was spontaneous combustion.

Cabra Road: At 7.17 pm on 1 July 1899, a fire broke out in cattle sheds located at 4, Cabra Road. An extended line of hose was needed to run from the hydrant. The fire was brought under control, with damage estimated at £150. The fire had occurred outside the Municipal area.

Many fire brigade call-outs were for chimney fires. In the tenements of Dublin in the 1890s and early 1900s, the brigade might have to tackle up to a dozen chimney fires in one tenement house. As at Church Street, common cause of fire

McKee Barracks, early 1900s (Courtesy Lawrence Collection, NLI)

was from spontaneous combustion in haysheds – before the advent of the motor car, many middle-class houses had stables at the rear.

McKee Barracks

McKee Barracks is an imposing and unique military structure dominating Blackhorse Avenue. It was constructed between 1888 and 1892 on a 45-acre site, chosen for its proximity to the city railway stations and port and the training facilities for cavalry in the adjoining Phoenix Park. Its design was by Lieutenant Colonel J.T. Marsh, BE. The site cost the British War Department £15,000, or £333 per acre. The buildings, of brick and in the French chateau, Elizabethan, Queen Anne and Tudor styles, were grouped on three sides of a 120-yard-long barrack square. The plans were carried out under the supervision of Major Barklie, Royal Engineers. The contractor was J.P. Pile and the building cost £80,000.

First occupied on 15 October 1891 by the British army's 10th Hussars, the strength to be accommodated was 862 men and as many horses. It was originally known as Grangegorman Barracks, until its formal naming, Marlborough Barracks, after the grandfather of Winston Churchill (Prime Minister of Britain during World War Two), who served as Lord Lieutenant and Viceroy of Ireland from 1876 to 1879. It is often mistakenly thought to be named after John Churchill, the 1st Duke of Marlborough. Commandant Andrew Shinnick, formerly of the 2nd Field Artillery Regiment, who hails from Ballyhooley, County Cork, is the current Commanding Officer of McKee Barracks.

The main entrance was on Blackhorse Avenue, and another led out to Marlborough Road, over a bridge spanning the connector railway line linking Heuston and Connolly stations. This entrance is now blocked off and the bridge is covered in grass and wild shrubbery. Marlborough Road is built on what was, in the 1870s, a field belonging to Miss Richardson. A cul-de-sac with a metal fence prevents access to the disused railway bridge. There are thirteen redbrick terraced houses on one side, built in the early 1900s; on the other side is the imposing Carndonagh House where James F. Gillespie lived in the 1920s. Facing it, in what was the former garden of the residence, is an apartment complex of fourteen units, constructed in the mid 1970s. A hill behind these apartments offers panoramic views towards the south of the city.

At the rear of the barracks the West Gate, still in use, leads directly into the Phoenix Park; this provided access to excellent cavalry training facilities. The following extract from the *Irish Times* of Friday 16 October 1891 refers to the initial occupation:

> On Thursday October 15th 1891, the headquarters of the 10th Hussars moved into Marlborough Barracks, Dublin, which had been prepared for their reception on the previous day. The under-mentioned officers of the 10th Hussars accompanied the headquarters from the Curragh Camp to Marlborough Barracks: Major Manners-Wood, commanding; H.R.H. the Duke of Clarence and Avondale, Captain Hon. A. Lawley, Adjutant; Captain Hon. J.H.G. Byng; Captain Hon. G. Bryan; Lieutenant Barkley, Lieutenant Brank, Lieutenant Molyneaux, Lieutenant Curzon and Captain Longhurst A.P.D., attached.

An article in the *Irish Builder* of 15 October 1891 gives a full appreciation of the architectural significance of the military complex. The article also dispels a much loved and still often quoted local myth that the plans were intended for a British military barracks in India and were by mistake used during the construction on Blackhorse Lane (Avenue). The riding school and stables are on the west side of the barrack square, with the billet blocks and married quarters on the east side and the officers' mess on the north. The block to the south was built in 1939.

At nine o'clock on the morning of 17 December 1922 the barracks was handed over by the British army to Comandant Bernard J. McMahon, E Company, 2nd Battalion, Dublin Brigade and was renamed after Brigadier Richard 'Dick' McKee (1893–1920). Dick McKee joined the Volunteers on its formation in 1913 and served in G Company, 2nd Battalion, Dublin Brigade; he fought under Thomas McDonagh at Jacob's Mills during the 1916 Rising. In 1918 he commanded the Dublin Brigade and was Director of Training. On 'Bloody Sunday', 21 November 1920, he was arrested by the British auxiliary force, the Black and Tans and taken to Dublin Castle, where he was murdered that night. A bronze bust of him by Laurence Campbell RHA is displayed in the hall of the Officers' Mess. The architecturally interesting mess building is crowned with an 86-foot-high pinnacle, erected in 1950.

McKee Barracks made an early entry into the Irish history books when, on 1 January 1926, Radio Éireann was established and its first call sign, 2RN, issued from the complex where the fledgling radio station had established its mast. Transmission from the barracks continued until 1931.

A pair of cannon positioned outside the Officers' Mess, manufactured in India, were captured at the battle of Gujerat in 1849 and were part of a presentation made to Field Marshall Gough on his retirement. They were originally displayed in the National Museum. A framed montage in the hallway of the Officers Mess outlines and records the history of the guns. There are many paintings on view throughout the barracks, including 'Manoeuvres Near the Gun Line' by Etienne-Prosper Berne-Bellecour (1838–1910), on loan from the National Gallery's Chester Beatty Collection. Items of interest include a pair of bronze Marley Horses in the foyer of the Officers' Mess, which came from the 1818 Paris sale of the effects of Marshall Ney, one of Napoleon's trusted generals; they are based on the celebrated 'Horse Tamers' by Guillaume Coustou (1677–1746), which forms the entrance to the Place de la Concorde from the Champs-Elysées in Paris.

Developments in recent years include the construction of the garrison church in 1957, which replaced a previous wooden structure. A special feature here is three stained-glass memorial windows by Stanley Tomlin; these honour sixteen artillery men killed on 16 September 1941 in an explosion in the Glen of Imaal practice range in County Wicklow. A new dining hall, built in 1996 on the site of the old one, incorporates the army's School of Catering and a new lecture theatre. A major conservation project was undertaken on the old Clock Tower block, completed in 1997 and officially opened on 26 February 1998. The painstaking restoration involved the importation of bricks from their original home in Suffolk, England. The total cost of these works came to €5.5 million. McKee Park, Blackhorse Avenue, was constructed in 1954 as purpose-built married quarters to a design by Captain Maurice A. Shanahan on a plot of land originally purchased in 1873. Restoration works were in progress at the barracks in 2016.

Retired Corporal Ronnie Daly from Annally Road, Cabra, is a local expert on the history of the Irish Defence Forces. Born in the Regina Coeli hostel on Morning Star Avenue, he lived there until the age of ten, when his family was housed. Joining the army in 1974, the final fifteen years of his career were spent at McKee Barracks. He made military history when, to his utter surprise, he was promoted to the rank of Corporal by General Beary, during the Easter Rising commemorations in the GPO in 2014. He was the first soldier to be promoted to the rank of Corporal in the GPO since the 1916 Rising, when Seán McLoughlin was promoted by James Connolly. Ronnie is a familiar figure in Dublin 7 and volunteers his time giving historical tours of the district.

Equitation School

The Equitation School, founded in 1926, was given the task of advertising the attributes of the Irish horse by competing in international events at home and abroad. The all-rank establishment, which in 2016 was commanded by Lieutenant Colonel Brian MacSweeney, exceeds one hundred personnel and the normal strength of horse numbers about forty. The Equitation School is the oldest unit in McKee barracks and has enjoyed continuous existence except for a short break during the Emergency (Second World War).

Over the past half-century many famous riders and horses have earned household-name status at home and abroad. In the period before World War Two the best known were Major Jed O'Dwyer, Lieutenant Colonels Fred Aherne, Dan Corry and Jack Lewis, riding famous horses such as Limerick Lace, Red Hugh, Duhallow, Shannon Power, Blarney Castle, Ireland's Own, Tramore Bay, Kilmallock and Miss Ireland. After the Second World War the equitation team was reformed and since then its most famous competitors have been Captains Colm O'Shea, Mick Tubridy and Louie Magee; Commandants Kevin Barry, Tom Finlay, Ron McMahon and Larry Kiely; Colonels Bill Ringrose and Jim Neylon and Lieutenant Colonel Ned Campion. Horses with many international wins to their credit during this period include Ballycotton, Ballyneety, Ballymonty, Bruree, Cloyne, Garrai Eoin, Inish Cara, Liathdrum, Loch an Easpaig, Lough Neagh and Red Castle. During the early 1980s Captain Gerry Mullins was in the top rank of international show-jumping.

In more recent years Captain John Ledingham has won the Highstead Derby on Kilbaha twice in succession, in 1995 and 1996; this is one of show-jumping's most prestigious events. Ireland's unprecedented run of success in the Nation's Cup at the turn of the last century saw Captain (later Commandant) Gerry Flynn and Lieutenant Shane Carey being major contributors to that achievement. Other successes included Captain David O'Brien and Captain Curran; notable horses include Carraig Dubh, Boherdeal Clover, Killossery and Kilkishen. Today riders from the Equitation School represent Ireland in World Championships. The history and tradition they represent is enormous, for there is little doubt that in the early years of independence, the school developed a huge international profile and made the Irish national anthem ring out throughout the world.

The first female officer to be assigned to the Equitation School was Dannielle Quinlivan from Kanturk, County Cork. Commissioned in 1998, she competed successfully on the national and international showjumping circuit until her retirement from the Permanent Defence Forces in 2002. The second female officer to join the Equitation School was Captain Sharon Crean, from Celbridge, County Kildare: commissioned in 2002, she also competed on the National Showjumping circuit. In September 2003 she transferred from the school in order to pursue third-level education at NUI Galway for a Bachelor of Civil Law. She is now the current Adjutant, officially titled Administration Officer, of the Equitation School. Jennifer Larkin joined the school in 2015 and is presently training for and competing on the national showjumping circuit while Charlene Kehoe, commissioned in January 2016, will join the Equitation School on completion of her military training in the Curragh.

2nd Lt. Jennifer Larkin and Sgt. Tommy Craig with Tullig Mor
(Courtesy Army Equitation School)

Horses have always been integral to barrack life at McKee and a special mounted escort was formed here for the Eucharistic Congress in 1932. Colourfully uniformed, it was popularly known as The Blue Hussars. They paraded at the inauguration of President Sean T. O'Kelly in 1945. This escort was disbanded around 1950. An earlier reminder of the equine inhabitants is a memorial inside the West Gate commemorating Mary, a bay Australian mare of the 5th Dragoon Guards; she served in South Africa and India. She arrived in McKee Barracks in 1907 and died there in 1909.

Memorial to Mary (Courtesy Roni Kwan)

A number of trophies won by the School are on display throughout the complex: in the bar the 1952 ARETE trophy, from Mexico; in the anteroom the 1937 Aga Khan Cup, 1951 Guecho, Bilbao Cup and 1932 Boston Horse Show Cup; and in the Chief of Staff's suite the 1946 Government of Ireland Cup, the bronze 1938 Governor of Rome trophy and various other trophies and honours. A history of the Equitation School remains to be researched and published.

Grangegorman Military Cemetery

Grangegorman Military Cemetery is located beside the Donard estate on Black-horse Avenue and was laid out in the early twentieth century for the burial of His Majesty's troops. Among the dead servicemen buried in the cemetry are 104 officers and men of the British army, including Lieutenant Commander George Richard Colin Campbell of the Royal Navy. With his wife Eileen Hester Louisa and only child Eileen Elizabeth Augusta, he perished on board the RMS *Leinster*, the Dublin Steampacket Company mail and passenger vessel, torpedoed by a German U-Boat in the Irish Sea just outside Dun Laoghaire. The incident occurred on the afternoon of 10 October 1918, a few weeks before the ending of the First World War. A total of 145 of those killed in the tragedy are buried here, including William Birch, the captain of the vessel. The *Leinster* had not been provided with a naval escort and this caused considerable controversy at the time. Nearly 600 lives were lost in the tragedy, a few hours after the vessel had left Dun Laoghaire. The Stop Press edition of the *Evening Herald*, circulated on Thursday evening, 10 October, carried the following news item:

> (From Our Correspondent) London, Thursday: The Press Bureau issued the following official statement this evening: The City of Dublin Mail Boat was torpedoed and sunk this afternoon in the Irish Sea. It is understood she carried a full complement of passengers, which are all believed safe.

This information was incorrect because of an error made in London. For publishing the data without official clearance, the *Evening Herald* was suppressed by British authorities and did not appear again until 15 October 1918.

British servicemen who died in lodgings in the Park or in Marlborough (McKee) Barracks are buried in the cemetery and the park gates opposite were known as the funeral gates; a crucifix is mounted above the gates, which are generally kept locked. Martin Doyle, who earned a Victoria Cross medal while serving with the British army in France on 2 September 1918, is buried in Grangegorman Military Cemetery. He was attached to the 1st Battalion, Munsters and later joined the Irish Free State Army. For his actions during the Civil War in a engagement at Ninemilehouse in 1922, while fighting against anti-Treaty forces, Lieutenant Colonel Tommy Ryan stated that he was 'worthy of an Irish equivalent should one exist'. He died on 20 November 1940 and is buried in grave number 222.

Henry Morris, born on 2 November 1921, was caretaker of the cemetery for many years and was to be seen every evening on his way down to the barracks to have dinner in the NCO's mess. This much-liked figure died on 3 March 2008 and is commemorated by a plaque in the McKee Barracks mess.

Beside the cemetery, in a field stretching from Blackhorse Avenue to Navan Road, stood the ruins of a plant used to manufacture bricks, some used in the construction of McKee Barracks. The main building had a 200-foot high chimney, demolished in the 1920s. The ruins remained until the early 1980s, when the present-day Donard housing estate of mixed local-authority and private homes was built. Up until 1978 cattle and sheep could be seen grazing in the field, a reminder that the agricultural days of Dublin 7 are not that distant a memory after all.

Cattle grazing in the field that is now Donard Housing Complex, with Grangegorman Military Cemetery in the background, 1976 (Bernard Neary)

7| Mater Hospital and Mountjoy Prison

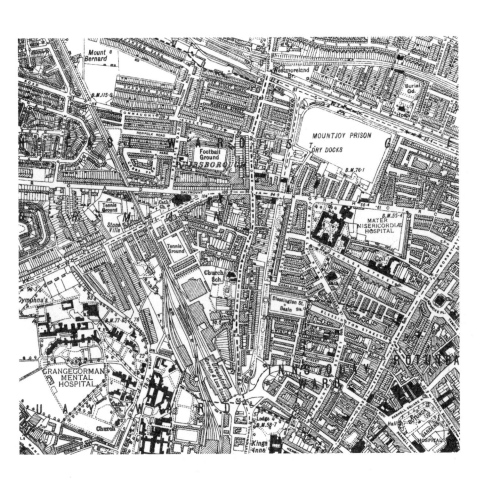

Catherine McAuley, born in Dublin in 1778, founded the Sisters of Mercy in 1831 in order to pursue a life of unremitting love and care for the poor. At this time Dublin was blighted by poverty, with many suffering due to the absence of education and shelter, a lack of food and bad health.

The following year, 1832, a severe epidemic of cholera broke out in Dublin, and an emergency hospital in Townsend Street was offered to Mother Catherine and her congregation. They did heroic work in combating that epidemic and decided that they should have a hospital of their own to cater for the medical needs of the poor.

In the 1850s they purchased a fifteen-acre site for the construction of a new hospital, the present-day Mater Misericordiae University Hospital. In that same year the congregation opened a hospital in Chicago, USA, followed by the hospital of St John and St Elizabeth in England – the first Roman Catholic hospital there since the time of Henry VIII. Architect John Burke of Charlemont Street was commissioned to prepare plans, inspecting hospitals in England, Scotland and Wales before designing the imposing building on Eccles Street that we still see today.

To avoid the burden of excessive debt, the Sisters decided to design and build their hospital in stages. On 24 September 1861 the first stage of the Mater Hospital was opened for its initial intake of patients, with an impressive stepped frontage onto Eccles Street, completed at a cost of £27,000. In 1866 the hospital was at the centre of another cholera epidemic and at its height 348 patients were treated during a six-week period, the great majority of them dying of the disease.

The new hospital quickly established itself and became known as the 'Palace of the Poor'. In 1868 work started on the east wing, based on Burke's plans, and this was opened in 1872. However, John Burke died suddenly in the house of Dr Thomas Hayden, Harcourt Street and did not live to see the work completed. The top floor of the east wing was reserved for infectious fevers. In a hospital publication in 1950, Dr Edward Freeman MD, for many years a senior physician at the hospital, recollected that half of that wing was still reserved for such purposes at the outbreak of the First World War in 1914. Further expansion became necessary and in 1884 construction began of the west wing, containing the convent, chapel and another block of wards. It was completed in 1886 under architect John Robinson at a cost of £68,000.

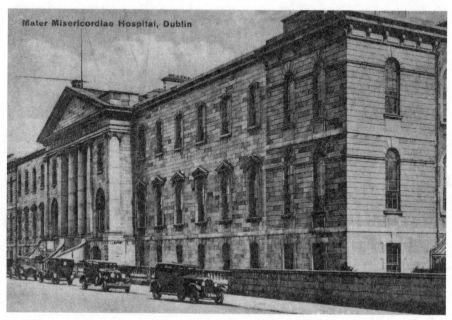

Mater Misericordiae Hosptial (Courtesy Old Dublin Society)

Number 38 Eccles Street was acquired in 1891, where a training school for nurses, which opened with twenty entrants, was established. The premises were soon too small for the expanding demands of the hospital and adjoining houses were gradually purchased for nurse training and a nurses' home. In the early years some nurses were accommodated in the mews at the rear of the houses. The first Matron and tutor at the training centre was Miss May McGivney, born in 1865 at Collon, County Louth, who came from the London Hospital. In his book on the Mater, printed in 1961, Dr Freeman remembers her fondly: 'Miss McGivney retired in 1920 after twenty eight years of devoted service, during which she established on a firm basis the training school of the Mater. I can recall her clearly – a slim, brisk, elderly lady in a grey silk dress, moving around St John's corridor.'

The hospital had 355 beds in 1912 and was 'open all hours for the reception of accident and urgent cases'. It received no government assistance and was supported entirely by voluntary subscriptions; at this time 'subscribers of one guinea (€1.34) per annum are entitled to recommend patients for admission'. During World War I hospital ships brought injured soldiers to Dublin to be treated at the Mater, and doctors and nurses from the hospital travelled to the front lines to treat injured soldiers.

In 1926 a nurses' home was built on the site of the gardens and stable yards of the Eccles Street houses which in time became overcrowded and unsuitable. The x-ray department was added in 1926, replacing the tiny unit in which one Dr Michael Hayes had worked for many years as "Medical Electrician' – the title under which he appeared on a staff list of 1907. In 1935 work began on a quad-rangle of buildings, including the construction of a chapel across its north end; the project was completed in 1937 under the supervision of architect Ralph Byrne. In 1936 the outpatient department, laboratories and residency, North Circular Road, were built. In 1954 the College of Nursing and Nurses Home, North Circular Road, was built to house 240 staff and student nurses and in 1955, in conjunction with UCD, a School of Physiotherapy with an extensive rehabilitation department was opened.

A significant moment in recent Irish history occurred in November 1960 at the Round Room of the Mater Hospital, for it was here that the Irish Wheelchair Association was established. One of the founding members was Leo St John Close, who was born in 1934 and became a paraplegic following an accident in France in 1955. He joined the Vincentians and was the first priest to be ordained in a wheelchair, on 14 June 1959. He represented Ireland in the Paraplegic Olympics in Rome in 1960, as part of a nine-man team sent by the Rehabilitation Tuberculosis Centre. They were unhappy with their treatment as competitors and, following their return home, Leo and four of the team subsequently met in the Round Room and set up the Irish Wheelchair Association. Leo represented Ireland again in the 1964 Paraplegic Olympics: subsequently appointed Head of Religious Studies at Dunedin in New Zealand, he was instrumental in setting up the New Zealand Wheelchair Association, for which he was honoured with an OBE (Order of the British Empire). He represented New Zealand in the Tel Aviv Paraplegic Olympics in 1968. He died in New Zealand in 1977.

In 1965 the hospital contained 433 beds and had an annual admission of 7118, with a daily casualty intake of 135 patients and a daily out-patient rate of 140. The community comprised sixty-four religious and the College of Nursing catered for 200 nurses. During the 1960s and early 1970s the expansion and development of the complex continued with the construction of the Child Guidance Clinic, cafeteria, Freeman Auditorium, a new Accident and Emergency Department, new operating theatres and a cardio-vascular diagnostic unit. In 1974, as a result of the recommendations of Comhairle na nOspideal, which was established in 1972 following the Fitzgerald Report, the government decided to develop six hospitals along the lines set out by the Comhairle. The Mater Hospital was one of the locations recommended for development. Interim reports were prepared and a report presented to the hospital's Board of Management in January 1977. The final development plan proposed the construction of a new hospital in four phases. The first phase began in September 1981 and the building was handed over to hospital management from February 1985 to June 1986, when it was fully completed at a cost of £30 million. It was brought into commission on 1 September 1989 and officially opened in November of that year.

A most recent development was the construction of the Whitty Building on North Circular Road, on the site of the former redbrick Nurses' Home. The Mater Misericordiae University Hospital currently has approximately 600 beds at full capacity, including day beds.

Eccles Street

Eccles Street is found on Dublin maps from as early as 1772; the name derives from Sir John Eccles, a Lord Mayor of Dublin who owned properties in the area. He lived in Mount Eccles on North Great George's Street and built St George's church, Hardwicke Place, for his Church of Ireland tenants. Completed in 1802 at a cost of £90,000, it is remarkable for its finely decorated spire and steeple of hewn stone.

During the early 1800s James Cuffe, Lord Tyrawly, lived at 18 Eccles Street. It was subsequently divided into two separate buildings and in 1835 was listed as a girls' boarding school. In January 1882 the Dominicans occupied the building and established the Dominican College there and next door in number 19. As the secondary school developed and flourished, a university education for women emerged in Eccles Street; female students, prepared by the Dominican Sisters, presented themselves for the degree examinations of the Royal University. Eccles Street became a true university centre. St Mary's University Centre, already under the auspices of the Dominican nuns, transferred to Eccles Street in 1902. In 1908 St Dominic's Training College for secondary teacher training for women was established and fulfilled its duty until Diploma Courses in Education began in 1911 in UCD. Over the years the college expanded into adjoining buildings and in 1928 Scoil Chaitríona, an all-Irish secondary school, was established. Scoil Chaitríona moved to Mobhi Road in Glasnevin in 1972. The Dominican College continued on Eccles Street and in 1983 it had 800 pupils on its rolls. With the new developments at the Mater Hospital in the 1980s, the Dominicans moved the college to Griffith Avenue, where it opened in September 1984.

The Dominican College Past Pupils Union was founded in 1914; distinguished past pupils include Margaret Sheridan and Mary Cummins. Margaret 'Margherita' Sheridan was born in Castlebar, County Mayo on 15 October 1889: her guardian, Canon Patrick Lyons, who had baptised her, arranged for her education as a permanent boarder in the college. She was accepted into the Royal Academy of Music, London and went to Italy in 1916, becoming a famous opera singer during the 1920s. She died in 1958; An Post marked her centenary with the issue of a postage stamp and the Italian Cultural Institute held an exhibition in her honour in 2008 entitled 'La Sheridan, Adorable Diva'. Mary Cummins developed an aptitude for languages while studying in the college. Upon leaving she went to Belgium, where she secured a post teaching English to the children of a Belgian countess. In the mid-1930s she began working as translator at the Canadian embassy. During the German conquest in the 1940s she became involved with the Belgian resistance movement; betrayed to the Gestapo, she was arrested, tortured and imprisoned in a concentration camp. At the liberation, she was released, weighing just six stone. She died on 20 June 1999, aged ninety-four.

The noted Jesuit priest Fr John Sullivan was born at number 41 Eccles Street on 8 May 1861 and was christened on 15 July that year in St George's Church. Shortly after that his family joined the flight of the gentry to the more fashionable Fitzwilliam Place on the southside. He shocked his family by converting to Roman Catholicism in 1896, for they never considered him to be in any way religious. Ordained a Jesuit in July 1907, Fr John Sullivan taught at Clongowes Wood College, County Kildare for most of his teaching life; he died on 19 February 1933 and is buried in the grounds there. Margaret Alyward, founder of the Sisters of the Holy Faith, established her first convent house, St Brigid's, at number 46. Number 58 was Clerkin's Hotel during the 1950s. The Eccles family owned number 59, the tallest house on Eccles Street; it was rented during the 1800s by Cardinal Paul Cullen, Ireland's first Cardinal, who personally appointed Henry John Newman as first Rector of the Roman Catholic University of Ireland, now UCD. It later served as a presbytery to nearby St Joseph's Church.

Sir Boyle Roche, soldier and parliamentarian, lived with his wife Mary (née Frankland) at number 63, and during the eighteenth century he was noted as the clown of the Irish Parliament, famous for his bulls and blunders – 'What has posterity ever done for us?' He died in this house on 5 June 1807, aged seventy-one. Frances Ball was born at number 63 on 9 January 1794. She was professed a nun in September 1816 at York in England and founded the Loreto Order of nuns in Ireland. In May 1822 she established Loreto School, Rathfarnham, and prided herself on never having to refuse a postulant due to lack of means. Her sister Anna Maria (1785–1871) established a house of refuge in Ashe Street in 1809; by 1814 it was inadequate and she moved it into larger premises in Stanhope Street, before handing it over to the care of the Sisters of Charity in 1815.

A conspicuous house on this street is number 64, with its inlaid sculptures, including a reproduction of Michelangelo's 'Moses' in the exterior walls. This was the home of Francis Johnston, renowned architect and first President of the

Royal Hibernian Academy. He designed the GPO, St George's church, Richmond Penitentary, Grangegorman and numerous other buildings around Dublin. Understudy to Thomas Cooley, the designer of Newgate Prison, Green Street, he had a small square tower erected at the rear of 64, which housed a peal of bells. On his death in 1829 he bequeathed the bells, then valued at £1300, to St George's church. Isaac Butt, lawyer and founder of the Home Rule movement in 1870, lived here in the mid-1800s; he died on 3 May 1879. For a number of years from the late 1800s the house was occupied by the Albert Retreat for Aged Females, established in 1831; in 1912 the Matron was Mrs Mumford and the honorary secretary and treasurer the Honourable Lady Smyly, who lived on Merrion Square. It provided lodging, coal, light and medical care for about thirty women and was intended 'principally, for servants past their work'. It was managed by a voluntary committee of ladies.

The noted entomologist and conchologist Mary Ball, born in Cobh, County Cork in 1812, lived in Eccles Street for many years before moving to Belmont Avenue, Dublin, where she died on 17 July 1878. She specialized in the collection of invertebrates and shells and was famous for her work in her chosen field; a mollusc and a seaweed were named after her.

On the corner of Nelson Street and Eccles Street is the location for the setting of the Brendan Behan play *The Hostage*. A little farther up, on the corner of Eccles Street and Berkeley Road, in the enclosed park adjoining St Joseph's Church stands a memorial to the Four Masters, Donegal Franciscan friars led by Michael O'Cleary, who between 1627 and 1637 chronicled the history of the ancient kingdom of Ireland. The memorial was erected in 1876. The Mater Hospital, in consultation with local interests, has made the site a park in perpetuity, and it is presently managed by Dublin City Council. Though it remains closed to public access, providing nature with its own exclusive haven, it may in future years be opened to the public.

Berkeley Road and Environs

Berkeley Road, which runs from North Circular Road to St Joseph's, and Berkeley Street, which runs from the church to Blessington Street, were laid out in 1825. Together, they were formerly called Somerset Place, after Somerset House on the corner of Berkeley Street and Nelson Street – now 37 Nelson Street.

St Joseph's Discalced Carmelite church replaced a wooden chapel obtained by Archdeacon James McMahon during his time as parish priest at Halston Street and erected on the site of the present-day presbytery in 1870. On 6 September 1874 the foundation stone for the imposing square-towered neo-Gothic Church of St Joseph was laid by Cardinal Paul Cullen. Designed by Messrs O'Neill and Byrne, architects of many fine churches in Ireland around this time, it was built by Messrs James McCormack using bluish granite from the Ballyknocken quarry in County Wicklow. The church was opened and dedicated by the Archbishop of Dublin, Dr McCabe, on Sunday 18 April 1880; the temporary wooden chapel was disassembled and relocated in Glasnevin. Archdeacon McMahon was appointed the first parish priest of St Joseph's and became a popular local figure; his funeral in January 1890 was one of the biggest the district had ever seen. He is interred in the church, in a vault below the Altar of the Sacred Heart.

Dubliner Matt Talbot (1856–1925) was a regular visitor to St Joseph's. Some of the beautiful stained-glass windows in the church were designed by the artist Harry Clarke. The parish priest in 1990 was Fr Eugene McCaffrey; the present parish priest is Fr David Donnellan. A long-serving sacristan here was Vivian Kavanagh; he served in that capacity from 1958 until 2006 and is commemorated by a simple plaque in the church. Bernie Meehan of Berkeley Road recalls his kindness to all, especially in times of need, stating that 'my husband John was the last person that Vivian buried'.

Nelson Street was built in 1810 and is called after the English naval officer and admiral, Lord Nelson following his victory over a French fleet at Trafalgar in 1805. The streets around this area, Fontenoy, Geraldine, Goldsmith, St Laurence, Shamrock and Sarsfield Street and O'Connell Avenue, were built around 1870 and are testimony to the increasingly nationalist composition of the City Council. The distinguished sculptor, Albert Power, lived at 18 Geraldine Street. O'Connell Avenue was originally called O'Connell Street (1870 to 1885), then Gerald Griffin Street in 1885, and further renamed O'Connell Avenue the following year. Just off Nelson Street is St Joseph's Parade and Place, given that name from the church on Berkeley Road. May's Cottages, a terrace of three small two-storey homes, are off St Joseph's Parade and its residents were probably the last in Dublin to draw their water from a water pump beside the street. May Furlong lived in the first cottage and she waved goodbye to the water pump when a water supply was connected to her home in January 1991. The pump was still in her garden up to 1996, but was removed shortly after that. May died on 12 January 2008, aged seventy-eight.

Directory maps from 1796 to 1840 and Tyrrell's maps of 1821 and 1831 outline a certain 'Royal Circus' at the top of Eccles Street. This was a proposed development that never materialized. It was envisaged at the end of the eighteenth century, a time when Georgian architects and town planners were turning their minds from the squares to curved forms, crescents and circles. This type of architecture may be seen in all its magnificence in Bath, England. The last of the great architects of this period, Francis Johnston, was entrusted with the plan for the fine elliptical circus to round off the unfinished Eccles Street, and it would have been the jewel in the crown of Georgian Dublin.

The plans envisaged a splendid range of private mansions surrounding a circle; the approach to it was to have been through any one of several grand streets, including Eccles Street and a proposed Elizabeth Street; the name probably referred to Elizabeth, daughter of Sir William Montgomery and first wife of Luke Gardiner, Lord Mountjoy. The street was to have started at the newly-built Synnot Place. An indication of the scale of this development is that it comprised present day St Joseph's church, Mater Hospital, Berkeley Road and all streets to the west of it to the linear park. It was intended to have included grounds beyond the North Circular Road, on the site of Mountjoy Prison. The only part of this massive proposed development to be physically executed, with possibly the exception of some houses actually constructed as part of the plan in Eccles Street, was Cowley Place. Built in 1792, it was named after Lieutenant General Cowley, who erected the buildings.

The Royal Circus was to have eclipsed Merrion Square. It was conceived by Luke Gardiner, who was born in 1745. He was a huge property developer and began building Mountjoy Square in 1792, which took its name from the Gardiner family title of Lord Mountjoy. Elected MP for Dublin from 1773 until 1789, he was supportive of a more lenient attitude towards Roman Catholics rights; Gardiner's Acts of 1778 and 1782 allowed Roman Catholics to acquire land and removed restrictions on conditions of worship and on clergy. He died during an ambush in the battle of New Ross on 5 June 1798. His son Charles John, born in 1782, succeeded him and was created Earl of Blessington. His family name and titles are commemorated in a number of Dublin locations, including Blessington Street and Basin, Gardiner Street, Mountjoy Prison and Mountjoy Square. The Royal Circus never materialized; circumstances such as the sudden death of Luke Gardiner, the growing popularity of the south side of the city as a desirable residential area and the Act of Union 1800, which created the United Kingdom of Great Britain and Ireland, impeded the plan. The Act of Union resulted in a flight of wealth, and of the wealthy, from Ireland.

Mountjoy Prison

Travelling up North Circular Road, approaching Phibsborough, one passes Mount-joy Prison, Ireland's premier committal prison. It was built at a time when central government began taking control of prisons and when a swing of public opinion from forced deportation to then inhospitable and remote places like Tasmania, was underway. This created the need for the construction of penitentiaries in Ireland.

Known to generations of Dubliners as 'The Joy', it houses prisoners for a wide range of purposes, from non-payment of fines to committal and penal servitude for life. Work began on the prison in 1847 and was completed in 1850. The engineer responsible for its construction was Colonel Browning. The complex was created using artisans from Europe, descendants of Napoleonic prisoners, and ordinary convict labour. The style was based on that of Pentonville Prison in England, which was the 'model radial prison', with one prisoner to a cell and with in-cell sanitation – a rare luxury in the Victorian era. From the circle end of the Administration Block (Block E), the governor can observe every wing of the prison.

In 1887 the Prison Hospital, visible from Whitworth Road, was built by the Central Prisons Board. In the early 1900s the building was extensively renovated to house prisoners who had been formerly temporarily confined to the Curragh Military Camp. It has gained considerable mention in Ernie O'Malley's book *On Another Man's Wound*. The Prison Officers' quarters on North Circular Road were erected by the Central Prisons Board in 1894. A terrace of these was demolished during 1991 and the rest followed shortly thereafter; the Dóchas Centre today occupies the site. Major extensions and renovations have taken place throughout the years and in 1975 the new training unit, with a capacity for ninety-six trainees, was opened, receiving its first trainee on 29 October 1975. Over many years it ran a variety of AnCO and FÁS courses, including classes in metal fabrication and welding.

Recent major investments included the installing of sanitation facilities in each cell from 2005. The prison originally contained in-cell sanitation when it first opened in 1850, but during the War of Independence and the Civil War the toilets and wash-handbasins were ripped out and the piping destroyed. D wing was undergoing refurbishment in early 2016 and is expected to open later in that year, accommodating 160 prisoners.

Aerial view of Mountjoy Prison: note the Benthamite panopticon structures on the banks of the Royal Canal, where Brendan Behan's 'auld triangle, went jingle jangle'

The triangle, which Brendan Behan's *Quare Fella* heard 'go jingle jangle, along the banks of the Royal Canal', was hung in the Circle and sounded at unlocking time; it could be heard in all parts of the main complex. It still hangs in the Circle, but for display purposes only. The execution chamber is still in existence and in working order; it was at the end of D1 wing and the last person to be executed was Michael Manning, on the morning of 20 April 1954. Albert Pierrepoint (1905–92), Britain's long-serving and last hangman, was paid £20, including expenses for the task. Manning, aged twenty-five, was convicted of murdering 65-year-old Catherine Cooper of Barringtons Hospital, Limerick. After attacking and assaulting her, he dumped her body on the roadside. Brian Walsh, who later became a Judge of the Supreme Court, was the State prosecutor at the trial. He recalled the crime as 'totally irrational'. The murder was committed after the consumption of drink, possibly poitín. In an article in the *Evening Herald* the then Governor of Mountjoy, Seán Kavanagh, described him as 'the most saintly prisoner' he had ever met. The execution caused little stir — a notice was pinned outside the prison at 8.10 am, and the hanging was reported on page two of the next day's *Irish Press*; it ran to just three paragraphs.

Three years later, in 1957, Albert Pierrepoint resigned as hangman following a row with the British government over the payment of expenses totalling one pound. The hanging scaffold was refurbished in the mid-1970s, following the murder of the off-duty and unarmed Garda Reynolds during an armed bank raid in Raheny, Dublin by Noel and Marie Murray. British hangman Harry Allen stated that he was prepared to travel to Ireland to perform the execution of the Murrays; however, their death sentence was commuted to life imprisonment. They were released from custody in 1992. At the time of the killing of Garda Reynolds they were on bail pending trial for a foiled armed robbery in Donnybrook, Dublin.

Until recent years there were many workshops in the prison, including upholstery, carpentry, soft toys, tailoring, metal fabrication and hobby-shop, along with traditional prison employment like mailbag sewing. Inmates were particularly busy around Christmas time in the soft toys, hobby and carpentry workshop, supplying toys and craftwork for orphanages and other worthy causes. In the 1990s the engineering workshop was the main technical instruction activity: popular with prisoners, the activity was discontinued following the implementation of State-wide uniform health and safety standards. Today classes are conducted in the areas of art, computer skills and other educational subjects; a popular workshop is that of bricklaying, in which participants make decorative barbeques and other ornamental features. Some prisoners have succeeded in getting work from family and friends after their release, easing their reintegration into society.

Over the years prisoners in Mountjoy have engaged in many worthwhile community projects, ranging from work carried out on St Michael's House, Phibsborough, community centres in Hartstown and Ballymun, and in Glencree Rehabilitation Centre. They rebuilt the wall in St George's Cemetery, Whitworth Road, where the architect Francis Johnston is buried. Among other memorials, this cemetery contains the tomb of Dr Carmichael, an eminent Dublin surgeon, from whom the well-known School of Medicine got its name. He was drowned on the evening of 8 June 1849 in Sutton Creek, while attempting to cross it on horse-back at low tide from Dollymount to his home.

Today's capacity of Mountjoy Prison is 550; the present Governor is Brian Murphy and the Deputy Governor is John Quinn. The former Governor, John Lonergan, from County Tipperary, who retired in 2010, was probably the most popular and well-known officer to have served at the prison. Following the recommendations of a report of the Inspector of Prisons, the phasing out of St Patrick's Institution as a centre for the detention of young persons between sixteen and twenty-one began in mid-2015.

Over the years Mountjoy has been the subject of many songs and nursery rhymes. My mother Agnes Neary (*née* McDonnell) sang this one with her pals as a child on the streets of Dublin:

> There's no place in Dublin like the Mountjoy Hotel
> There's blinds on the windows and bells on the doors
> Beautiful carpets laid out on the floors
> I've been there once myself and I'm able to tell
> There's no place in Dublin like the Mountjoy Hotel.

Mountjoy Prison has often been mentioned in the memoirs of people incarcerated there. The Fenian leader Jeremiah O'Donovan Rossa in his book *My Years in English Jails*, relates that after his arrival in Mountjoy Prison, in December 1865, a 'warder escorted me to my cell, and, giving his command to two others, they came, one holding a candle and the other a razor ... my eyes fell on the face of the man who was holding the candle, and they began to swim in their sockets. It was the first time I got soft during my imprisonment, but when I saw the tears streaming down the cheeks of this Irish-hearted jailer who was holding the candle, I could not restrain my own from starting.' In more recent years, in her book *Kathy's Story*, Kathy O'Beirne from Clondalkin, Dublin 22, states, 'incredibly I remember my time in Mountjoy as one of the happiest periods of my childhood'. In Mountjoy Prison she felt free not only from the constant threat of, but actual, sexual abuse she endured while in the care and custody of institutions run by Roman Catholic religious congregations.

The Dóchas Centre, a new female detention centre adjacent to Mountjoy Prison, was built in the late 1900s and officially opened on 28 September 1999.

It replaced the accommodation previously provided on one floor in D wing of the male prison; this was totally inadequate and subject to constant over-crowding. In 2016 it had a capacity of ninety-eight and the present Governor is Mary O'Connor. There are numerous workshops in the centre offering skills training to prisoners, which include leathercraft, hairdressing, beauty care, sewing and hand crafts.

The Choir of the Irish Prison Officers, most of whom were based at Mountjoy, Cloverhill and Wheatfield Prisons, was formed in 1980 by the energetic and well-known Tony Lang. Called the Irish Prison Officers Male Voice Choir, it had a wide repertoire of songs, including classical pieces and numbers from popular shows. It rose to prominence and fame during the 1980s, when it came under the musical directorship of the internationally renowned Moira Griffith-Reid. During this time it performed several concerts in a variety of venues, including St Peter's Church, Phibsborough and appeared on national television, including RTÉ's *Late Late Show*. After a low point in the mid-1990s the choir was revived in 1998 by John Ward, now retired and practising as a barrister but then based in the training unit in Mountjoy. It is no longer active, although Wheatfield and Cork Prisons presently boast active and entertaining choirs consisting of both male and female officers.

Synnott Place

Synnott Place dates from 1795 and is called after a family of that name, originally from Wexford, who owned property here. Mark Synnott of Drumcondra Lane, now Dorset Street, was Sheriff of the County of Dublin in 1742. An unnamed laneway connects Synnott Place to North Circular Road. At the end of this laneway is a four-storey house where the playwright Sean O'Casey lived prior to his departure for England; it was in this house that he wrote *Juno and the Paycock* (1925) and *The Plough and the Stars* (1926). Other noted plays included *The Shadow of a Gunman* and *The Silver Tassie*. He was born just around the corner on 30 March 1880 at 85 Upper Dorset Street. His father died aged forty-nine and the family then moved to 9 Innisfallen Parade, which runs from Dorset Street to Glengariff Parade, parallel to the North Circular Road. A plaque commemo-rates the O'Casey connection on the wall of each of these three houses. The first two houses on Innisfallen Parade, numbers 1 and 2, are distinguished by intricate brickwork; the O'Casey home is a small single-storey cottage, and they lived here from 1882 until 1889, when they moved to East Wall.

Seán O'Casey worked as a labourer with the Great Northern Railway from 1902 until December 1911, when he was dismissed for joining the Irish Transport and General Workers' Union. In the mid-1920s he went to London and married actor and author Eileen Reynolds Carey, spending his final years living in Torquay on the south coast of England until his death on 18 September 1964. His wife Eileen died on 9 April 1995 at Denville Hall, a house for retired actors, in Northwood, London.

Between Mountjoy Prison and Lower Dorset Street the names of the streets, built in the mid-1800s, recall the beauty spots of Kerry and the names of Roman Catholic saints. These are Valentia, Innisfallen, Muckross, Derrynane, Glengariff and Killarney Parades, St Ignatius Road and St Benedict's Gardens. There is a small statue of the Blessed Virgin Mary in St Benedict's Gardens, which can be seen as one passes along North Circular Road. Behind St Benedict's Gardens, just off St Ignatius Avenue, is a relatively new, gated and well-kept cluster of two-storey houses, a sign of the revitalization of the area.

Number 4 St Benedict's Gardens was the home of James Edward Hernon, born here on 28 November 1910. In 1924 he won the boys' diving event at the Táilteann Games and came third in the senior event, behind Olympic champion Dick Eve and Irish champion Charlie Batt. He won thirty-four Irish national titles in senior competition and the Amateur Swimming Association's British open high-diving championship in 1933. A popular athlete, Herman attracted a crowd of 5000 to an exhibition at Foynes, County Limerick, in 1940. His huge medal collection was stolen from his Blackrock home in December 1984. He died on 23 April 1985 and is buried in Shanganagh Cemetery.

The Cluskey family lived on St Ignatius Road; May Cluskey, a famous actor, was born on 18 May 1927. A well-known performer, she played the part of Queenie Butler in Telefís Éireann's (RTÉ) first soap opera, 'Tolka Row', which ran from 1964 to 1968. She performed regularly at the Eblana Theatre in Busáras, Store Street and in the Dublin Theatre Festival. A member of the Abbey Theatre Company, she played supporting roles in several films, including *Young Cassidy* (1965) and *Ryan's Daughter* (1970). May died on 15 May 1991. Her younger brother Frank, born on 8 April 1930, started out life as an apprentice butcher and joined the Labour Party at eighteen; he was a Labour TD for a total of twenty-three years, and held ministerial office and served as party leader from 1977 to 1981. He attended St Francis Xavier's School, Dorset Street, and St Vincent's CBS Glasnevin. His father Francis (1890–1955) was also a butcher by trade, as well as an active member of the Worker's Union of Ireland, and friend and associate of Jim Larkin. The houses on the Cluskey's end of the road, with two top-floor windows, are bigger than those on the Glengarriff end of the road and the adjacent St Ignatius Avenue.

Behind St Ignatius Road is the Royal Canal, and a small laneway leads to a pleasant track bordered by grass and the canal. There is a building facing the track, once occupied by Spain and Company, furniture manufacturers. Similar premises behind the houses on the south side of St Ignatius Road are evidence of the time when residents and manufacturing workers lived and worked cheek-by-jowl. The factory of the well-known soft-drinks manufacturer Savage Smyth was located here. Around the corner is St Francis Xavier Schools, Dorset Street, founded by Rev. John Gaffney SJ in 1850, which occupies the site of an older building called Kellett's School. The school's name is carved out in the granite stone on the front wall of the building; it now serves as a community centre.

8| Phibsborough

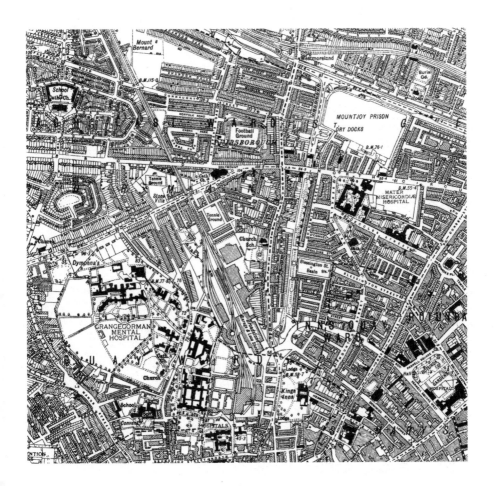

There is some doubt regarding the origins of the place-name Phibsborough. Sir Frederick Falkiner in his *History of the Royal Hospital* says that the name Phibsboro was given to the area from the people who lived at the confines of the wood Salcuit, or Salcock, which extended from Oxmanstown near to the locality that is today known as Phibsborough. They were called 'Phipoes' or 'Fairpoes'; Anglo-Normans, they were deemed 'vast grabbers of Ostman lands'. The Rev. C.J. McCready, in his book *Dublin Street Names* dates the name from 1792 and so called from Edward Phipps, fourth son of Richard Phipps of Kilmainham, who bought property in the locality in the 1780s; it is more than likely that he gave his family name to the district. It is a coincidence that the name resembles that of the ancient freebooters who dwelt there in earlier times, according to Falkiner.

In the early 1800s Phibsborough was home to thousands of people living in misery and squalor. Their homes were of mud-huts and the incidence of disease, lawlessness and crime was rampant. However, from the mid-1800s, with the arrival of the railway, the district became a thriving, industrious centre on the fringes of Dublin city, between the Broadstone Railway Station and the Royal Canal. Now a busy commercial, business and residential centre, it is home to one of north Dublin's premier landmarks, St Peter's Church.

St Peter's Church

In 1822 the Roman Catholic authorities were concerned about the poor educational facilities in the district and a group of laypeople formed a committee to establish a school. In October 1822 work began on a site at the junction of North Circular Road and New Cabra Avenue and in September 1826 the school opened for catechism classes, on Sundays only. The following February a schoolmaster was engaged and a day school established for boys and girls; within two months there were 230 boys and 160 girls on the rolls. The committee then persuaded Reverends Young and Carroll to take over the project. They converted the upper storey of the building into a chapel, with adjoining accommodation for two priests, a sacristy, lending library, and a schoolmaster's kitchen and room. The first Mass was celebrated in the chapel on Trinity Sunday 1827.

The following extract from *Ireland Illustrated*, which contains original drawings by G. Petrie RHA, W.H. Bartlett and T.M. Baynes, with descriptions by G.N. Wright, gives an early account of the church:

> Saint Peter's Chapel stands at the divergence of the New Cabra Avenue and the beautiful and fashionable ride to the Phoenix Park, called the North Circular Road. The Chapel consists of a Porch and Chancel eighty feet in length, by forty in breadth, very neatly and unostentatiously finished. The exterior is in Milner's second order of Gothic Architecture, very correctly executed, and built of the impure limestone found in the County of Dublin. The floor of the Chapel is much elevated above the exterior surface, which gives an opportunity of introducing a beautiful flight of steps, with broad landings in front, and admits of a spacious apartment beneath, used as a free-school, where the poor children of the district are educated.

In the print by G. Petrie (1831) accompanying the extract, G.N. Wright points out that 'at one side of the Chapel a vehicle peculiar to Ireland and called an 'Outside Car', is represented and at the other, a character with which Ireland is unhappily too familiar, the mendicant, catches the attention'.

In 1838 the Archbishop of Dublin handed over the management of St Peter's to the Vincentians, who appointed Fr McNamara, Fr Hand and Fr Scully to run the new undertaking. Fr Thomas McNamara was one of the co-founders of the Cabra schools for deaf boys and girls. Fr Hand left after a short while to devote his energies in other directions and in November 1842 he founded All Hallows

St Peter's Church and School, Phibsborough, circa 1840
(*Ireland Illustrated*, Courtesy NLI)

College, Drumcondra. Shortly afterwards the small building proved inadequate for the ever-increasing needs and in 1841 they started to look towards the expansion of the facility.

A public meeting, presided over by the city's first Roman Catholic Lord Mayor in over two hundred years, Daniel O'Connell, proved a financial success. The occasion was remarkable because it was the first public meeting of Dublin Roman Catholics for a charitable purpose. As a result forty-three feet was added to the length of the church. This was done by the vacating of the ground floor housing the school, removing the ceiling and upper flooring, leaving a large area 35-foot high compared to the previous twenty-five, for use solely as a church. These works began in 1843 and as part of the improvements new schools were built to the rear of the site. The new school served the community until 1891, when it was transferred to a new building on St Peter's Road. An inscription carved into the granite stonework in the old school building is a reminder that the school was formerly housed within the church complex. It reads: *St Peter's National School* and can be seen from the Elmo, a shop on the corner of St Peter's Road and Cabra Road.

In 1845 Fr McNamara introduced the Society of St Vincent de Paul to Phibsborough, their second Irish branch. During the mid-1800s the neighbour-hood of Phibsborough improved vastly and church numbers grew apace. In 1862 Fr McNamara put on the drawing board a 'really grandiose gothic edifice that bid fair to outdo all previous efforts in church building'. The chancel and transcepts were erected, together with a great central tower. The construction of the tower was a controversial affair, however, and resulted in long and costly litigation, initially between the builder and the architect and eventually with the involve-ment of Fr McNamara. On foot of a court order the tower had to be dismantled and the materials were subsequently re-used in the construction of some local buildings, including the former Allied Irish Bank and the John Doyle pub, both located at Doyle's Corner. Often at odds with church authorities, Fr McNamara was appointed Superior to the Irish College, Paris, in 1867 without achieving his dream of completing his magnificent church. He returned to Ireland in 1890 to live in St Joseph's, Blackrock, where he died in 1892; his funeral took place at St Peter's Church, in which 400 deaf children assisted.

Further major improvements started in the early 1880s, including the construction of a new school on present-day St Peter's Road, and the incorpo-ration of the old school into the extended church building. Lawrence Flanagan, a carpenter then living in Balbriggan, County Dublin, was appointed Clerk of Works for the project and took up residence at 34 Munster Street in 1882. He lived here for many years, with his wife and family, including their daughter Jane, who was born on 1 June 1875. Just six years old when they moved, she was educated locally. She adopted the Gaelic form of her name, Sinéad Ní Flanagáin, because she was interested in folklore and the Irish language.

In January 1910 she married Eamonn de Valera. One of the leaders of the 1916 Rising, he later became Taoiseach and President of Ireland in that order. Following her husband's imprisonment after the Rising, and with no personal income, she was forced to return to her family home at Munster Street, at a time when she was pregnant. She gave birth to her son Rauri in November 1916. She cared for her invalid sister and for her ailing mother, who died in January 1917. Her other children, Máirín and Vivion, joined her here. Vivion later repre-sented the district as a Fianna Fáil TD. After her husband was released from prison, and when their economic circumstances had improved, they moved to

Greystones, County Wicklow. She died on 7 January 1975.

In 1902 Fr Joseph Geoghegan set about the task of completing the church and on 19 April called a great public meeting at which Dr Walsh, Archbishop of Dublin, presided. The meeting was attended by Joe Mooney JP of Cabra Lodge and other notable dignitaries. In the course of his appeal the Archbishop stated that 'it is creditable to us that, in the midst of the general advancement and improvement that is to be seen all around us here, there should be upon a site, which is, in many respects, the most prominent site in all this district, a building such as this; a building containing as it does, in painful incongruity, comparatively old work and comparatively new work, representing no style at all'. The haphazard nature of various church extensions was then all too apparent to the eye. The response was remarkable and work was able to commence shortly after the archbishop's appeal. The following account in the *Irish Builder* of 12 February 1903 describes some of the work subsequently carried out:

> The work, which has been in progress for some time, consists of new nave, aisles and tower. The site being about the highest in the city, the new tower will form a commanding feature and will rise to a height of over two hundred feet to the top of the spire, the dimensions at the base being about thirty-four feet square. The principal entrance is in the front, which consists of double doors, deeply and richly recessed with Newry granite columns and molded jambs. The Belfry windows are handsomely treated, and have gables with crockets, and with standing angles between. The octagonal turrets on either side of the tower will give access to the organ gallery and upper stages of tower, and will, at the same time, give an appropriate finish to the nave, which will be carried on to the full height of the existing chancel.
>
> The new aisles will be about four feet wider than the old and will be groined throughout, the confessionals being in arched recesses, and each bay being lighted with two single-light windows. It will be of interest to know that Irish materials and workmanship are employed throughout. The amount of the contract will probably run into £25,000, and close on this amount will be spent in Ireland, with the exception of the internal stone for the nave piers, which has been got to match as near as possible to the old stone in the chancel. The work externally will be built throughout in limestone. The design for the work was entrusted to the eminent architect, Mr G.C. Ashlin, FRIBA., and the contract to Mr James Kiernan, Talbot Street.

St Peter's Church, *circa* 1912 (Courtesy Lawrence Collection NLI)

Work began almost immediately, although it was not until April 1911 that the steeple was completed, presenting Dublin's northside with one of the finest examples of church architecture in the city. Phibsborough was then a fairly wealthy parish, for the preacher of the day, the Vincentian Bishop of Elphin, was able to relate that the church was 'totally free of debt'. Local folklore has it that the Australian Cardinal Moran in 1905, while staying with Archbishop Walsh in Drumcondra, remarked, as he looked out his bedroom window, that he could see no steeple of a Roman Catholic church in sight and the next time he came to Ireland he would like to see one. As a result of those comments Archbishop Walsh gave an additional £400 – he had contributed £100 at the public meeting – and work on the spire commenced in 1907. Recent developments and improvements include the addition of a new sacristy and parish office. Fr Brian Doyle served as parish priest in the 1990s; he was from the district and served as an altar boy in the church during the 1940s. His brother Eamon taught at St Declan's, Cabra for many years.

St Peter's Church, early 1900s (Courtesy Lawrence Collection NLI)

St Peter's contains a wonderful collection of Harry Clark stained-glass windows; it consists of the large Sacred Heart window, together with a set of four two-window panels, in the mortuary chapel, all dating from the 1920s. These underwent conservation work in Germany in 2014, with financial assistance from Dublin City Council. Also of interest are the later addition of icons of St Vincent de Paul, St Louise de Marillac and Blessed Frederick Ozanam by Ferghal O'Farrell.

A number of plaques in the church include one to the deceased missionaries of St Peter's 1849 to 1952. A memorial plaque outside two confessional boxes marks their donation by the Rathborne family of Cabra Villa, 'in memory of Miss Rathborne, her father Robert St George and mother Grace Rathborne'. There is also a pictorial display about the life of Frank Duff, born nearby in 97 Phibsborough

Road on 7 June 1889; a commemorative plaque alludes to this, one of the surprisingly few in the district given its wealth of history. The founder of the Legion of Mary, a Roman Catholic lay organization that presently has three million active members in over 170 countries, Frank Duff was responsible for the establishment of the Morning Star Hostel (1927) and the Regina Coeli Hostel (1930), located on Morning Star Avenue, North Brunswick Street. Both hostels cater for the needs of the city's homeless men and women. He died on 7 November 1980.

Outside the church, beside the small wall supporting the iron railings on Cabra Road, was a stone marker denoting the height of the ground above sea level; it existed here until quite recently.

St Peter's Road and Environs

The construction of new national schools for infants, girls and boys, on St Peter's Road, was completed in 1891. It was formerly called St Peter's Terrace, and a stone-carved nameplate denotes this fact on a terrace of houses opposite the school. In 1999 all three schools, the infants' and girls' school on the ground floor and the boys' school on the first floor, were amalgamated into one, with a total of 303 pupils on the rolls. A huge redevelopment, at a cost of around €8 million, started in 2006 and the school moved into temporary prefabricated units in the church grounds nearby. It reopened in September 2008 and in 2016 it had 450 children on its rolls; the current principal is Joan Quinn, from Castleisland in County Kerry, who began her teaching career at the school.

A famous past pupil is the entertainer Jack Cruise, born in the family home at 14 Arranmore Avenue, Phibsborough on 9 August 1913. Arranmore Avenue is located beside the old schoolhouse at Blacquire Bridge and consists of just twenty-three single-storey terraced houses, with interesting decorative iron railings and granite steps leading up to the front doors. He joined the Fr Matthew Players, Church Street in 1936, becoming their star performer and appeared regularly in the Theatre Royal; his first appearance in the Gaiety Theatre was in 1946 in *Arsenic and Old Lace*, directed by Hilton Edwards. He became Director of the Olympia Theatre in 1964, producing a total of twenty-seven Christmas pantomimes. He married Jean McKevitt in 1940 and they lived for many years on Croaghpatrick Road, Cabra before moving to Castleknock. Jack Cruise died in 1979, after which his wife Jean moved into an apartment beside the railway bridge on the Old Cabra Road.

Another noted pupil is James 'Jimmy' Bourke from Nelson Street, born on 16 March 1912, who changed his name to the Irish form, Séamus de Búrca, in later life. He wrote *The Soldier's Song* (1957), a biography of Peader Kearney, his uncle and author of the Irish national anthem, and *Brendan Behan, A Memoir* (1971). Brendan Behan was a cousin as their mothers, Margaret and Kathleen Kearney, were sisters. Desmond Connell, who is from the district, is also a past pupil. He became Archbishop of Dublin and a Cardinal of the Roman Catholic Church. His handling of the issue of child sexual abuse within the Church during the 1990s tainted his episcopate.

Opposite the school is Norfolk Road and Cabra Park. Arthur V. Healy was the Secretary of the Rathmines and Rathgar Musical Society, and during the 1940s he ran the Society's office from his home at 2 Norfolk Road; numbers 1 and 3 have distinctive bay windows, facing onto St Peter's Road. The houses here were constructed at the end of the nineteenth century, with the exception of the two terraces of houses in the cul-de-sac at the very end of Norfolk Road. These display a very unusual crest on the wall over the front doors depicting Cú Chulainn, the Irish mythological hero. The terrace on the right-hand side was built in 1936 and those facing the railway line to Broadstone Station were built in 1939. Margaret Smyth, the longest resident here, told me that her parents Margaret and John were the first to move in, during 1936, adding that 'the Sweetmans moved in the next day, and then Bernard Wafer; he ran a brass foundry off Church Street and they were the first to have a car. The land once belonged to CIE and we paid our ground rent to them for many years.'

Most of the houses on Cabra Park are three storeys high. In order to prevent Bulmer Hobson carrying out the orders of General Sean MacEoin and thereby implementing the cancellation order for the 1916 Rising, he was detained in a house here by Martin Conlon, Michael Lynch, Con O'Donovan, Maurice Collins and Seán Tobin, from the Saturday night before the Easter Rising until hostilities broke out on Easter Monday. Síle O'Neill, whose father-in-law Michael O'Neill fought in the Rising, identifies the house as 75 Cabra Park. A grocer, Michael O'Neill lived at 69 North King Street in 1916, where he sold coal by the stone and tea by the ounce. He fought in the GPO during the Rising and was later interned in Frongoch Prison Camp in Wales. He married Agnes Fagan, whose family was one of just three living on Peck's Lane, Castleknock, where they ran a small farm. She provided food and provisions to the insurgents in North King Street during the Rising.

Síle recalls that during the War of Independence, Agnes and Michael were travelling out to Dun Laoghaire on the upstairs of a tram when it was boarded by the Black and Tans; he had a pistol in his possession and slipped it to Agnes: 'it was lucky that he did, as they searched him and although she hid it in her knickers they didn't search her.' Michael Collins hid in a wardrobe in a bedroom over the grocery shop during 1920 after he was chased by British soldiers; he evaded arrest during a search of the house. The wardrobe is today a prized family possession. The O'Neill family later moved to Cabra Park; Agnes died on 18 March 1963 and Michael died on 18 September 1976. Síle married their son Peter in the 1950s and, at the request of Michael and Agnes, moved in with them. Peter became the Sports Editor of the *Sunday World* and covered the famous Irish odyssey in the 1990 World Cup campaign Italia '90, when the national team was under the stewardship of Jackie Charlton. Peter died in 1998.

There was a cast-iron Victorian letterbox opposite 10 Cabra Park during the early years of the twentieth century, removed many years ago – joining the vanishing street architecture as the city and suburban landscape slowly changes. Not far from Cabra Park, on the church side of Cabra Road, at number 24, was the home of Louise Gavan Duffy, who lived here during the early part of the last century. Louise was born in Nice, France, on 17 July 1884, the only daughter of Sir Charles Gavin Duffy and Louise Hall; she was fluent in Irish and attended the Gaeltacht in Tourmakeady, County Mayo. In 1907 she joined the Gaelic League and founded Scoil Bhríde, Ireland's first Gaelic school for girls. She was a member of the Provisional Committee of Cumann na mBan and its joint secretary along with Molly Maguire. The sister of George Gavan Duffy, Minister for External Affairs in the first Dáil, she attended UCD from 1908, when she lived in the Women's College, Dominican Convent, Eccles Street. She worked as an assistant in education at St Dominic's Training College, also on Eccles Street, from 1915 to 1916. On Easter Monday 1916 she went to the GPO where she asked to see Pádraig Pearse, later stating that she told him that she 'wanted to be in the field but that I felt that the rebellion was a frightful mistake, that it could not possibly succeed and that it was therefore wrong'. Pearse suggested she should help out in the kitchens, and she agreed since it was not active service. She remained in the GPO until its evacuation. She died at her home 7 Kenilworth Square, Rathgar, on 12 October 1969.

Phibsborough

There are many approaches to Phibsborough, but the principal routes are via Berkeley Road, Broadstone, Cabra Road, Eccles Street and North Circular Road. The oldest of these routes is from Broadstone, where the stretch of road to Glasnevin was formerly known as Finglas-road. In the late 1800s it became known as Phibsborough Road. The busiest approach is along North Circular Road, built in the late 1700s and opened in 1800.

Phibsborough Post Office, North Circular Road, was built in the late 1800s. The contractor was John Pemberton and construction was completed in 1883; it was a single-storey, three-bay brick structure with a distinctive gable-fronted exterior. The public office included a seat underneath the windows and a bench for writing telegraphs opposite the public counter. The area behind the public counter included a fireplace, a bench, cupboards with a benchtop and a telegraph receiver box. In an era before race-clocks, pigeon fanciers would bring their pigeon tags into the post office after Saturday races to be recorded by telegram. The district sorting office was at the back of the building, accessed through a small laneway off the main road. It closed down when this activity was transferred to Bannow Road, Cabra West in November 2013. The present two-storey modern building bears no resemblance, either inside and outside, to the original structure.

Between the Post Office and St Peter's stands the old Baptist church, which now serves as the office of F.H. O'Reilly & Company, Solicitors; it was carefully renovated by the firm about twenty-five years ago. The integrity of the original interior was preserved under the supervision of Michael Mohan, a Raheny-based architect. For years a hole in the outside railing, the result of British army shelling during the Easter Rising, wasn't visible due to a hoarding erected by the next-door fruit and vegetable shop, formerly called The Orchard. When that business closed down the hoarding was removed and the evidence of the shelling could be seen again for a short period of time. In 2016 it housed a motor parts business, SPPumps.ie, who erected a storage space against the railing, so that it is again impossible to see the hole. John Harney of Aughrim Street, recalling his memo-ries of the Easter Rising, pointed out the hole to me during a tour of the area in 1971. He remembered seeing the British army guns shelling Volunteer positions in Phibsborough in 1916.

Next to the post office is a laneway, locally referred to as 'the Cut' or 'the Gut'; this is Phibsborough Avenue, location of the original manor house, Phibsborough House, built in 1790 and demolished in the 1970s. Adjacent to this was The Turret, built in 1772 and forming part of the original village of Phibsborough. It was so called from the distinctive turret-room on the roof of the house. The last owner of The Turret, Richard Lawson, failed in his efforts to preserve the premises and, riddled with dry-rot, it was compulsorily demolished in 1979. There are still some interesting Georgian houses here, including number 19, Anna Lodge, with its tiny garden. The concrete bollard in the middle of the laneway, installed to prevent cattle from bolting down the narrow opening as they were driven to the docks from the nearby Dublin Cattle Market, is a reminder of that bygone era.

The Turret, Phibsborough, 1976 (Courtesy David McKeon)

Phibsborough Road cuts through North Circular Road at Doyle's Corner. The imposing former Allied Irish Bank branch is located on the south side of Phibsborough Road; the original occupier's crest adorns the wall of the building, bearing the initials MB, denoting the Midland Bank. Not far from here is St Peter's Court, which contains a cluster of single-occupancy Dublin Corporation housing units. Formerly called Lynch's Place, it once led from Phibsborough Road to Royal Canal Bank. There is no throughway now and the old nameplate for Lynch's Place, still on the wall in 1993, has disappeared. In the nineteenth century it was called Pinchgut Lane, probably as a result of its narrow form. Next to this is Weaver Lane, evidence that not all the Dublin weavers were based in the Liberties area. Farther down the road opposite All Saints Church, a nameplate on the wall of the first house, built around 1985, indicates King's Inns Court; older residents still call it Kelly's Lane.

Royal Canal Bank runs along the old branch of the canal, which went from Cowley Place to the canal terminus at Broadstone. A few of the original houses survive. Number 39, demolished during the 1980s, was the home of Leslie Mary Price, born there on 9 January 1893. The daughter of Michael Price, a blacksmith, and Mary Price (*née* Hamilton), she was an active member of the Gaelic League and of Cumann na mBan and reported to the GPO on Easter Monday. During the Rising she delivered dispatches between the GPO and the headquarters of Ned Daly in the Fr Matthew Hall, Church Street, and was later imprisoned in Frongach, Wales; her two brothers, Seán and Eamonn, were also imprisoned there. Upon her release she was appointed full-time Director of Cumann na mBan and travelled the country establishing a communications network. She married Tom Barry, whom she met while in Cork in August 1921 and took the anti-Treaty side during the Civil War.

Withdrawing from politics in the 1930s, she joined the Irish Red Cross Society upon its inception in 1939, becoming its chairperson in 1950. A tireless humanitarian, she represented the Society at international level for many years. She was also National President of Gorta, an overseas aid charity and a founder member and president of the Women's Industrial Development Association. She was the recipient of many awards for humanitarian work, including decorations from the Irish, Dutch, German and Italian governments, and received the Henri Durant Medal in 1978, the highest award conferred by the International Committee of the Red Cross. She died on 9 April 1984 in St Finbarr's Hospital, Cork.

The State Cinema

The Phibsborough Picture House, located at 374 North Circular Road beside Blacquire Bridge, was opened in May 1914. It was built by William King of Belcamp House, Raheny, County Dublin and was managed by his brother Jack. Within a month of opening, it was in the news; on 4 June 1914 a riot broke out during the screening of *In the Shadow of the Throne*, when a number of men, objecting to the perceived anti-Catholic scenes in the film, started a riot during which they threw ink at the screen, thereby damaging it. Some ink landed on the blouse of a lady musician in the orchestra, staining it 'beyond use' and 'yet more ink splashed on the music-sheets of the cinema's orchestra, thereby destroying them'. A number of men were arrested and subsequently appeared in court, where they were each fined the sum of one shilling. The protests ensured that the film run was extended and shown to a packed picture house each night.

It was later renamed the Blacquire Cinema and became run-down by the early 1950s. Lilly O'Brien, now living on Navan Road, remembers having to leave the cinema during a screening: 'I was in the Blacquire one night when a sudden downpour drenched the picture house and we all had to leave. The manager apologized to us on the way out and he gave us our money back.' It was demolished in 1953 and re-opened on same site, as the State Cinema, on 24 April 1954; the first screening was *West of Zanzibar* starring Anthony Steele and Sheila Simms. With a capacity for seating 850 patrons, it was managed by William D. King, son of the aforementioned William. The picture house was typical of the 1950s style of architecture, and became a popular evening entertainment spot until 1980. It was the first purpose-built Cinemascope picture-house in Europe and formed part of the Odeon group of cinemas. Louis Elliman was the Chief Executive of the group and a promoter of the Ardmore Film Studios in Bray. In the late 1950s the State often held yo-yo competitions there, hosted by the famous yo-yo practitioner Billy Panama.

Weekend pictures once had to be pre-booked in order to get a seat and queues were a common feature, running along the side of the cinema and down the steps that lead to the linear park. In 1952 there were 965,000 admissions to the country's 238 cinemas each week – one third of the population of just fewer than three million people then living in the Republic. Cinema admissions in 1954 totalled 54.1 million – over one million patrons per week. Bookings were generally carried out by schoolchildren on Thursday or Friday afternoons for the working lads, who took their girlfriend or 'the mott' to the pictures on a Saturday or Sunday night. This was a common source of pocket money for schoolchildren in the district.

The last film screened at the State Cinema, on 29 June 1974, was *The Assassin* starring Ian Hendry and *And Now for Something Completely Different* with John Cleese. This was in the days when the picture-goer was offered two films, giving good value for money. The State also hosted concerts, including Noel Pearson's production of *Jesus Christ Superstar*. The famous rock band The Ramones played there in 1978. During the 1960s and early 1970s Ren Tel Ltd operated a TV rental business from a shopfront beside the cinema entrance and many local families secured their first television, a rented set, from here. The building was acquired by Des Kelly in 1982 and operated as a skating rink from then until 1987. It is currently used as a furniture warehouse and retail outlet. The original roof was replaced around 2011 and the projectionist's room still exists.

Beside the State Cinema a bridge carried the North Circular Road over the canal spur, which ran from the canal proper near Cross Guns Bridge to the terminal at Broadstone. Called Blacquiere Bridge after a Director of the canal, the view of Dublin city from here during the 1800s was a most imposing one and was described by George Petrie in 1831:

> The view from this bridge is one of the most commanding that can be
> obtained of the City of Dublin … The fine dome of the Four Courts,
> the spire of St Patrick's Cathedral, the towers of Christchurch and of
> the other principal churches of Dublin are seen in the distance.

With the conversion of the terminal into a railway station this spur became disused and was filled-in during the 1930s; it is now a popular and much-used linear park managed by Dublin City Council. In December 2015 the Council restored the statue commemorating the Easter Rising, at Blacquire Bridge, and created a public opening here leading into the linear park.

Long before a picture house appeared, an old police guardhouse stood on the site. In 1824, when lawlessness and crime was 'rampant in the poverty-stricken area of Phibsborough', local people petitioned the authorities to set up a police station in an unused guard house at Blacquiere Bridge. Police headquarters coldly retorted that 'the area was not paying any watch tax, and, even if it were, that it would come to no more than £25 a year, a mere tithe of what a police party would cost'.

Phibsborough Library

For many years the library needs of the Dublin 7 district were served by the Public Library in Capel Street. The extension of the city boundaries under the Greater Dublin Act of 1930 brought within the municipality a number of suburban areas and as a result the Dublin Corporation Library Service expanded considerably. Shortly after the passing of the 1930 Act, Dublin Corporation earmarked a sum of £20,000 for the building of new libraries; plans were developed for a chain of small libraries throughout suburban Dublin. Based on similar libraries then being constructed throughout urban England, it became the intention of Dublin Corporation to produce ones that were simple in form, pleasing in design and economical to build and maintain. The first of these was constructed at Blacquire Bridge, Phibsborough, on a site formerly occupied by the city spur of the Royal Canal. Opened in December 1935 at a total cost of £4900, within two years it became the busiest library in Dublin, issuing approximately 800 books per day and 1500 on Saturdays and Mondays.

Due to the success of the Phibsborough library, the Corporation reserved a site on Annamoe Road for a Cabra library, and also considered plans to build a similar library on Broombridge Road, Cabra West. None of these proposals materialized and the considerable demand for library facilities in Cabra and Ashtown was met, from the 1970s to the late 1990s, by a Mobile Library. It served the entire district, operating from sites at the Seventeen Shops and the church grounds on Fassaugh Avenue. The new library on Navan Road, next to Cabra Cross, which opened in 2001, is a now showpiece facility for the benefit and enjoyment of the citizens of Dublin 7 and beyond.

Doyle's Corner

The stretch of road from the library at Blacquiere Bridge to Doyle's Corner is called Madras Place, a fitting setting for the well-known Koh-I-Noor Indian restaurant, which operated here for a number of years up to the end of the last century. Doyle's Corner is perhaps the most famous landmark in Dublin 7 and the Bohemian Lounge was originally called Doyle's. This was John Doyle's pub, whose initials can be seen on the upper brickwork 'JD 1906'; through also owning the pub on the opposite corner, he indelibly stamped his family name on the intersection, which up to the early 1900s had been named Dunphy's Corner. The Doyle family sold the pub in October 1963. The proprietor in 1990 was Ted McGeough; the present proprietors are Seamus and Alan McGeogh. The John Doyle was formerly called the Sir Arthur Conan Doyle, appropriately named to associate it with the intersection; prior to that it was called Murphy's. The licensee in the 1980s was Cavan-born Aidan McGovern; the present proprietor is Thomas McLoughlin.

Doyle's Corner was a chronic traffic bottleneck during the 1960s, until its single overhead traffic control light, called the 'Winking Willie', was replaced by more modern traffic lights. This helped to ease the flow of vehicles passing through. Children of the area assembled at Doyle's Corner when workmen were maintaining the Winking Willie and would dive on the disused graphite stick left by them at the roadside. It was great for chalk. Just around the corner is The Hut, a distinctive public house noted for its Victorian interior and trick mirror outside, offering passers-by a distorted view of themselves. Donegal-born Colm Mohan called 'time' here in 1992. Today it is his son Ed Mohan who now performs that ritual.

Doyle's Corner, Phibsborough, early 1900s
(Courtesy Seamus Kearns Postcard Collection)

Facing The Hut is Phibsborough Shopping Centre, built on the site of the former tramway cottages, and some bungalows, which had well-kept gardens fronting onto Phibsborough Road. These ran from number 71A to 88, and were demolished around 1968. Peader Healy lived at number 86; a member of A Company, 1st Battalion, he was a ticket collector at Broadstone Railway Station; he came home, as usual, for his dinner on Easter Monday and only then heard news of the outbreak of hostilities. He took up a position as a sniper on the roof of Moore's Coachbuilders on Church Street, and later moved to the Four Courts. Imprisoned in Frongoch, he was released in 1917 and ordered to live in exile in Oxford. When neighbours complained to the local authorities about an Irish insurgent living in their midst, the order was lifted and he was allowed to return to Ireland in 1919. He died that year in the Spanish flu epidemic.

The Dublin United Tramways Depot and terminus, or the tram shed as it was called locally, was close to Doyle's Corner, at 345 North Circular Road. It was the only Dublin tram depot with a traverser to turn the trams, due to the cramped nature of the location. The last Dublin tram to leave Phibsborough depot did so in July 1949; some of the original walls still exist and can be easily seen by the passer-by. The trams entered and exited the transport system from North Circular Road. The entrance was positioned between the domestic dwelling at 343, which featured in one of the many State public tribunals involving payments to politicians, and the present-day Mr Tubs Launderette, which in the days of vinyl during the 1970s was the Phibsborough Record Store; next to this was Connolly's shoe shop.

The houses between Doyle's Corner and St Peter's were built during the mid-1800s. Those directly across from the church, at Dalymount, were built in 1870. In one of these houses James 'Jim' Boland was born in Manchester, England, in October 1856 and came to Ireland during the 1880s, where he started work in the paving department of Dublin Corporation. He lived at 6 Dalymount Terrace, where his son Henry James 'Harry' Boland was born on 27 April 1887. When he was made an overseer in the paving department the family moved to 9 Phibsborough Road. He died in the Mater Hospital on 11 March 1895 from a head injury and the family moved to Marino in 1914. Harry Boland took part in the 1916 Rising and later fought in the War of Independence. He took the anti-Treaty side in the Civil War and was shot dead in Skerries in 1922.

Tramshed, Phibsborough, early 1900s (Courtesy Seamus Kearns Postcard Collection)

Bohemian Picture House

The now-disappeared Bohemian Picture House was next to Doyle's Corner, on Phibsborough Road. Together with a few nearby shops, it occupied the site of the present-day Boots chemist, Woodstock restaurant and the apartment complex to the rear. Deriving its name from the nearby football club, it opened its doors for the first time on 8 June 1914 with *In the Hands of London Crooks*. The advertisement for this first showing referred to the new venue's 'refinement', together with 'good music and clear steady pictures' and admission cost 3*d.*, 6*d.*, and one shilling. The Boh, as it was universally known, made Irish cinematic history when it premiered the first film produced in Ireland by an Irish film company and featuring Irish actors. Made in 1916 and entitled *O'Neill of the Glen*, the screenplay was adapted by the Irish film director W.J. Lysaght and was based on a novel by the famous Ulster novelist, M.T. Pender. Starring Fred O'Donovan and Nora Clancy, the film was shot entirely on location in Ireland by The Film Company of Ireland Limited, whose headquarters was located in Dame Street. A Cinderella compared to the State cinema around the corner, the Boh, also called 'the hopper house', closed its doors on 30 March 1974, its last screening being the epic *War and Peace* starring Audrey Hepburn and Henry Fonda.

Dalymount Park

Long before Dalymount Park came into existence, the space now occupied by the hallowed soccer stadium was a large field known to locals as 'the Pisser Dignam's field'. It formed part of the Monck Estate and as such was private property. However, the attractive green space was more or less common land, with the residents of Phibsborough cultivating vegetable plots on one side and local youths using the other side as a playground.

In 1900 officials of Bohemian Football Club opened negotiations that led to the acquisition of the site and on Saturday, 7 September 1901 the ground was officially opened, the first match being a Bohemians *vs* Shelbourne tie. The ground was then no more than an ordinary field, with a corrugated metal surround to keep eager fans at a safe distance. The 'changing room' was a tent pitched at the tramway end of the ground. Within a couple of years the club made such great progress in developing the ground that the then Irish Football Association allocated the 1903 Cup Final to Dalymount Park. In 1904 the ground hosted its first international match, when Ireland played Scotland in a one-all draw.

FAI Cup Final, 1950. Shelbourne *vs* Cork Hibernians (Courtesy Bohemian FC)

Further developments included the widening of the pitch, ancillary drainage works, and the erection of large wooden stands behind the goals, the 'popular' and reserved terrace of the ground, in 1908. These improvements sufficed up to the mid-1920s, when the amenities on offer became inadequate to meet demands. In 1927 a new steel stand was erected at a cost of £5833. In 1931 another section was added to the stand and new exits built at the rear. The plans for these developments were drawn up by Archibald Leitch, a noted architect with a proven track record – he had previously designed such famous soccer stadia as Anfield, Ibrox, Hamden Park and Goodison Park.

The next major step in the conversion of Dalymount Park into the premier soccer stadium in the State took place in 1953 when, on Sunday 15 March the Minister for Defence, Oscar Traynor, officially opened the new terracing on the Connaught Street or unreserved side of the ground. Oscar Traynor was born in 1886 and was educated in St Mary's Place CBS, Dublin 7. He was in charge of the Metropole Hotel garrison during the 1916 Rising and later served as a Fianna Fáil TD from 1932 until 1961.

Unlike most of his party colleagues, who traditionally only supported Gaelic games, he had a great interest in soccer and played for Belfast Celtic from 1910 to 1912. He was President of the Football Association of Ireland from 1948 until his death on 14 December 1963. He resisted the efforts of Dr John Charles McQuaid, Roman Catholic Archbishop of Dublin, to ban an international soccer match at Dalymount Park between Ireland and Yugoslavia in October 1955 on the grounds that Yugoslavia was a communist country that had kept a Cardinal under house arrest.

A significant development was the installation of an ambitious floodlight system, which was switched on on 7 March 1962, marking another milestone in both the history of the ground and Irish soccer. The initiative allowed for European Cup, European Cup Winners' Cup and European Fair's Cup fixtures involving League of Ireland clubs to be played in the evenings at Dalymount Park, bringing huge excitement – and expectation – to the premier Irish soccer ground.

During the 1970s, due to lack of funds, Bohemians were unable to invest in the upgrading of the ground and as a result Lansdowne Road, spiritual home of Irish rugby, became the regular venue for Ireland's international soccer matches. 'Dalyer' had a brief reminder of former glory days when in September 1989 'Jack's

Lads', the Irish team, turned out on the once-hallowed turf in an Ireland *vs* Morocco International friendly. Cheered on by 'Jack's Army', as the Irish supporters were called during the Ireland tenure of Jack Charlton, the former English and Leeds United player, the famous 'Dalymount Roar' was again to be heard, wafting into the Phibsborough night air, urging the team on. The opening of the new Aviva Stadium at Lansdowne Road, in a joint multi-million euro programme between the Football Association of Ireland and the Irish Rugby Football Union, has secured that venue's position as the new home of Irish soccer. For many years now that venue has also hosted the FAI Cup Final.

In 2000 the old wooden stand was demolished and the present Jodi Stand, a safe concrete and iron structure, was erected. With generous sponsorship from a local business, the school end, called 'The Shed' was renewed and seating installed. In 2015 Dublin City Council acquired Dalymount Park and further improvements are planned for the stadium as the overall standard of League of Ireland facilities continues to rise to meet today's requirements. This development will hopefully ensure the continuation of League of Ireland football at Phibsborough for years to come.

The celebrated Irish boxer Jack Doyle, the 'Gorgeous Gael', whose amateur record was twenty-eight wins (all except one being knockouts), fought Mullingar blacksmith Chris Cole in front of a huge crowd at Dalymount Park for the heavy-weight championship of Ireland in 1943. His defeat effectively ended his boxing career. He married Mexican actor Movita, who divorced him in 1945 and then married Marlon Brando. Jack ended up homeless on the streets of Dublin after the Second World War, and for a period slept in the back of a broken-down taxi in Henrietta Street. His later moved to London, where he died on 13 December 1978. He is buried in his native town of Cobh, County Cork.

During the 1970s and 1980s the ground was the venue for rock concerts and in 1977 hosted Bob Geldof and the Boomtown Rats; three years later Bob Marley performed there. Other concerts included Heavy Rock specialists Meatloaf and Black Sabbath, on 13 June 1982 and 28 August 1983 respectively; the ticket price for Meatloaf was £10.50 (€13.44).

Bohemian Football Club

Bohemians are synonymous with Phibsborough and Dublin 7, and has given its name to many local businesses, including the Bohemian Lounge, the Bohemian Cafe and the former Bohemian picture house. It was at Bell's Academy, a civil service college in North Great Georges Street, that the seeds were first sown that led to the formation of Bohemians. Since 1887 soccer had been played at the Academy at a time when few people in the city either heard much of or cared even less about the game that would one day sweep the world. Rugby football was the game that really mattered in those days and devotees of the Association were treated with considerable condescension. Soccer players found great difficulty in arranging fixtures, which were mostly played among members of Bell's Academy and their immediate friends. As the popularity of the game spread and outsiders began to take up the sport, it became vital for the Academy, with its bulging outside membership, to change its name. The title finally decided upon was Richfield F.C., which met for its first general meeting on Saturday, 19 October 1889. A.P. Magill was appointed first Honorary Secretary and H.P. Bell Honorary Treasurer.

Without realizing it, these pioneers were the founding fathers of the club, for in 1890 Richfield changed its name to Bohemians, thereby creating a famous Irish sporting institution. The birth of the new club led directly to the formation of the Leinster Senior Football Association in October 1892, following a meeting in the Wicklow Hotel, Dublin. The club also played a significant role in the founding of the Football Association of Ireland and the Football League of Ireland in 1921, when it was the first club to signal its intention to join.

Bohemians' first trophy was the Leinster Senior Cup in 1894, which they went on to win in each of the next five succeeding years; their first major trophy was the IFA Cup in 1908. They were league champions on eleven occasions and the FAI cup winners on seven occasions, which includes the League and Cup double in 1928, 2001 and 2008. The club's most successful season was that of 1927/28 when, as a fully amateur team, they won the Irish Free State League, the Irish Free State Cup, the Shield and the Leinster Challenge Cup. They won the Setanta Sports Cup, a competition involving League of Ireland and Irish League teams, in 2009/10. Other successes include the League Cup (three times), League of Ireland Shield (six times) and Leinster Senior Cup (thirty-one times). The present club president is Matt Devaney and its secretary is Stephen Lambert. The official club historian is Stephen Burke who lives in Pinehurst, Rathoath Road. He is currently compiling a history of the club. The club's first international player was John Fitzpatrick, who captained Ireland in 1895; its first Ladies international was Sharon Boyle, capped in 1994.

Perhaps the most famous player in the history of the club is John 'Jackie' Jameson, born on 27 March 1957 in Cashel Avenue, Crumlin. He started his playing days with Lourdes Celtic and came to Bohemians in 1980 via Shamrock Rovers and St Patrick's Athletic. He scored on his league debut on 13 September 1980 against Sligo Rovers, and became a legend to Bohemian supporters. He was the team's top scorer during his first four seasons at Dalymount, scoring forty-nine goals. Jackie Jameson had a placid temperament and once he got possession of the ball it was difficult to take it from him. His most memorable game was against Glasgow Rangers in a UEFA Cup Winners Cup tie at Dalymount, when he mesmerized the Rangers defence and in the process set up a famous 3-2 victory for Bohemians; they lost the return fixture at Ibrox to two late Rangers goals and were eliminated from the competition 4-3 on aggregate. In the mid-1980s injuries took their toll and on 28 January 1990 he played his last game, a 1-0 home defeat to UCD in the League of Ireland; he retired from the game at the end of that season. He was such an exciting player that many neutral spectators came to Dalymount Park just to witness him playing. Tragically, he drowned in Dun Laoghaire in 2002, aged just forty-five. One of the three function rooms at Dalymount Park, the Players' Lounge, is named in his honour.

During 2015 the Club established the Bohemian Foundation as an independent non-profit organization tasked with improving the health and well-being of its north Dublin community. Offering a focal point for community involvement, it collaborates with Dublin City Council and has to date worked in partnership with a number of bodies including Age Action, Special Olympics Ireland and the Garda Youth Diversion Project. It also provides football coaching throughout the year in Mountjoy Prison. The president of the foundation is Thomas Hynes from Killala Road, Cabra West.

Model Railway Shop

Not far from Dalymount Park, at Number 18 Monck Place, was the Model Railway Shop, operated by well-known train enthusiasts Ciaran and Gerry McGowan. They lived on St Peter's Road, Phibsborough. The brothers' interest in model railways began when their father bought them a train set in 1939 for Christmas. They took to the hobby and a number of years later had expanded it by constructing an O-gauge model railway in the back garden of their home. Neighbours, impressed by the huge outdoor layout, started asking them to repair engines and train kits. Their mother suggested that they set up a repair business, such was the demand for their skills, and with her encouragement they opened the Model Railway Shop in Monck Place on 19 January 1950.

The brothers built up a successful business and many customers became close friends over the years. Andrew Flynn, one of those who lamented the passing away of the unique Model Railway Shop, cherished happy memories: 'It was the only shop in the area which was a social meeting place. You could always pop in for a chat. Often, you would drop in just to see who you would bump into.' The brothers were commissioned to make the bogeys for the Dart and coaches and diesel engines for the Fry Model Railway display at Malahide Castle, since removed to make way for a retail and restaurant chain. It is said locally that the entertainer Frank Sinatra, who performed at the RDS during the 1980s, visited the brothers during his stay to discuss and get advice about model railways. They stayed in business until their retirement in January 1992 after over forty years, bringing to an end another unique aspect of Dublin life. They presented their shop sign to the Old Dublin Society.

Next to the old Model Railway Shop, the houses on Great Western Square are of solid red brick with heavy eaves. These were built for employees of the MGWR at Broadstone. Consistent with the thoroughness of railway construction, red brick is used throughout. The houses overlook a pleasant green, now railed-in, managed and maintained by Dublin City Council; it was not always so, as in the 1950s and 1960s it was just a field, which also served as a football pitch. Des Abott, a former pupil of St Peter's school and a local travel agent, grew up in Great Western Villas, and recalls some great football being played on the green, with many League of Ireland stars displaying their skills. His father was a train driver based at Broadstone: 'The drivers were housed in the Villas, which are smaller homes, and the inspectors and equivalent grades were housed in the square. All the tenants eventually bought their house from the company.'

Nearby, at 268 North Circular Road, lived John and Elizabeth Flynn, who established Grafton Publications in the late 1920s. They published the widely read women's magazine *Model Housekeeping* that ran successfully from 1928 until the mid-1960s. The couple also established the *Monument Press*, a Bray-based printing company, which gave employment to fifty people. John, originally from Athlone, was President of the Irish Master Printers' Association and was deeply involved in wartime negotiations to secure printers' supplies of rationed paper; he died in 1953 and the family disposed of all of their businesses in 1970. Their son Andrew is a well-known barrister who grew up in the district and now lives in Drumcondra.

Blacquiere House

At the top of the present-day linear park at Phibsborough, where the spur, or the 'City Branch', cut away from the Royal Canal to connect with a harbour, wharfage and storage facility at Broadstone, stood Blacquiere House, near the Fourth Lock at Cross Guns Bridge. Built in 1791, it was named after Sir John (Lord) Blacquiere, born in 1732 and of French Huguenot origin. A Director of the Royal Canal Company and a member of Grattan's Parliament, representing the Borough of Charleville, Tipperary Riding, this wealthy man used his considerable resources to buy influence. He was appointed bailiff of the Phoenix Park with a sinecure that paid £40 per annum, which he later had increased to £500. He built the Chief Secretary's Lodge – now home to the Ambassador of the United States of America – in the Phoenix Park, earning him the nickname 'the King's Cowboy'. He died in 1812. Taylor's 1828 map indicates the location of Blacquire House, then important enough to be connected to North Circular Road by an extension of Cowley Place; it was demolished in 1977. His name is remembered through the terrace of houses at Blacquire Villas nearby. The former printing works of Dakota Ltd was situated opposite Blacquire Villas; the only reminder of the thriving 1960s firm is the modern apartment development on the site, Dakota Court.

The Basin and Environs

'The Basin', an enclosed water mass, provided the north city area with its water supply in the 1800s and is entered through a door in the granite wall alongside the linear park. It was constructed in 1810 as a reservoir for the storage and distribution of water to the city. Its water was drawn from the Royal Canal, through pipes running from the canal inlet at the 8th Lock, Reilly's Bridge, Cabra, through iron pipes. The water percolated through a gravel and stone filter before being pumped into the city's water supply. The Gothic-style gate lodge at the Blessington Street entrance was built in 1811 as a residence for the water-keeper. In 1860 the authorities eventually recognized that the canals provided an unsafe, as well as an inadequate, water supply and the Waterworks at Vartry, County Wicklow, were put in train during that decade, ending the need for the Basin as a reservoir. It continued to supply the distilleries in Smithfield, from the 1860s up until the 1970s. There was a granite structure beside a centre island in the basin and this formed part of the water supply works; further remains of the works can be seen just inside the Blessington Road entrance to the park.

Basin Lodge, Phibsborough, 2016 (Courtesy Ed Bowden)

This unique piece of the past was preserved and incorporated into a quiet city park. In 1993 it was refurbished, with extensive planting of new trees and shrubs, construction of decorative iron railings to replace old fencing, installation of new seating bays and the restoration of the old stone walls. It is now a much-loved public park, managed and cared for by Dublin City Council and is also a haven for a variety of interesting wildlife. On warm sunny days it is not unusual to see patients from the nearby Mater Hospital resting in the park with their visitors.

Nestled to the west of the Basin are Mytle Street, Primrose Street, Shamrock Street, Wellington Street, Fontenoy Street and Auburn Street. Seán Heuston, one of the executed leaders of 1916, stayed at his mother's home in 20 Fontenoy Street before taking part in the Easter Rising. Successive editions of *Thom's Directory* list her at this address as 'Mrs Heuston'.

Blessington Street was built in 1795, its name deriving from the owner and developer of the surrounding lands, Luke Gardiner, whose family held the titles Lord Mountjoy and Earl of Blessington. The writer Jean Iris Murdoch was born at Number 59, on 15 July 1919. Her parents met by chance on a tram they both boarded in the city centre; her mother was going to choir practice in the Black Church when they exchanged glances. Her family moved to London in 1922. Iris Murdoch went on to write twenty-six novels, her first one being *Under the Net*, published in 1954. Her novel *The Red and the Green* was set in Dublin during the Easter Rising. She won the Whitbread Prize in 1974 for *The Sacred and Profane Love Machine* and the Booker Prize in 1978 for *The Sea, the Sea*. She died in Oxford on 8 February 1999.

Barrister and politician Randal Kernan, born in 1774, lived in Enniskillen, County Fermanagh, but maintained a residence at 25 Blessington Street for many years before his death on 30 January 1844. His brother Edward Kernan was the Roman Catholic Bishop of Clogher. The headquarters of BATU, the building and allied trades union, is located at 13 Blessington Street. Formerly the Ancient Guild of Incorporated Brick and Stonelayers, its iconic General Secretary Richard O'Carroll (1876–1916) was a Volunteer during the Easter Rising in 1916; he was arrested by British forces on Camden Street, disarmed, taken to the back of a building and shot dead.

Flour Milling in Phibsborough

The mill at Cross Guns Bridge was originally built as a flour mill and was owned by John and Robert Mallet. Known locally as 'Mallet's folly', it was on a site containing two roods and twelve perches. According to the *Primary Valuation* of 1850, the premises, including stores, workshop and a garage, were valued at £36. This former flourmill lay idle for some years due to a dispute over water rights from the adjacent Royal Canal. With the advent of the railways, Mallet converted it to an iron mill, employing over forty blacksmiths.

Born on 3 June 1810 in Ryder's Row, Dublin, in 1831 he married Cordelia Watson and in 1836 they moved into Delville House in Glasnevin. Robert was considered the father of instrumental seismology: he invented and patented buckled plates (1852), used to floor Westminister Abbey. He also invented a metal bed, with one leg, for use in prison cells. He lived in some style and the fact that he 'held a special day's feast and dispensed beer to all employees on the occasion of the coronation of Queen Victoria' gives some indication of his wealth. The ironworks produced the railings surrounding Trinity College, recorded by the inscription on the base of the iron railing on that part of the wall from College Green to Nassau Street: *I & R Mallet, Dublin*. The company also supplied fire engines, the castings for the first Fastnet lighthouse, and supplied steel for the Dublin and Kingstown, Great Southern and Western Railways.

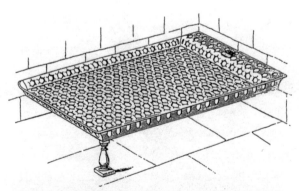

225. Design for a cast-iron bedstead by Mallet of Dublin, illustrated by J.C. Loudon in 1833 as suitable for a ploughman's room. They were also used in prison cells (see Plate 289).

Cast-iron prison bed by Mallet's Foundry, Phibsborough
(Courtesy *English Vernacular Furniture 1750–1900*)

Due to a shortage of contracts, Robert closed down the mill at Phibsborough in 1860 and moved to London, working as a consultant engineer and a writer. He also contributed to the science of earthquakes, detonating explosions on Killiney Beach to measure shock waves and coining the term 'seismology'. He died on 5 November 1881 and is buried in Norwood Cemetery, Surrey.

Murtagh Brothers acquired the premises that same year and began one of the worlds oldest crafts, that of flour milling. Under the trade name of the Dublin North City Milling Company, they initially operated with nineteen millstones and a kiln for drying corn. The power for the plant machinery was steam-driven and the company had what was believed to be the largest single-stroke condenser steam engine in Ireland at the time, with a 28-foot diameter fly-wheel. The mill chimney was the highest in the city. The company also used the waters of the Royal Canal as a source of energy. In 1947, however, the mill was connected to the National Grid and their steam power plant became obsolete, and another famous city landmark, the high mill chimney, disappeared forever.

Demolition of Chimney Rank's Mills, Phibsborough, 1947 (Courtesy *The Irish Times*)

The destruction of the chimney in 1947 was recorded for posterity by the *Irish Times*. A Dubliner who worked for many years at the plant, Maurice Butler, told me of a former colleague who had spent his entire life working at the mill and who, on hearing that the chimney was to be demolished, remarked that when it came to be torn down, he would go down with it. On the very day that the old chimney was demolished, the mill worker was being buried in Glasnevin Cemetery nearby.

In the early 1950s the mill ceased using the waters of the Royal Canal for the transport of wheat and in 1952 sold off their canal barges to a scrap dealer. However, the purchaser never collected his new acquisitions and they lay idle for nearly forty years, slowly rotting away beside the banks of the Royal Canal. Viewed from Cross Guns Bridge they provided a silhouette, reminiscent of a Turner painting, against the canal background, hinting to the onlooker that the waterway did once serve a useful economic purpose. In 1991 the barge wrecks were removed by the Office of Public Works (OPW) during canal improvement works.

Dublin North City Milling Company was taken over by Ranks in 1957, who installed new machinery and upgraded the transport fleet. Originally a six-sack mill, on its takeover Ranks increased production to sixteen sacks and when it closed in the mid-1980s it had a forty-sack capacity, that is, five tons of flour per hour. The railway spur to the side of the mill from the Glasnevin Cemetery section of the main Dublin-Galway line continued to be used by the new owners. This railway siding, which crossed the canal by means of a metal bridge at Shandon Park Mills, was used by Ranks until 1964 when the company expanded its transport fleet and concentrated fully on road haulage. The metal bridge was removed in 1992 by the OPW.

Ranks pulled out of the flour-milling business in the early 1980s and this heralded the closure of the plant, which involved considerable controversy and a long and bitter workers' sit-in. However, the former plant continued its association with flour milling, in that a portion of the complex was taken over by Modern Bakery, managed by Kildare-born Joe O'Brien. To expand the bakery he purchased a section of the mill and moved the company's operations from a smaller factory nearby. From here they manufactured a variety of bread and cake products and supplied a large market segment of the city, from institutions like hospitals to small voluntary-run Day Care Centres, from supermarkets and shops to domestic customers. The brands were well-known, and included 'The Granary' and 'Old Mill'. One of the employees at Cross Guns was James Hartnett, who had previously spent over thirty years at the old Ranks mill, where he served his time. Modern Bakery continued selling flour-milling products in the Phibsborough area until it ceased trading around 2008, ending a long tradition of milling at the site. Johnston Mooney & O'Brien acquired Modern Bakery's 'The Granary' brand, still in use today. The old bakery building became disused and was derelict in January 2016, with a planning permission sign for a proposed housing development posted at its entrance.

A large section of the old mill, constructed in the 1800s, was renovated and converted into apartments in 1992; one side of this development faces out onto the restored Royal Canal. The front portion of the former mill, constructed in the 1970s, served as office headquarters for ADT Ltd from the late 1980s; it lay vacant in 2016.

Shandon Park Mills

Shandon Park Mills, a distinctive north city landmark, was located at the back of the former Ranks Mills, with a road entry from Shandon Park and adjoining the Royal Canal. Built around 1800, it was acquired by the Midland Great Western Railway in 1848. They used it to store logwood until 1885, when they converted it into a manufacturing plant for pins and rivets. In the early 1900s the railway company disposed of the plant, following which it lay idle for some years; it is described on the 1908 Ordnance Survey map as a disused pin factory. In 1928 the property was acquired by William Blake of Macroom, County Cork, who initiated the manufacture of bread rusk for use in sausage making.

On 7 May 1943 the mill was completely gutted by fire and the following is an account of the incident, from the *Irish Times* of Friday May 7 1943:

> A large quantity of valuable machinery, which it will probably be impossible to replace, was destroyed when fire gutted the main portion of the Shandon Park Mills, Phibsboro, last night. The only mill of its kind in Dublin, it employed twenty-two workers and manufactured spices and meal for sausage filling. The fire started when a dust explosion ignited a drying room in which a quantity of rusk meal was drying. The origin of the flame which caused the explosion is not known. Mr William Blake, the proprietor of the mill, said that he did not know the value of the machinery destroyed or of the stores lost

Fire at Shandon Park Mills, 1943 (Courtesy *The Irish Times*)

William Kelly, the only employee on the premises at the time of the outbreak of the fire, gave the alarm immediately on hearing the explosion, which occurred at ten past six in the evening, only five minutes after William Casserly, the mill foreman, had left for home following his usual inspection tour of the building. The fire appears to have spread rapidly. The flames and smoke were seen over a great distance and as a result crowds converged from a wide area. Four sections of the Fire Brigade, under Major J. Comerford, Chief Superintendent, fought the blaze, assisted by units of the Auxiliary Fire Service.

An *Irish Times* photograph of the aftermath of the fire recorded the extent of the damage to the mill, which was reconstructed in its original form afterwards. However, the fire led to the demise of an ancient source of energy obtained from the waters of the Royal Canal. This powered the turbines located in a basement. The turbines, and mill race along which the canal waters were diverted, still existed up until 1990, though hidden from view by a metal floor installed in 1944 to cover the disused machinery. I was given a tour of the premises by the company in 1985 to view the old turbine equipment and machinery.

On the death of William Blake the company passed on to a firm called Stokes and Dalton, which in turn was acquired by Ranks, Hovis & Mc Dougall. When the mill began production in 1928, the company employed eight people. In the mid-1940s it employed twenty-five. In the early 1980s there were fourteen workers. In 1979, due to cheap flour imports, the company stopped making bread rusk and concentrated on the production of pepper and spices, importing its raw materials from exotic places like Sarawak, Jamaica, Zanzibar and Madagascar. The firm produced for industry requirements only.

The construction of houses in Shandon Park started during the 1930s. Shandon Crescent was built during the war and the houses were advertised in the Golden Jubilee booklet issued by Bohemians to celebrate fifty years of the Club in 1940. A compact, quiet estate, it has a unique little pitch-and-putt course behind the back gardens, complete with a small clubhouse. Next to Liam Whelan Bridge and behind the old shops, which were converted to flats in the 1990s, stood Mount Bernard House. One of the old great houses that once dotted the Cabra countryside, a Mrs Mary Anne Sheridan lived here in 1870. Vacant in the late 1900s, it was demolished and the fine, present-day Mount Bernard Park now occupies the site. This beautiful, well-kept public park, with three fenced-in tennis courts and a basketball court, is owned and maintained by Dublin City Council.

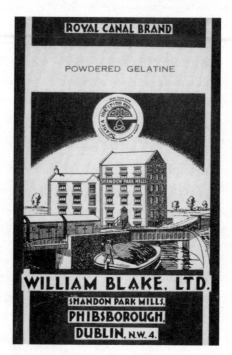

Poster of Shandon Park Mills
(Courtesy Shandon Park Mills)

Cross Guns Bridge

Built in 1791 and named Westmoreland Bridge, from the early 1800s it was more commonly known as Cross Guns Bridge. It was modernized and widened in 1912, and until 1930 it marked the northern boundary of the city. A bronze plaque from the bridge, manufactured by W. Curtis of 98 Middle Abbey Street and donated by City Hall to the Dublin Civic Museum, was located just inside the entrance on South William Street until the closure of the museum in 2003. The plaque bore the following inscription:

> *Westmoreland Bridge, Built by the Royal Canal Company in 1791. Widened, improved and rebuilt by the Municipal Council 1912. Rt. Honorable Lorcan G. Sherlock, L.L.D., Lord Mayor. James J. Kelly, High Sheriff. William F. Cotton, Alderman, D.L., J.P., Chairman, Paving Committee. Francis Keegan, Alderman, Christopher Monks T.C., James Cummins T.C., John Thornton T.C., Representatives of Glasnevin Ward. Henry Campbell, Town Clerk. John G. O'Sullivan, Boro' Surveyor.*

In his *Guide to Historic Dublin*, Adrian McLoughlin states that the name for this bridge comes from the name of a village in Glasnevin. Indeed there is a place called Cross Guns near present-day Hart's Corner, marked on John Rocque's 1756 map of Dublin; it is also very clearly marked on John Taylor's 1816 map of the city and surrounding area. It is quite possible that this village could have derived its name from the fact that the nearby fields were a duelling ground.

Next to Whitworth Road where the Charleville Lawn Tennis Club is located, a celebrated duel took place in 1826. John Bric, a young Kerry-born barrister and an ardent supporter of Daniel O'Connell, was shot dead. On Christmas Eve 1826 he quarrelled outside the GPO with William Hayes, a Cork solicitor and a relative of the conservative candidate in an impending Cork city by-election. John Bric challenged Hayes and the duel was fought two days later, at ten o'clock on the morning of St Stephen's Day, with fatal consequences. John Bric was shot in the lungs and died within fifteen minutes. William Hayes, the victor, lived into his nineties. Duels were a common occurrence at the time; in a duel fought in County Kildare on 3 February 1815, Daniel O'Connell shot and killed John Norcot D'Esterre (1797-1815) when he (D'Esterre) issued a challenge after O'Connell called Dublin Corporation 'beggarly'.

Beside the bridge is O'Loughlin's dental practice, established in 1953; the

Cross Guns Bridge, early 1900s (Courtesy Edwin Mitchell)

late Kevin O'Loughlin told me in the early 1970s that a retired army man living locally stated that it was here on the bridge that soldiers escorting important funerals to Glasnevin reversed their arms, approximately one mile from the cemetery, and so the bridge was given its name. Kevin operated his dental practice for close on forty years and originally shared the building with Billy Bushe, a doctor and the son of Michael Bushe, former proprietor of the next-door pub. Kevin's brother Brian now runs the practice; he is a past president of the Irish Dental Association and of the Association's Metropolitan Branch. Bushe's pub next door was originally called the Cross Guns, a name that appears on the side wall of the building in early twentieth century photographs of the area. In the 1990s the proprietor was Michael O'Mahony and under his management it became a favourite GAA meeting place, possibly due to its convenience for those parking nearby while attending Croke Park, although it could also be the fact that Michael was a former Tipperary hurler; a mirror in the entrance foyer is inscribed with 'The Hurler's Poem'. Michael died in 2006 and the pub was bought by T.P. Smith from County Cavan, who renamed it 'Smith's'. In 2015 he renamed the premises to 'Bushes'.

Cremona String Band

Next to Cross Guns Bridge and beside the dental practice, at 117 Phibsborough Road, is the former home of a well-known early twentieth-century Irish musical family. In 1910 Joseph and Gussie 'Albert' Mitchell formed the Cremona String Band, which consisted of piano, fiddle and cello. They became a popular travelling band, performing throughout Ireland until the 1930s. During the weeks leading up to Lent each year, the band performed outside Broadstone Railway Station to attract the attention of the gentry, hoping to secure bookings to play in their stately homes. This was at a time when dancing was frowned upon during Lent by the Roman Catholic Church and dancehalls therefore closed for the seven-week period. They would also be offered full board by the gentry for the duration of their services.

Zandra Mitchell went to London in 1928 where she purchased a saxophone from the famous Shaftsbury Avenue music shop of Alexander Byrne. Byrne later saw her perform in the Theatre Royal in London and persuaded her to join the Irene Davis Ladies Band. Her career blossomed, with performances in Switzerland followed by a regular engagement in Selfridges, the London department store. On the demise of that band, Zandra joined the Russian Ladies Band, touring mainland Europe. She subsequently employed a personal manager, Mr Reinhold, and formed her own band, Baby Mitchell and her Original Queens of Jazz, which was an instant international success. She became a household name in Europe and beyond, performing in Ireland, England, Holland, Belgium, Germany, Spain, Switzerland, Italy, Sicily and North Africa. She spent the war in Berlin before retiring to Ireland to the tranquillity of County Donegal.

Edwin Mitchell played with Flynn's Band, Roscommon, from 1926 until 1932, when he formed Edwin Mitchell and His Girls band. He toured the country, enjoying considerable success and fame. The band was popular during the 1940s and continued to perform until its break up in 1961. Edwin later retired from the music business and lived reclusively in Phibsborough. His house was a local landmark, decaying and covered by a large, shady tree and a wild garden. An old Morris Minor stood in its driveway for many years, undriven. A brass plaque, always polished, took pride of place on the railings outside his house. It bore the following inscription: *Cremona String Band*. Edwin died in the mid-1980s and the house was sold and renovated.

Big bands were in demand from the 1920s through to the late 1950s, and the Cremona String Band was just one of a number of popular acts in the district. The Billy Manahan Band was founded by Waterford-born Billy Manahan, who lived at 258 North Circular Road performed at functions such as hunt balls and toured the country, being as famous in their day as the Clipper Carlton and Miami show-bands of the 1960s. Manahan's wife Kay Fagan was a well-known light-classical singer and was probably the first person to sing on 2RN, Radio Éireann.

Next to Edwin's house are the small cul-de-sacs of Enniskerry Road and Royce Road. Rory O'Hanlon was born at 14 Royce Road on 11 April 1923, the third son of journalist Terence O'Hanlon and Mary O'Hanlon (*née* Halley). He was appointed a Judge of the High Court in 1981 and, retiring in 1995, he spear-headed the NO campaign leading up to the divorce referendum of November that year. He died in 2002.

Phibsborough was a great retail hub during the 1900s and people from the surrounding areas of Cabra, Grangegorman and Navan Road went there for all their shopping; it always had a great festive atmosphere, especially at Christmas-time. It began a long period of decline from the early 1980s; however, the strong local community spirit and the many resident initiatives, such as the annual Phizz Fest, bode well for the area's future.

9| The Royal Canal

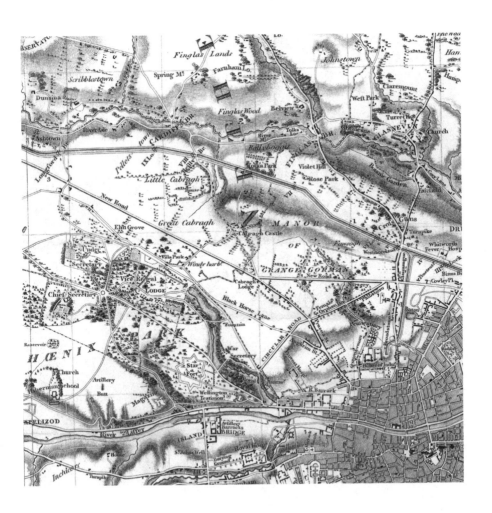

Flowing through Ashtown, Cabra and Phibsborough on its way to the Irish Sea, the Royal Canal is where many youngsters in Dublin 7 learned to swim the hard way, prior to the advent of the indoor swimming pool. It provided hours of enjoyment for thousands of children during school holidays before organized children's activities became the norm. Today the canal is appreciated as an amenity and keen canoeists have now replaced the youngsters of yesteryear with their makeshift rafts. All year round the familiar figure of the angler graces its banks.

With regard to the construction of the Royal Canal, the following extract from *Illustrated Ireland* (George Wright, 1831) gives the reader a good description of the extent of the undertaking and the nature of the massive works involved:

> In 1789 a company was incorporated by Royal Charter and to them extensive powers were committed. Their object was the collection of subscriptions for the purpose of opening a grand line of canal, from the north side of the city to the upper part of that noble river, the Shannon, a distance of eighty-six-and-a-half English miles. In this great length, which is terminated at Tarmonbury, or Richmond Harbour, in the County of Longford, an elevation of 307 feet above the sea-level is attained by means of twenty six locks while the descent,

on the west side, to the river Shannon, is accomplished by fifteen. The supply of water, which is indeed never-failing, is derived from a natural reservoir called 'Lough Ouil' in the County of Westmeath, an area of about 2,856 English acres, whose aqueous resources are altogether internal and independent, being solely supplied by springs. The average height of the surface of this beneficial lake is about two feet above that of the grand summit level at Coolnakay, and consequently 309 feet above high-water in Dublin Bay. The too-great liberality exercised in the formation of the Royal Canal rendered the termination of the design unfortunate and of course unprofitable; and tends, in no remote degree, to engender a disgust towards that useful mode of obtaining funds for the promotion of national works – public subscriptions.

The dimensions of the Royal Canal are 24 feet at the bottom and 44 feet at the surface, having a depth of six feet; the eastern extremity is terminated by a series of floating docks, communicating with the River Liffey, fourteen-and-a-half feet in depth and capable of containing sixty sail; and the western end opens into the river Shannon at Richmond Harbour, already mentioned. In the execution of this extensive design two errors, of a nature almost fatal, were committed; first, the dimensions were too great for any probable state of commercial prosperity and should rather have followed than led an improvement of trade; secondly, these two noble canals, originating at Dublin, are carried through nearly the same district and for many miles run nearly parallel; the first error can never be redeemed, but a remedy is suggested for the second, viz., a union of the two main trunks through the medium of Lake Belvidere. A very considerable trade, both in corn and fuel, is carried on with Dublin by means of the Grand and Royal Canals, and very probably they may yet render Dublin a most important emporium for the exportation of grain; the barges or boats which navigate both are rated from forty to sixty tons burden.

The first reference to a proposed canal from the northwest end of Dublin city to the River Shannon dates from February 1756 and is found in the *Journals of the Irish House of Commons*, when a Mr Cole presented a Bill for forming such a waterway. The proposal was not acted upon, however, as it seems that the supporters of the Grand Canal, or southern line, won the day on that occasion. It was not until thirty years later that the matter was again raised. As a result of a

Royal Canal at Reilly's Bridge, Cabra, 1975 (Courtesy Larry Maher)

quarrel among the directors of the Grand Canal Company one of the members of the Board, John Binns, deemed himself to have been insulted and declared in a fit of anger that he would build a rival canal that would eventually take all the traffic. Due to his considerable height he was called 'Long John Binns' by his supporters and the 'devil's darning needle' by his enemies. He is unique in that two bridges are called after him, over the Royal Canal at Drumcondra and the Grand Canal at Robertstown, County Kildare. Born in 1730, he moved to Dorset Street in 1797 and died there in May 1804. This rich and successful silk merchant was a friend and associate of the patriot James Napper Tandy, who was an investor in the canal.

Petitions were presented to the House of Commons in 1789 seeking aid to build the newly proposed canal and on 24 October the Charter of the Royal Canal Company was established. Subscribers, including the Duke of Leinster, the Earl of Carhampton, Lord Longford, Sir John Blacquiere, Sir William Newcome, John Hatch MP and John Binns, promised the sum of £134,000 in total. Work commenced in 1790 and by 1806 the canal had reached Mullingar. One of the most costly items in connection with the construction of the waterway was the great aqueduct over the valley of the Rye Water in Leixlip, County Kildare, which cost £30,000. By the time the canal had reached Kilcock, a distance of only twenty miles from Dublin, almost £200,000 had been spent. Consequently, more capital had to be raised.

Following its official opening, the canal began to attract traffic, with toll revenue of £15,000 for 1810, representing a through tonnage of 52,600 tons; goods carried included grain, potatoes, dung, coal, turf, iron, bricks, gravel, sand, stones and flags. Trade was quite small, however, when compared with the rival Grand Canal, which in that same year saw a throughput of over 200,000 tons. The income derived from the business was not enough to pay the interest on the debt and carry out the task of completing the canal.

The debt had risen to £826,000 by 1810, when, after several investigations, the Royal Canal Company was dissolved by statute and all its property vested in the Board of Directors General of Inland Navigation, which in 1815 was authorized to complete the canal. In 1817 the fully constructed waterway was then vested in the New Royal Canal Company.

View of the City of Dublin from Blacquire Bridge, Royal Canal Spur, 1831
(*Ireland Illustrated*, Courtesy NLI)

The construction of the canal had cost £1,421,954 - almost £15,000 a mile; no less than eight Acts of Parliament were necessary to complete the job. After the establishment of the new management company the canal continued to increase its traffic, although tonnage figures never reached those of the Grand Canal. A lucrative passenger business was introduced in the early nineteenth century using new 'fly boats' and proved popular, considerably reducing the time taken to travel between destinations. The passenger trade was eroded by the onset of the railways in the 1850s. The following advertisement, which appeared in the *Sligo Journal* in 1823 under the heading 'Expeditious Travelling', gives an idea of what travelling long distances was like then:

> Royal Canal – cheap, secure and expeditious travelling to and from Dublin to Sligo. A boat will leave Dublin every day at 3 o'clock pm and arrive at Tenelie at nine o'clock the following morning, whence a most comfortable caravan starts and arrives in Boyle that evening at five, passing through Longford, Rouskey, Drumsna and Carrick-on-Shannon. The following morning a car will leave Boyle for Sligo and return to Boyle the day after. The fares of the boat, caravan and car from Dublin to Sligo, a distance of 110 miles Irish, is only sixteen shillings.

During the 1830s the annual profit shown by the canal was around £12,000. Both canals vied strongly with each other for trade but by 1844, when the Royal carried 91,000 tons compared to the Grand's 239,000 tons, it became obvious that it would never be able to compete. The canal was sold to the Midland and Great Western Railway Company (MGWR) in 1844 for the sum of £300,000. The MGWR, having acquired the canal, set about building their railway line from Dublin to Mullingar on the land alongside it. The railway company, although bound by a statutory obligation to maintain navigation on the canal, reduced upkeep on it to the bare minimum, allowing it to deteriorate. In 1871 the railway experimented with horse-drawn cargo boats and from 1875 to 1886 had four steamers operating; however the commercial tonnage carried continued to fall rapidly, from 95,000 tons in 1853 to 11,000 tons in 1921.

In 1906 a Royal Commission on Canals and Waterways found against the MGWR with regard to the maintaining of water levels, weed cutting and dredging and suggested the removal of the canal from the railway company's control.

Royal Canal from Cross Guns Bridge, 1982 (Courtesy Coleman O'Donovan)

A similar Dáil Éireann Commission came up with the same findings in 1923 but nothing was done and after the passing of the Transport Act, 1944, the canal was vested in Córas Iompair Éireann (CIE). Although some improvements took place over the following years, the canal saw further neglect and what could have been a great amenity never materialized.

During the war years of 1939 to 1945 the canal served a useful purpose, when during that era of fuel shortages horse-drawn barges transported turf to Dublin from the Midlands. Shortly after the war only a couple of dozen boats remained working on the canal. Ranks Flour Mills, Phibsborough, was one of the last companies to use the facility, their barges bringing in wheat from the port of Dublin, a short journey that took ten hours. Willie Leech of Hyde Park, Killucan, was the last trader to use the canal, ceasing operations in 1951; the end of an era came ten years later when the Royal Canal was officially closed to navigation.

In the mid-1970s, as a result of greater public awareness and the establishment of a voluntary organization called the Royal Canal Amenity Group, new life came back to the once-great inland waterway. Developments carried out in

Blanchardstown and the Iona district of Glasnevin heralded a brighter future. Lock gates were constructed and installed through AnCO, the Industrial Training Authority of the time.

The control and management of the canal passed to the OPW in 1986 and a new impetus was given to its development as both a valuable resource for everyone, young and old, rural and suburban and a haven for plant, bird and animal life. In 2015 the towpath from Ashtown to Blanchardstown was upgraded, and public lighting and CCTV cameras were installed. This opened the amenity to wider use, including young families and cyclists.

Fisheries Development

The continuing development of the Royal Canal by the OPW is carried out in close cooperation with relevant statutory bodies and interested groups such as angling clubs and the Royal Canal Amenity Group. Canal user groups have acknowledged the dedicated work of the OPW and its remarkable achievement in developing the waterway since its takeover; for its part the OPW has highlighted the work and commitment of bodies such as the Central Fisheries Board and other groups in its literature and through platforms such as the Boat Show or the Spring Show in Dublin.

Since its inception in 1980 the Central Fisheries Board conducted surveys and restocking programmes and introduced effective weed control. Fish life in the canal includes bream, carp, eels, loach, minnow, perch, pike, stickleback and tench. Angling clubs avail of the amenity and some, like the Leixlip and District Anglers Club, have held competitions on the canal; other groups to have used the canal include the Dublin Coarse Anglers Club.

On 1 July 2010 Inland Fisheries Ireland was created, following the amalgamation of the Central Fisheries Board and the seven Regional Fisheries Boards into a single agency, and the Royal Canal now falls under its remit. There is now a greater emphasis on the monitoring of water quality, and Inland Fisheries Ireland provides a rapid response unit to deal with any pollution problems affecting the canal.

Royal Canal Amenity Group Limited

The Royal Canal Amenity Group is a voluntary organization dedicated to the preservation and use of the Royal Canal for the benefit of all. Founded in 1974 by Dr Ian Bath, a lecturer in Trinity College who had just moved into Castleknock, it developed a strong base in Dublin 7. Dr Bath, an honorary life president of the group, now lives in Monkstown, County Dublin. Ned Slane from Kinvara Drive and Ted Galway from Navan Road spent years tirelessly serving the group in various capacities. Initially consisting entirely of volunteers drawn from the Navan Road area, it began to clear the towpath, overgrown and in disrepair, on the Blanchardstown to Clonsilla stretch. They persuaded CIE to make a set of breast gates for the Twelfth Lock at Blanchardstown by cannibalizing the middle and deep lock gates there. This resulted in a seven-mile stretch being restored to full water. The first fruits of their efforts were the successful attraction of canoe-ists, anglers and walkers to the canal.

In 1977 the group organized the construction of its first lock gates at Lucan Vocational School, installed on the Thirteenth Lock by CIE in 1979. This spurred it to greater efforts and in conjunction with AnCO they established a lock-gate manufacturing unit at Watling Street in premises made available by Guinness Brewery. Between 1980 and 1990 the unit manufactured almost all the new lock gates for installation between Dublin and Mullingar. The scheme, taken over by FÁS as successor to AnCO, expired in 1990. The last leader of the project was Paddy Brennan. Developments undertaken from 1990 to 1992 included the opening of a picnic and canal-side recreation area with a boat slip and boathouse, and the creation of a picnic area at Pike Bridge, Maynooth, near the tiny harbour, built for the Duke of Leinster who was a Director of the Royal Canal.

The organizational structure of the Royal Canal Amenity Group was modernized in recent years and in 2016 it consisted of seven branches, including ones in Dublin, Enfield and Mullingar, and a total membership of 350, consisting of 200 life members and 150 ordinary members. In 1992 it had a membership of 850 and during the early years raised funds through raffles, dances, walks and concerts; this money was augmented by amenity grants from Dublin Corporation (Inner City Group), and Dublin and Kildare County Council. Membership is open to all, with an annual subscription of €20 per individual or family. Until recently the group issued a quarterly newsletter containing information on all aspects of the canal, including ecology and development; such information is now disseminated electronically.

The present chairman of the group is Matt Kennedy from Maynooth; the vice-chairman is Niall Spaine from Martin Savage Park, Dublin 7; the Secretary is Niall Slane (son of Ned Slane, who died in 1992) and the treasurer is Brian O'Donoghue from Enfield, County Meath. A former Dublin Branch Committee Chairman was Charlie Hayden of Finglas, Dublin 11, who had Dublin 7 links in that he was attached to McKee Barracks for many years. As Commandant Hayden he was well known to countless young men in the district who came in contact with him though membership of the FCA at McKee Barracks. In particular, many a former pupil of St Declan's College, Cabra, will remember him, as he presided over their own unit, A Company, 7th Battalion, Declan's Platoon, during the 1960s.

Royal Canal, Phibsborough, looking toward Dakota Court and the city, 2016
(Courtesy Lar Boland)

Now promoting heritage rather than restoration, the Royal Canal Amenity Group has inaugurated regular, guided canal walks, led by Peter Clarke, Royal Canal historian, author and retired lecturer, DIT, Bolton Street; these are conducted during summer months. During Heritage Week 2015 the group ran seven guided walks that were well supported and attracted many from around the city and beyond, continuing and fostering an appreciation of the canal.

10 | Smithfield, Stoneybatter and Environs

The Stoneybatter and Smithfield district is one of the oldest areas in the city of Dublin. The areas are so overlapped that it is probably best to treat each area as one unit. Prior to 1765 Prussia Street and its extension into Cabragh was called Cabragh Lane. On John Rocque's 1756 map of Dublin City it is described as 'Cabragh Lane or Prussia Street'; it received its name after one of the most powerful European personages of the day, Frederick the Great of Prussia. Manor Street was then part of Stoney Batter, Bóthar na gCloch, the stony road; the street received its present name in 1780 from the Manor of Grangegorman. Grangegorman Manor survives and is located at 42 Manor Street. Stoneybatter, though now just a very short stretch of thoroughfare, gives its name to the surrounding district. Three hundred years ago it was very lively area close to the original Dublin cattle market in Smithfield and was littered by small businesses and tiny cottages, interspersed by fine period dwellings. There were numerous candlemakers in the district, including James Grant, a tallow-chandler who operated from his home at 13 Stoneybatter around 1800.

Manor Street

On the Primary Valuation of Tenements, 1850, Grangegorman Manor House with the garden and lands was valued at £33. In 1926 it was adapted for use as a Garda Station, with the first contingent of Gardaí moving in during the month of November. In the 1940s the Gardaí were transferred to alternative accommodation on nearby Green Street. During the 1980s the building was set out in self-contained flats for the elderly. Today, it houses the Phoenix Community Resource Centre, a crèche and other local social services. Evidence of past days of grandeur, when the house served as a coach-house, was visible in the courtyard at the rear of the house during the late-1990s. This courtyard was at one time a popular handball alley. Comprising four storeys over a basement, it is easily distinguishable to the passer-by.

Gardai at Manor Street Garda Station, 1932
(Courtesy Neil Ward and *Garda Review*)

Manor Street is noted for its many small, family-run businesses. Perhaps the best known of these are the Pender and Grant families. Grant's, a supplier of children's school uniforms, can be found at 8 Manor Street. The present proprietor is Jim Grant; his great-grandfather Thomas Pender started out as an apprentice military tailor. With plenty of custom from the two nearby military complexes, McKee Barracks and Collins Barracks, he was never short of work. His grandfather Richard Pender continued in the military tailoring business and opened the first family-run shop in 1922 at 3 Manor Street, building up a business that at one time employed up to forty tailors. Later that year, with business expanding, Jim's grandmother Mary B. Pender opened a children's clothing, school uniform and haberdashery shop next door. Throughout the 1950s Jim's mother Agnes Grant (*née* Pender) worked in the shop. Agnes served her time as a draper in Arnott's; she married Tom Grant from County Wicklow and in 1965 they opened their own shop, now managed by Jim, her son, who began working full-time in Manor Street in 1983.

Grants is one of those shops where customers enjoy the chat that goes with making a purchase; Jim recalls a customer in nearby Kirwan Street, who while in the shop in September 2015 remarked that a baby was born on the street, and that two more were due within the following two months, the first new babies on the street in forty-two years. Nearby Richard Pender traded until early in the present century; also specializing in military uniforms, he served his time in Savile Row, London. Unable to compete with overseas suppliers, he closed his shop in 2006.

Another local business was that of Séan Kelly's bicycle shop. Seán's mother ran her own shop, Atkinson's, in St Mary's Abbey, before her marriage to his father Michael; they both lived and traded on Manor Street from the late 1930s. Seán Kelly informed me in 1995 that his father told him that 'in those days, few people cycled for pleasure, using their wheels solely for transport and cyclists who raced were regarded as being somewhat eccentric'. An old IRA veteran, Michael's door was smashed in by the Black and Tans during the War of Independence. Michael died in 1967 and the business passed on to Seán, who carried on a lively trade with people from Dublin 7 and beyond. However, his shop was too small to compete with the newer, larger stores operating in the city and he stopped trading in 2005.

Joseph Cashman was born in Blackpool, Cork City in 1881, and became a photographer, working with the *Freeman's Journal* from 1912 until its closure in

1924. Noted for the iconic photographs of the police baton charge on protesters in O'Connell Street during the 1913 Lockout, he also took many photographs of the Easter Rising and its aftermath. Oisín Kelly's statue of Jim Larkin on O'Connell Street was inspired by his photograph of the trade union leader. In 1931 Cashman became manager of the *Irish Press* processing, engraving and photographic departments. He married Lora Jones of Glanmire, County Cork and after her death in 1947 lived at 13 Manor Street until his death on 1 January 1969. Joseph Cashman's photographical archive was stored in the garden shed, where it remained in a remarkable condition. An album of his photographs, edited by Louis McRedmond and titled *The Revolutionary Years: Photographs from the Cashman Collection, Ireland 1910–1930*, was published in 1992.

At the junction of Aughrim Street and Prussia Street stands the familiar turreted, landmark building of Kavanagh's public house, although most locals only know it as 'Cotters'. This was formerly occupied by the Cotter family and was built according to Mr Cotter's personal specifications. Its style of architecture, with its Rhine-valley type turret, is eye-catching. Noel Peacock, the present proprietor, took it over from Gerry Kavanagh. The Victorian interior is striking; a mural painted on the wall above the bar is of more recent vintage. According to longtime local Ray Kelly the mural 'was painted forty years ago by college art students; there is a preservation order on the pub so I am stuck with looking at that forever'.

Nearby, at 60 and 61 Manor Street, was the old Manor Cinema. The site was purchased in 1919 and work began immediately on the construction of a picture-house, which opened on 10 May 1920 with accommodation for 630 patrons. The first screening, *He Comes Up Smiling* starred Douglas Fairbanks and Marjorie Daw. It featured one of the cinema world's smallest orchestras, this being the era of the silent movie, consisting of a piano, a cello and two violins; the manager was Thomas Fagan. For one week beginning on 4 March 1929 the Manor Cinema hosted a local talent competition open to 'singers, dancers, musicians etc, children and adults'. Entrance to the competition was free. Shortly after this it closed down, it was then renovated and reopened as The Palladium on 1 September 1929 under the management of the Dublin Cinema Enterprise Company. The screening on this opening night was *The Circus* with Charlie Chaplain. A popular staff member was Willie Tierney of Kirwan Street. In 1935 it again changed hands and was renamed The Broadway; still operating under that name, it closed its doors for the last time on Saturday 11 August 1956. Even today it is known in the district as 'the Manor'.

The building was then taken over by its next-door neighbour, Thomas Dunne of 59 Manor Street, where the Dublin Cooperage Company was located; it was then used as a cooperage for a number of years before being converted into FÁS community training workshops. It continues to operate as a local community training centre under the auspices of the City of Dublin Education and Training Board and a student team from the centre won the overall runners-up prize in the senior category of the Irish Cancer Society 2015 awards for their short anti-smoking film presentation entitled *No*, providing a connection to the cinematic history of the Manor.

Terry Walsh (*née* Morris) from Ivar Street recalls all her brothers going to the Broadway: 'I only went to the Manor a few times myself. It was considered a bit of a flea-house then.' She is the third generation of her family to live in the area; her grandmother was the first tenant of 35 Mulcahy Road, where her own mother, Gertrude O'Hara, grew up. Terry went to Stanhope Street National School in the 1950s and started work in Mulcahys, making Bear Brand stockings; she later moved to the Castlehoisery factory on Blackhall Place, which manufactured nylons and knitwear. She recalled that there was 'an entrance to the factory through a door in a wall on Arbour Hill, next to the Lilliput Stores'. Lilliput Stores took its name from Lilliput Press, originally housed alongside it in Rosemount Terrace; in the 1960s the proprietors of these three shops were the Byrnes, Dorans and Quinns. Terry remembers buying sweets in the shops on Manor Place, around the corner at the top of Sitric Road: 'There was Carton's, which sold groceries, Gilhooley's and Madden's, which sold papers and sweets, then a different Carton's, which sold hardware and sweets. The 72 bus stopped right outside Gilhooley's.' The number 72 bus route, which formerly served Oxmantown Road and O'Devaney Gardens, was withdrawn from service during the 1970s and Gilhooley's shop is now the famous Maureen's; Maureen McGuinness, from Enfield, County Meath, has been running the shop for the past thirty-six years, and is known far beyond the confines of Cowtown for her unique style of shopkeeping.

At the top of Prussia Street stands the City Arms Hotel, formerly the town-house of the Jameson family, who built the present-day imposing residence. In the late 1700s the premises was occupied by H.S. Reilly, a director of the Royal Canal after whom the bridge at Ratoath Road is named; he is the same Squire O'Reilly of Burton's strange topographical romance, entitled *Oxmanstown*. John Jameson is shown as the occupier of the premises in the Primary Valuation of 1850 when the house, together with out-offices and yard, on an area of over seven acres, had a listed valuation of £126 per annum. An interesting resident of Prussia Street during the late 1700s was William Wenman Seward; he was admitted to King's Inns, Dublin in May 1776, and came to live in Prussia Street in 1782, conducting his legal practice there. He was famous for his topographical writings, and published *Hibernian Gazeteer* (1789) and *Topographia Hibernica* (1795) which even today are highly sought after by collectors due to the quality of the illustrations. He moved to James's Street around 1800 and died in 1805.

James Collins's *Life in Old Dublin*, published in 1913, shines a spotlight on the history of this area of Dublin. In it he relates how, when Robin Hood and his merry men were dispersed in England around 1265, some of his followers, including his companion Little John, made their way to Ireland and settled in the Arbour Hill/Aughrim Street area. Little John is said to have entertained the natives with his amazing archery skills, standing on the present-day bridge at Queen Street and discharging from his bow an arrow that reached a hillock on Oxmantown Green, some considerable distance. The redoubtable hero is said to have been hanged on the hill, then used as a place of execution. According to old records, this hanging place was called Gibbet Glade. Dermot O'Hurley, Archbishop of Cashel, one of eighteen Irish martyrs elevated to sainthood by Pope John Paul II in September 1992, may have been executed here on 19 June 1584; there are other accounts citing St Stephen's Green as his place of execution. A famous alehouse called The Half Moon later stood on the site during the late 1600s.

Joseph Ashbury, born in London in 1638, lived in Bowling Green House, on the edge of Oxmantown Green. He was an actor for fifty-eight years and managed the Smock Alley Theatre in Dublin for forty-five years. A prominent teacher, he launched the careers of many a young actor of the day and was the first to produce plays by George Farquhar and William Phillips. He arrived in Ireland in 1662 with the assistance of the patronage of the 1st Duke of Ormonde, then Lord Lieutenant. He died in Bowling Green House on 24 July 1720 and is buried in St Michan's, Church Street.

Aughrim Street

The apex of a triangle formed by two streets at the north end of Manor Street marked the site where a village existed long before the city of Dublin had extended out that far. Prussia Street was on one side and Blackhorse Lane was on the western or left-hand-side of the triangle. In 1780 the portion of Blackhorse Lane from this apex to North Circular Road was renamed Aughrim Street, as a memorial to the battle of Aughrim, which saw the defeat of the combined Irish-French forces under the command of the French General St Ruth. St Ruth was slain during the battle on 12 July 1691.

The fine, Gothic-style Holy Family Roman Catholic church was built in 1880. The marble pulpit was built by Messrs Early of Camden Street and donated by a Mrs Donnelly, who lived nearby on North Circular Road. On 4 August 1895 the church organ, built by Messrs Telford of St Stephen's Green, Dublin and donated by the officers and men of the Royal Irish Constabulary, was blessed and commissioned at the ten o'clock Mass. According to the *Freeman's Journal* 'a large congregation of Constabulary and Military' were in attendance. At this time, and up to the foundation of the State, many police and military personnel lived in the general Oxmantown area. The church contains some excellent stained-glass windows, especially those of St James and St Columba. The present parish administrator is Fr Paddy Madden from Mostrim in County Leitrim.

The church grounds was the scene of one of the biggest *grushees* seen in the district for many years following the wedding of Debbie Lawless and Noel Mooney in August 1990. There were three separate grushees outside the church, with a good sprinkling of pound coins in the mix. A tradition for many years in the city, a grushee occurred following a wedding; the altar boys would alert the local children to an impending marriage and these children would gather outside the church after the ceremony in their droves, sometimes numbering up to sixty or seventy. They would shout 'We want a grushee, we want a grushee. Throw it out. Throw it out.' The best man would then throw coins in the air, leading to a big scramble. In the ensuing melee, bigger boys would sometimes stand on a young child's hand and press gently until the hand was removed, leading to the exposure of a coin, and pick it up and walk away with it – a grushee was not for the faint-hearted. On occasion there would be some washers among the coins. As the grushee was in progress, the bus containing the wedding party would leave the church and often the guests, caught up in the moment, would throw any small change that they had out of the window, prolonging the euphoria of the children.

Dublin Cattle Market

Dublin Cattle Market, located behind the City Arms Hotel between Aughrim Street and Prussia Street, was previously based in Smithfield. In the late 1850s it became necessary to relocate the market as Smithfield was inadequate to meet the demands of both a growing population and an expanding cattle industry. The original blueprint for redevelopment involved the transfer of the market to the North Wall area, which then 'had facilities for ample pasture' and stated to be an ideal location due to its 'contiguity to the Liffey Branch of the Midland and Great Western Railway and to the packets for shipment to England and elsewhere'. This proposal was controversial at the time.

View of Cattle Market looking towards North Circular Road, early 1900s
(Lawrence Collection, NLI)

The City Engineer, George Hemans, prepared a report on a proposed new junction of the city railways with a cattle depot located at the North Wall. An extract of that report, published in the *Dublin Builder* on 1 February 1861, drew strong criticism. A letter published in the newspapers of the day by Messrs Ganly, Sons and Parker, 'eminent salesmasters', condemned the report, stating that 'share in a market at the North Wall for sale of cattle would be difficult to turn into cash' and that, if the project did go ahead, it would 'require a new Carlisle Bridge [O'Connell Bridge] of treble its present breadth' to be built. The letter requested that those engaged in the sale of cattle be left where they were, 'in the fields'.

In December 1861 an application was made to Parliament for leave to introduce a Bill

> to incorporate a company for the purpose of establishing, erecting and maintaining a new Market, to be called the Metropolitan Cattle Market, for the sale of cattle, horses, sheep, pigs, hides, skins and other marketable commodities; such proposed market being situate in the North Lotts, immediately adjoining the Liffey branch of the Midland Great Western Railway and extending from the Dublin and Drogheda Railway to the East-road and Sheriff-street, all in the townland of North Lotts, in the parish of St Thomas and county of the city of Dublin. And power will be taken to erect suitable offices, counting-houses, sheds, stores for the sale of provender, dwelling houses, shops, weighing machines, water tanks, stalls, pens, slaughter-houses, with all other necessary buildings suitable for the purposes of such proposed Market.

On the 9 December 1861 a lengthy and lively discussion took place at a general meeting of Dublin Corporation concerning the relocation of the market. Mr O'Brien opened the debate by referring to the Act of Parliament sought for the transfer proposal and tabled a motion opposing the move:

> It is the opinion of this Council that such an Act, if passed into law, would seriously injure that portion of the City in which the present cattle market is situate, and considerably depreciate a large extent of the property of this Corporation, and that it would be prejudicial to the interests of the public at large; therefore, that a special Committee of this Council be now appointed to take immediate steps to place the Municipal Council in a position effectively to oppose the passing of such an Act ...

Opposition to the North Wall relocation gained momentum. In July 1862 advocates for the retention of Smithfield gathered support in order to defeat the plans of Hemans. They secured, through guaranteed subscriptions, money required for the erection of a suitable market on a desired site. A list of subscribers is set out on page 178 of the 15 July 1862 issue of the *Dublin Builder*. Their efforts paid off and on 26 November 1863 the new cattle market was officially opened. It remained in business for over one hundred years. During the 1920s it was the busiest of its kind in Europe; throughput in one year numbered nearly three-quarters of a million animals and included 182,627 fat cattle, 368,756 sheep, 47,000 store cattle, 14,697 dairy cattle, 47,995 pigs and 3833 calves.

During the late 1960s business at the markets started to decline as railway cattle-wagons were replaced by road-transport vehicles and provincial markets grew. The prominence enjoyed by the Dublin Cattle Market in the meat industry began to decline and finally in the early 1970s it ceased operations. However, the death-blow that the closure was forecast to bring to the area, known locally as Cowtown, never materialized. In 1979 Dublin Corporation started to build on the site and what was once 'the Market' is now the Drumalee estate, a modern local authority housing development of redbricked homes, complementing the materials used in the nearby houses built in previous centuries. Drumalee estate has given a new impetus to everyday life in the general area.

City Abattoir

At the junction of North Circular Road and Blackhorse Avenue the Corporation Abattoir and Dead Meat Market, or City Abattoir, was located. Built by Dublin Corporation, its foundation stone was laid on 1 November 1880 by the Lord Lieutenant, Earl Cowper, after whom Cowper Street is named. Construction was completed in 1881, and the slaughter of livestock began in 1882. The site of the abattoir, consisting of ten acres and five perches, was acquired in fee-farm at the rent of £318 15s. 0d., and plans prepared by Mr Parke Neville, the Borough Engineer, connected the building to the Dublin Cattle Market by a tunnel under the North Circular Road. The contractor was Mr Kelly of Thomas Street and the cost of construction came to £15,000. The development was a most welcome one at the time as private slaughter houses, which then numbered nearly one hundred, were 'a disgrace to Dublin and a danger to public health' according to the *Irish Builder* edition of 15 November 1880. A plaque from the abattoir was on display inside the entrance to the Dublin Civic Museum until its closure in 2003:

> *The first stone of this Abattoir was laid by His Excellency the Rt. Honorable Earl Cowper, Lord Lieutenant, on 1 November 1880. The Rt. Hon. Edmund Dwyer Gray M.P., Chairman of the Public Health Committee. It was declared open on 11 April 1882. The Rt. Hon. Charles Dawson M.P., Lord Mayor. Parke Neville Engineer.*

In 1977 the abattoir followed the same fate as the cattle market and was closed down. A small, architecturally-interesting mix of Dublin Corporation and private housing was built on the site. Both here and in the general district there is still a throwback to times past, as many local people refer to the immediate area as the 'cattle market' and 'the abattoir'. Indeed the schoolchildren at St Gabriel's nearby refer to Drumalee as 'the cattler'.

Hanlon's Corner to the Phoenix Park

The closure of the Cattle Market was the catalyst for the new Park Shopping Centre, with Quinnsworth, later Tesco, as anchor tenant. It led to the revitalization of local businesses, with new shopfronts and a refurbishment carried out on Hanlon's pub, a well-known north-city landmark. The proprietor in the early years of the last century was John Hanlon of Cremore House, Terenure, who gave his name to the iconic corner. On 8 August 1928 his daughter Helen Clarissa Hanlon married Charles 'Charlie' Casey, whose family home was at 34 Upper Ormond Quay. Born in 1895, Charlie studied law at King's Inns and qualified as a barrister in 1923. Appointed Attorney General on 21 April 1950 by the then Taoiseach, John A. Costello, he became a Judge of the High Court in June of the following year, and died on 6 November 1952; Helen died in 1997. Still retaining the name of Hanlon's, in 1992 the proprietors were Jim and Tom McCormack. The present proprietor Michael Brazil took over the premises in late-2014, and the present manager is Jim Dunne, who previously managed the pub for the Hanlon family, from 1979 until 1984. For many years William Arthurs from Finglas was a friendly and familiar presence outside the pub; a paper-seller since 1948, he held his 'pitch' here for many years, having previously spent most of his career in the cattle market itself, selling his '*Herald, Mail or Press*'. In 2016 the pitch was manned by his son Willie.

Behind Hanlon's pub, and with entrances off Annamoe Terrace and Cabra Road, a huge lock-up yard and garages operated during the early to mid-1900s; schoolchildren used to hang around here on Saturdays to look at the fancy cars such as a Daimler and a Rolls-Royce as they were taken out for the weekend. The yard also served as a depot for the Blue Cross veterinary ambulance service. The Irish Blue Cross was established in 1945 and introduced its first mobile animal dispensary onto the streets of Dublin in the early 1950s. Since then, the charity has treated, vaccinated and arranged surgeries for well over 600,000 small animals through its mobile clinic service, and subsidized welfare schemes run in cooperation with veterinary practices. Its mobile unit is to be seen each Monday evening on Fassaugh Avenue, Cabra West and on Wednesday evenings at Smithfield. At least 18,000 treatments and vaccinations are carried out at the mobiles each year. The service is intended for genuinely needy pet owners unable to afford private veterinary fees and is dependent on the goodwill of volunteer drivers, helpers and vets. It is presently headquartered in Goldenbridge Industrial Estate, Islandbridge.

North Circular Road looking towards Phoenix Park and the Wellington Monument, early 1900s (Lawrence Collection, NLI)

Opposite Hanlon's a private housing development called Rathdown Court was completed in 1993 on another 'Cowtown' site, cattle lairage yards, on the corner of Prussia Street and North Circular Road. The houses on the stretch of the North Circular Road from Hanlon's Corner towards the Phoenix Park were constructed in the late 1800s, and though not on the scale of the old Georgian dwellings of the rich around the city centre, they were nonetheless fine, imposing homes typical of upper-middle class habitation of the time. Houses were then graded in the census of the period from 'first-class' to 'fourth-class' according to their size and the construction materials used. Red brick was a feature of new buildings of the period, attested to in dwellings throughout the area. Houses were generally constructed using high-quality natural materials including slated roofs, granite sills and wooden sash windows. Iron railings, and stained glass and tiles, not only for the hall and kitchen area but for the porch and garden pathway, were also in fashion at this time.

Margaret Collins-O'Driscoll, the eldest of three daughters and five sons of Michael Collins, a West Cork farmer, and Mary Anne Collins (*née* O'Brien), was born in 1878 and was the eldest sister of General Michael Collins, who led the War of Independence from 1918 to 1921. A primary schoolteacher, she married Patrick O'Driscoll, a journalist, on 8 September 1901. They moved to Dublin in 1922, and lived at 147 North Circular Road; here they raised a family of five sons and nine daughters. Margaret taught at the West Dublin Model Schools from 1922 until 1928 and was opposed to corporal punishment. She entered politics and in the General Election of 1923 was elected Dublin North TD, representing Cumann na nGael, the forerunner of today's Fine Gael. She was a sitting TD for ten years. During that time she contested no fewer than five general elections, and was elected vice-president of Cumann na nGael in 1926. Margaret was the only female member of the Dáil between 1927 and 1932 and died on 17 June 1945 aged sixty-eight. Her husband Patrick, who predeceased her, also died at age sixty-eight, on 20 August 1940. She is buried across the footpath from Michael Collins, in Glasnevin Cemetery.

Michael Collins was a regular caller to the house prior to his death in August 1922. An interesting article by Margaret's grandson Pól Ó Murchú, published in the 2002 Commemorative Edition of *The West Cork People*, refers to one such visit: 'Michael in the front room [of 147 North Circular Road] standing at the fireplace, talking, telling stories, laughing and playing with the younger children.'

Adjacent to Margaret O'Driscoll's is the home of Tommy Hodnott; Tommy is well known throughout the locality for his annual Christmas coffee morning, where the visitor can enjoy a cup of tea or coffee with cakes and marvel at the interesting display of mechanical festive decorations. The monies raised on the day go to an animal welfare charity.

Around the corner on Ellesmere Avenue, Dick Hearns, in his day a famous Garda boxer, lived all his married life. Taking up the sport in the 1930s, he became Irish Light Heavyweight Champion. Commentators of the sport believe that he would have won Gold in the Berlin Olympics of 1936, for he had well beaten Roger Michelot, that year's Olympic Gold Medallist in Germany, in the British Open Amateur Boxing Championship. However an objection was raised by Britain to the Irish team taking part in the Olympics and the Olympic Committee, in a highly controversial decision, upheld that objection and in doing so deprived Ireland of what looked certain to be a gold medal. Hearns retired from the ring as reigning national Champion in 1939, the same year as his colleague and friend Jim 'Lugs' Branigan also retired from the sport; they both maintained their friendship, being regularly in touch with each other, until Jim's death in 1987. Dick Hearns continued to train Gardaí in the sport at the Garda Depot, Phoenix Park, until his retirement in 1964.

Frankie Byrne was born on 27 December 1921 in a nursing home at 7 North Frederick Street. She and her two sisters were reared by maids from infancy at 23 North Circular Road in an unconventional, bohemian household. Her first job was that of a secretary in the Brazilian consulate in Dublin, which introduced her to a wide and influential circle of people. After twelve years she secured a position in McConnell's advertising agency, becoming a leading pioneer in public relations in Ireland and establishing her own firm, Frankie Byrne Limited, in 1963. She secured a contract for Jacobs, the biscuit manufacturer, and in 1963 she began hosting *Woman's Page* on their sponsored programme on Radio Éireann, now RTÉ, during which she answered listener's letters, interspersed with Frank Sinatra songs. Her opening line to each programme began with the words 'welcome to Woman's Page, a programme for and about you'. Frankie Byrne became a household name and Ireland's first 'agony aunt', and played a key role in the inauguration, promotion and presentation of the Jacob's Awards for Broadcasting, which was screened annually on RTÉ. Launched in 1962, it was a longtime major social event and ran until her retirement in 1990. During the 1980s she wrote a weekly column in the *Evening Press*. She lived in a cottage in Donnybrook with her sister Esther and died on 11 December 1993.

Next door to the Byrne family, at 21 North Circular Road, was the Dromid Hotel, long since gone out of business but operating as late as 1962. On the opposite side of the road, Kingscourt, 48 North Circular Road, was the home of Harry Clarke, Ireland's renowned stained-glass artist. His greatness was recognized when he was commissioned by Harrup to make forty full-page illustrations for Hans Christian Anderson's *Fairy Tales*; his illustrations also appeared in *Tales of Mystery and Imagination* by Edgar Allan Poe. He lived here from 1922 to 1925 when he went to live beside the company studios on North Frederick Street, founded by his father Joshua Clarke. Harry Clarke married Margaret Crilly in 1914: she was born in Newry, County Down on 29 July 1888, and studied under the artist William Orpen, who greatly admired her work. After the death of Harry Clarke on 6 January 1931 in Switzerland, where he was receiving treatment for tuberculosis, Margaret moved back and spent the rest of her life on the North Circular Road. She is recorded as Mrs Clarke, living at 48 North Circular Road, in the 1956 edition of *Thom's Directory*.

Next door, at number 50, was St Paul's Parsonage, the residence for the Church of Ireland vicar attached to St Paul's church, North King Street; a simple plaque denoting 'St Paul's' on the front railing today alludes to the previous occupiers. In 1916 Rev. E.J. Young occupied the parsonage, succeeded by Rev. James Poyntz; finally from the late 1950s until his retirement in 1976, Rev. George D. Hobson occupied the vicarage. He died in 1985; his daughter Anne Cadoo, who lives in Castleknock, recalls Mrs Clarke living next door and remembers the fine stained-glass window at the front of the house. She also recalls a larger-than-life sized Marian statue lying in the back garden of Kingscourt for many years, a company commission that was never inaugurated.

Behind these houses is O'Devaney Gardens, a complex of Dublin Corporation flats earmarked for redevelopment as part of a public/private partnership in 2007; the project failed to materialize following the economic crash of 2008. Many of the flats have been demolished in stages over the past number of years and in 2016 just four blocks remained. Between O'Devaney Gardens and Infirmary Road lie Aberdeen Street, Sullivan Street and Black Street. These houses were built by the Artisan Dwellings Company Limited, who requested the Earl of Aberdeen to perform the official opening of Aberdeen Street in 1886; he duly obliged, the street consequently being named in his honour. Black Street, built in the same year, was called after Gibson Black, a director of the Artisan Dwellings Company who died in January 1889, while Sullivan Street was called after Dr Sullivan, a one-time Lord Mayor of Dublin. Infirmary Road takes its name from the military hospital, which was then located in the grounds of the former headquarters of the Irish Defence Forces, now occupied by the Chief Prosecution Solicitor.

Black Street is the home of Anna Maria 'Nancy' Noone, who is typical of many of those whose families have resided in the area for generations. Nancy's grandfather, Patrick Noone, worked on the railway and lived at 14 Black Street; from this address his son John left, aged just fourteen years, to join the Royal Army Medical Corps, later being assigned to the Royal Artillery. During the First World War he was wounded in the foot and suffered gas poisoning. He was awarded the Great War Medal and the Victory Medal and was de-mobbed in 1919. His parents moved into a bigger house, at 29 Aberdeen Street, around 1916, and it was to this address that John returned to live after the war, joining the Post Office and working in the GPO; he later became a postal sorter on the Dublin to Cork train. He married Nancy's mother Jane and they moved into Black Street, where Nancy was born, in 1930. He died in 1956 aged just fifty-six; he never fully recovered from the gas poisoning.

Collins Barracks (previously named The Royal Barracks) circa 1924

Educated in Stanhope Street Convent schools, Nancy got a job in Hargreaves & Ashmore in Ship Street, where she met Frank Taylor, who hailed from South Summer Street and was a tailor by profession. They started to go out together and went to the Bohemian Cinema every Sunday night, having booked it the previous Thursday. Midweek they went to the Broadway Cinema, still known in the locality as 'the Manor' and she recalled that 'in those days they showed two films and a trailer'. A trailer was a short preview of a forthcoming film. They lived at 60 Arbour Hill following their marriage in Aughrim Street in 1954 but two years later moved to Black Street because 'my dad had just died and mam was on her own. My mam, dad and husband all died in the house on Black Street.' Nancy recalls the gas lights on North Circular Road: 'There was a gaslight outside our own house too and me mam often told me about a policeman who used to sit on our window-sill every night, reading a newspaper under it.' Nancy's house was also gaslit; the fittings were removed in the late-1940s.

Finbarr Flood

One of the most successful people from the area in recent years is Finbarr Flood. A local legend, he was born in Ross Street in December 1938 and attended Stanhope Street National School and Brunswick Street CBS. Though encouraged by his teachers to go on to secondary school, he had to leave at fourteen to get a job. At that time a job in Guinness was an enviable one and Finbarr had to queue to collect an application form to sit the messenger's exam, which he successfully passed. He started work in 1953 and his duties included the counting of casks coming into and out of the brewery. A lover of soccer who played football against a gable wall in Ross Street, he joined Shamrock Rovers in 1958, winning a Minor Cup Final runners-up medal with them; a competent goalkeeper, he later joined Shelbourne and was on the team that won the FAI Cup in 1960, when they defeated Cork Hibernians 2-0.

With that success he came under the watchful eye of cross-channel talent-spotters, eventually signing for Morton, a Scottish Second Division side that had previously played Shelbourne in a friendly. He secured a term in his contract that Morton would fly him to Scotland at weekends, returning to Dublin on Sunday night so he could continue in his work as a messenger at the brewery. He spent two years with Morton before signing for Irish League side Glentoran. Finbarr finally finished out his soccer career playing League of Ireland football with Sligo Rovers, retiring from the game in 1966 following an injury.

When Harry Hannon expanded promotional opportunities for Guinness staff, Finbarr was successfully promoted to an indoor messenger position, although not everyone agreed with the new flexibility. His new boss informed him that he would 'go out on pension as a messenger from this office'. Appointed Road Transport Manager in the early 1970s, in 1977 he was assigned to the Personnel Division, rising to become first Personnel Manager and then Personnel Director. He was appointed Managing Director of the brewery in June 1989, a post he held for a number of years, running a brewery that then covered sixty acres of the city of Dublin, had a staff of 1100 and exported over 40 per cent of its annual production. Finbarr Flood left the brewery and became Chairman of the Labour Court, a position he held until his retirement. He died in 2016.

The well-known radio and TV presenter Pat Kenny grew up on Infirmary Road; his father Jimmy attended St Gabriel's National School in Cowper Street and became an assistant lion-keeper in Dublin Zoo in 1933, when his own father James was in charge of the elephants. In mid 1903 the Duke and Duchess of Connaught presented a young elephant called Padmahati to Dublin Zoo and it was James who was sent to Portsmouth in southern England to collect it in May 1904: he trained the elephant in the art of giving rides and subsequently received a commission from the income derived from this activity.

During the 1950s and the 1960s Jimmy was in charge of the elephants and a pictorial plaque in the zoo shows him giving elephant rides to children; this was when there was little emphasis on either animal welfare or health and safety. He retired from Dublin Zoo in April 1976. At the River Liffey end of Infirmary Road, next to the Kennys' home, is the little cul-de-sac called de Burgh Road, probably the smallest road in the district. It consists of just seven houses, and in 1917 four of them were inhabited, by W.J. Doak, Richard Maher, Thomas Garland and Philip Gummer, with their respective families.

Arbour Hill

Before Collins Barracks, formerly Royal Barracks, was built in 1706, Arbour Hill was a densely wooded area much frequented by children from the surrounding villages. It was a well-known retreat for bandits and robbers and there are accounts of labyrinthine caves beneath the hill where stolen property was said to have been hidden. Newspaper reports in 1775 tell how part of a pavement collapsed, revealing traces of the caves. When the foundations for Arbour Hill Prison were being dug further evidence of the caves came to light. There are still a number of old dwellings located here, such as the imposing triangular building at 49 Arbour Hill. A recently constructed apartment block adjoins this house and beside it is a small terrace of four houses, called Temple Villas, built during the 1930s.

Across from Arbour Hill Prison, rows of stables with wooden ventilation shafts enclosed a forage yard that extended to the rear of Collins Barracks. A tunnel, now bricked up, connected the prison building to the Barracks. Bartholomew Teeling and Matthew Tone were detained and executed at Arbour Hill following the defeat of the French forces that landed in Killala Bay, County Mayo, under General Humbert in 1798. On 2 October 1798 *Faulkner's Dublin Journal* ran the following:

> Matthew Tone, convicted of treason in serving his majesty's enemies, was on Saturday last hanged on a gallows at Arbour Hill. He died with great hardihood, cursing the executioner for his awkwardness and avowing his attachment to the French.

Both men were buried in the Croppies Acre following their execution.

On 8 November of that same year, Theobald Wolfe Tone was taken to Dublin Castle from Derry Gaol. From there he was removed to Arbour Hill, where on the night of 11 November he used a penknife to pierce his throat. He died from his wounds on 19 November 1798. After the 1798 Rising there was an apparent falling-off in the number of prisoners held at Arbour Hill and in 1820 the prison authorities were asked to provide custodial accommodation for civilian inmates by Dr Trevor, the medical officer of Kilmainham Gaol. The building of the new Detention Barracks in the style of a Benthamite panopticon, the church and Warden's quarters began in 1845 and this was when the Arbour Hill complex we know today came into being. The work was completed in 1848. Subsequently there were no further admissions to the old provost prison, which was converted to an NCOs' mess.

During the Fenian revolt of 1866/67 Arbour Hill Prison housed those captured 'on suspicion of treasonable activity'. During a raid on Pilsworth's public house in Thomas Street a number of Irishmen serving in the British army were arrested by Colonel Fielding (the 'Major Sirr' of the 1867 period), among them John Boyle O'Reilly, who at twenty-one years of age was sentenced to death. Following a period of detention in Arbour Hill he was transported to the infant state of Western Australia. There he left an indelible mark on the history of that State before escaping to America in spectacular fashion aboard the Boston-registered whaling ship *Catalpa*. Settling in Boston, he embarked on a highly successful career in journalism. When his cell was vacated, the following was found scratched on the wall:

> *We have borne with scorn and insult*
> *But the Saxon yet shall feel*
> *The strength of Irish vengeance*
> *And the points of Irish steel*
> *The foremost men to strike the foe*
> *In freedom's glorious war*
> *Shall have worn England's scarlet*
> *And the blue of the hussar.*

One of the most famous visitors to the district was John F. Kennedy, President of the USA. During his visit to Ireland he laid a wreath at Arbour Hill on 28 June 1963 in memory of the executed leaders of the 1916 Rising. He described John Boyle O'Reilly as his 'favourite poet' and on one occasion, making a speech about freedom, told how 'John Boyle O'Reilly, who came to Boston by way of a penal colony in Western Australia, understood this [freedom] as few men have'. He concluded by quoting the poet: 'Freedom is more than a resolution – he is not free who is free alone.'

The prison church was originally dedicated for Anglican worship, it being the garrison church for the British army. There are records dealing with the lack of facilities for Roman Catholic prisoners in Arbour Hill, a matter that was taken up by Fr J.A. Burke prior to the foundation of the State. He entered into correspondence with the British Officer Commanding and as a result a structure was erected within the prison yard, which served as a small chapel at some stage.

The correspondence on the subject is now in the National Library of Ireland.

The leaders of the Easter Rising were buried in the exercise yard, which lay within the Arbour Hill Military Cemetery, following their execution at Kilmainham Jail in May 1916. In 1922 the complex was taken over by the Irish Army and during the Civil War the prison held some notable figures, including Eamonn de Valera. When visiting the complex in the late 1950s, he pointed out his former cell, 113, on the west landing. During the 1940s the prison saw an influx of IRA prisoners, including the author Brendan Behan. The Detention Barracks was in use as a military prison until 1964. Renovated during the early 1970s, Arbour Hill now serves as a civilian prison. Ralph Lee, who lived all his married life on Conor Clune Road, Dublin 7, served as Governor of Arbour Hill for a number of years during the 1970s.

In 1927 the garrison church was altered and restored by the Free State authorities; it was then made available for Roman Catholic worship and was consecrated to the Sacred Heart by the Archbishop of Dublin, Dr Byrne. The altar of the church in Kilmainham Gaol was removed and underwent restoration at Arbour Hill in the early 1970s. A plaque beside the altar commemorates the wedding in Kilmainham Gaol of one of the leaders of 1916, shortly before his execution:

> *At this altar also, Joseph Mary Plunkett, one of the seven signatories to the Proclamation of the Republic, was married to Grace Gifford on 3 May, 1916, the eve of his execution. Pray for the souls of those who died for Ireland.*

The church was the resting place for the repatriated remains of Roger Casement: thousands filed past as they lay in State at Arbour Hill before internment in Glasnevin Cemetery in February 1965. This Irish patriot, poet, revolutionary and nationalist was born in Dublin on 1 September 1864, spending his early childhood in Doyle's Cottages, Lawson Terrace, Sandycove. He was involved in a plot to import arms into Ireland during the Easter Rising. The plot failed and he was arrested on 21 April 1916 at Banna Strand, County Kerry, and taken to Arbour Hill Prison. Transferred to London, Casement was tried and executed by hanging at Pentonville Prison on 3 August 1916 and his body buried within the prison confines until 1965. Arbour Hill is now a designated National Memorial.

At the back of Arbour Hill, in the former Schoolmaster's House, built in 1848, is the Irish United Nation's Veteran's Association. It was founded in Dublin in

1989 by former army personnel who had served on overseas missions with the UN. Association member John Condon, who joined the army in 1959 and saw service in Cyprus in the late 1960s, recalls its establishment: 'We were provided with the use of this building for a meeting place in 1992. Everybody got involved and we proceeded to decorate and transform it. Our next step was to develop the little park attached to the building, which once served as allotments during the Emergency.' With assistance from Dublin City Council Parks Department, it has been transformed into a small memorial park, officially opened on 8 November 1998 by the President of Ireland, Mary McAleese. It commemorates all Irish citizens and not just military personnel who died overseas while on UN service. For many years the gardens were voluntarily tended by Michael Prince, who lived nearby on Murtagh Street.

The headquarters, unofficially called Niemba House, provides a safe and comfortable meeting place for members of the Association to talk with colleagues who have shared similar experiences while serving on UN missions, sometimes in violent and dangerous circumstances. Members regularly make up food parcels for distribution to those in need and for dependents and widows of deceased members. The Association also runs bingo sessions, patronized by many older people from the area. An annual wreath-laying ceremony takes place on the Sunday nearest to Peacekeeper's Day, 29 May.

Arbour Place joins Arbour Hill to Manor Street; formerly Chicken Lane, it received its present name early in the last century. A former resident recalls chickens, pigs and horses being kept on this street as late as 1967; the 1962 edition of *Thom's Directory* records a horse-dealer, a cement block manufacturer, a metal store and stables. In 1870 there were thirty small houses, in tenements, on Chicken Lane; the brickwork on the double-fronted house at number 11 and the wrought-iron decoration on the windowsills of number 23 provide an interesting aspect to the streetscape.

Montpelier Hill

Due west of Arbour Hill is Montpelier Hill; the Duke of Cambridge, Prince George, grandson of George III and first cousin of Queen Victoria, lived here around 1850. He was assigned to the Royal Barracks as an Officer of the British army and later served as Commander-in-Chief for many years and saw action in the Crimea. While living in Montpelier Hill he married an actor, Louisa Farebrother, in Arbour Hill Garrison Church. As the marriage was contracted without the consent of Queen Victoria, it was contrary to the Royal Marriage Act (coincidentally passed during the reign of, and at the behest of, George III) and was always regarded as morganatic; the eldest son of the marriage, Colonel Fitzgeorge, did not succeed to the title of Duke of Cambridge. Remarkably quite a few houses on Montpelier Hill have survived redevelopment. While many new houses and apartments were constructed in the past thirty years, some notable houses still exist, such as number 26, Montpelier House, built in the late 1700s and now occupied by Paramount Distributors Dublin Ltd.

The streets around Montpelier and Arbour Hill take their names from the fact that the district was formerly a Scandinavian or Viking settlement – Olaf Street, Oxmanstown Road, Viking Road, Ostman Place and Sitric Road. The Lilliput Press is located at 62-63 Sitric Road: founded by Mullingar man Antony Farrell in 1984, it moved to Arbour Hill in 1989 and in 1993 it transferred to its present location. It has published hundreds of titles over the years, ranging from art and architecture, autobiography and memoir, biography and history, ecology and environmentalism, to essays and literary criticism, philosophy, current affairs and popular culture, fiction, drama and poetry. As well as the work of more established writers The Lilliput Press has also exposed the talents of new and unpublished authors to the public, such as essayist Hubert Butler, naturalist Tim Robinson,

62-63 Sitric Road, Arbour Hill, Stoneybatter. Home of the Lilliput Press since 1993
(Courtesy The Lilliput Press)

philosopher John Moriarty, and novelists Donal Ryan and Rob Doyle. It drew inspiration from the townland of Lilliput on Lough Ennell in County Westmeath, where Jonathan Swift visited during summer months.

The building was established in the late 1900s as a depot to teach local women how to scald milk during the scourge of tuberculosis, when Dublin had one of the highest infant mortality rates in Europe; Lady Aberdeen the viceroy's wife was one of its patrons. In the 1940s the Dublin Bread Company occupied the premises; it was more commonly known as Kennedy's Bread, and its registered name was Peter Kennedy Ltd. Children through to the 1960s sang this ditty, which could be heard across the city, from Cabra to Dolphin's Barn and Killester to Inchicore:

> Don't eat Kennedy's bread
> It sticks to your belly like lead
> Your mother will wonder
> Fart like thunder
> So don't eat Kennedy's bread.

Beth Lawler, who lives up the road on the same side, recalls constant visits to the bakery to buy a loaf of bread for her mother, and tearing the 'skin' off the side of the loaf and eating it on the way home. She is the third generation of her family to live on the street; her grandfather Frederick Greaves, who was born in Stratford-upon-Avon in England, was in the British army and fought in the Boer War. He was stationed in the Viceregal Lodge and the family lived in a gate lodge within the grounds. This is where her mother Elizabeth grew up, attending the little school in the Phoenix Park; in later life she married Anthony Cullen from 80 Prussia Street, moving in with her in-laws. The Cullen family was staunchly republican; Beth's uncle Liam Cullen was one of Michael Collin's lieutenants and was imprisoned in Frongoch after the 1916 Rising. Collins was a visitor to the house during the War of Independence. In 1960 Beth married a neighbour, John Lawler, who also grew up on Sitric Road.

St Bricin's

Probably as a result of its proximity to Collins Barracks, Arbour Hill was chosen as the site for a military hospital and provost prison, completed in 1797. The hospital stood on the site of the present St Bricin's and was originally called Arbour Hill Hospital. Entry is gained from Montpelier Hill, just off Infirmary Road. It was rebuilt and renamed King George V Hospital in 1912. It was built of brick with a slate roof, and cost the British War Department £13,919. Handed over to the Irish Free State in February 1923, custody of the hospital was received by Major General Hayes, appointed Director General, Medical Services, by General Michael Collins on 1 August 1922. It was then renamed and called after St Bricin, who had a school of medicine at Belturbet, County Donegal, in the seventh century and is credited with having performed a successful trepanning operation on the Irish scholar Ceannfhaolaidh, wounded at the battle of Moira in AD 634.

Brigid Lyons, from Northyard, Scrumogue, County Roscommon, was a nurse and after the War of Independence was given a commission in the newly formed Irish national army in 1922 by General Michael Collins. The only female officer commissioned in the Irish army until 1981, Brigid was given the responsibility of planning a new administrative direction for St Bricin's Hospital. She was based there for fifteen months, and assisted in forming the Nursing Corps and establishing a team of medical orderlies. She married Edward Thornton in 1925 and died in 1987.

The hospital was extended during the 1920s; the building to the south of the hospital, known as 'the Wing', was erected in 1944 for TB patients. It was closed down in 1974 and adapted for use as offices. The motto of the Medical Service is 'Comraind Legis'. Roughly translated, it means 'impartial treatment of the wounded'. A wing of the hospital is today reserved for use as emergency accommodation for the homeless, in a programme managed by the Salvation Army.

Smithfield

Smithfield was the home to a sixteenth-century bandit named Scaldbrother, whose habit was to ambush and rob the people of Oxmantown. He was believed to live with his gang in caves located near Arbour Hill, where it was rumoured that he stored his ill-gotten booty. Some of the houses built in Queen Street are believed to have been built over vaults formed from these caves. Smithfield occupies a site formerly covered by Oxmantown Green and was laid out in the early 1700s as an enclosed cattle market. During the eighteenth century Smithfield was the home of the Earl of Bective, ancestor of the Marquess of Headfort.

William Murphy resided at 48 Smithfield; born in 1771, he was listed at this address, with the occupation of cattle salesmaster, in 1795. A businessman and political advisor, he was a member of the United Irishmen and fled to France following the arrest of Lord Edward Fitzgerald in May 1798. He was prominent as a member of the Catholic Committee, and he amassed such a vast fortune that in 1820 he gave financial assistance to those Irishmen who volunteered to travel to South America to join the army of Simon Bolívar in his fight for freedom from Spanish colonialism. He died in 1849.

A notable resident on this street was Richard Jones (1810–40) who was born in Franey, County Monaghan. He came to Dublin in 1825 to live and work with his uncle, Mr Clarke, a hay, straw, corn and potato factor who traded from his residence at 13 Smithfield. Employed as a clerk and later as a junior salesman, he attended the Corn Exchange twice weekly from 1830. He joined the Ribbonmen around 1828 and dominated the movement's Dublin section during the 1830s, when it was led by Andrew Dardis, a publican who lived at 32 Constitution Hill. Ribbonism was a mostly rural movement of poor Roman Catholics agitating against landlords and their agents. Richard Jones took part in the destruction of the statue of King William, located in College Green, in 1836 and was put on trial in June 1840 on charges of membership of a secret society and detained for a time in Newgate Prison. Upon his release he left the area.

In the early part of the twentieth century Smithfield was noted for agricultural activity, despite it being in a city centre. Moira Lysaght, former Public Health Nurse and historian, was born on 25 May 1902, and grew up in Smithfield. She went to a small private school run by the Misses Tighe at their home in Manor Street. She gave a wonderful description of life in the heart of Smithfield during the first two decades of the last century in a talk delivered to the Old Dublin Society on 7 November 1984, later published in the Society's *Dublin Historical Record*:

> To me it resembled a country town except for the cobble-stones which contributed a far greater amount of noise … an earlier shattering of the brief silence of the nights on Thursdays when the lowing of cattle and the padding of their hooves were rounded off by loud 'ho, hoo hos' from their drovers en route to the cattle market on the North Circular Road. Haymarket days, which were held in Smithfield, created a hum of

Smithfield Markets, early 1980s (Courtesy Tom Mulligan)

industry, the horse-drawn carts heavy with hay adding their fragrance to the picturesque scene. In the top end, adjoining North King Street, grainwash from the nearby Jameson's distillery was shoveled from big vat-like lorries into farmers carts for animal feed. Tinkers (as they were then termed) dealt in horses, asses and mules. Farmers strode along with their whips tied in bandolier fashion over their shoulders; all to me now only spectres of the past.

Large business premises such as Bergin Brothers, suppliers of seeds, feeding-stuffs, E. & D. Carton for forage, hay and such. Bolton Murphy, chemist for animal medicinal curatives; tea, wine and spirit merchants; licensed premises, coach builders, harness makers and farriers – many with living quarters over their premises. Unpretentious restaurants and sleeping accommodation was to be found to facilitate visiting farmers and dealers.

Run-down by the mid 1960s, Smithfield was the location for the celebrated film *The Spy Who Came in from the Cold*, based on a John Le Carré novel about double-agentry. The film was shot on location in London, Germany and Ireland during the winter of 1964/5 and directed by Martin Ritt, whose successes included *The Outrage* (1964). The cast included Richard Burton and Claire Bloom. A meticulous job was done converting Smithfield into Checkpoint Charlie, the East/West Berlin border crossing, with the replica receiving widespread critical acclaim for its authenticity. The district was buzzing at the time, as Richard Burton's wife, the world-famous actor Elizabeth Taylor, was by his side on location. The caravan serving the film location was the subject of much media and local interest. During filming, scores of schoolchildren could be seen anxiously seeking a glimpse of the legendary couple.

Checkpoint Charlie, Smithfield, in *The Spy Who Came in from the Cold*, 1964
(Courtesy British Film Institute)

Distilling is synonymous with Smithfield and in 1783 there were several distilleries in the area, including that of John Swan at number 52. Edmund Grange had two nearby and John Stein ran a distillery in nearby Bow Street. John Jameson came to Dublin from Alloa, Scotland, with his sons John (born August 1773) and William, and obtained an interest in the business of the aforementioned John Stein. In 1802 the young John married Isabella, daughter of John Stein, and in the process took over the Bow Street distillery. He grew the business, which soon covered several acres in the adjoining district. Using on-site wells as a water source and building his own workshops for coopers, wagon-makers and coppersmiths, by 1833 production had risen to such dramatic levels that the distillery was paying an annual duty on over 330,000 gallons of whiskey. He purchased a site on the then outskirts of the city, building himself a fine house at 55 Prussia Street, and died on

31 July 1861. Andrew Jameson was born in 1855 and guided the distillery during the last century. He was a managing director of the business from 1905 until 1941 and at one time a director and Governor of the Bank of Ireland. Closely involved in the Irish National Memorial project at Islandbridge, he died on 15 February 1941. In 1971 the Dublin distillery was closed down and relocated to Middleton, County Cork. However, Jameson's have maintained their link with the district and the Jameson Visitor Centre on Bow Street is today a major tourist attraction in the city. In 2015 it drew 280,000 visitors into Dublin 7.

Smithfield has changed dramatically since the late 1900s, when it incorporated fruit and vegetable markets, the Dublin Metropolitan Road Traffic Courts and Children's Court, Linder's motors factors, Tully Tiles, Duffy's scrapyard, some decaying buildings and a distinctive vehicle-load weighing scales set into the street. After a complete transformation in the present century it is now a fashionable area dominated by apartment blocks, hotels, the Lighthouse Cinema, cafes, pubs, the Jameson Distillery Visitor Centre, and Distillers Building, which houses the Smithfield Business Centre.

Smithfield horse market was famed throughout Ireland and farther afield, attracting tourists from all over the world; it has existed here for centuries. Traditionally held on the first Sunday of each month, new middle-class attitudes towards its existence hardened and activity ceased in 2015. It was partially resurrected in early 2016, a shadow of its former glory, with licences and 'chips' demanded of the traders, and is confined to a corner of what was once one of the city's most beautiful open public plazas. Nearby is the once elegant thoroughfare of Haymarket, the name a melancholy palimpsest of the rural activity that once dominated the economic life of the area. Only one old house exists on the thoroughfare, on the corner of Burgess Lane, occupied by the Proper Order Coffee Company.

North King Street

North King Street, facing Smithfield and linking Manor Street in the west to Church Street in the east, was once called Abbey Green. There was a King's Lane in Oxmantown in the early fifteenth century; the name of King Street, Oxmantown, dates from at least 1552.

St Paul's Church was constructed in 1824; established as a parish in 1697, and part of the Church of Ireland diocese bounded by St Michan's to the east, the church replaced an earlier one that first opened in 1704. When St Paul's closed down as a place of worship in the 1980s the building suffered spates of vandalism and many of its fine stained-glass windows were destroyed. In the late 1980s it was given over for community use by the Church of Ireland and renovated by FÁS, and on 13 September 1990 it was officially opened as a centre for business startups by the Minister for Labour, Bertie Ahern TD. Operated by SPADE Enterprises, there are currently fifteen small businesses operating in the church section, with a total of forty-five units beside the church and at other city locations. The three houses inside the church railings date from the early 1800s. The graveyard at the back is now a car park. The vaults of St Paul's are another rumoured burial site for the body of Robert Emmet, but past searches for his remains did not meet with any success.

An interesting tablet on the outside back wall of the church commemorates the deaths of three British soldiers on the night of Robert Emmet's rebellion:

> *This Memorial was erected by non-commissioned Officers and Privates of His Majesty's 21st Royal North British Fusiliers in Memory of James Chapman, James Wogdon and Daniel Patton, soldiers in the above regiment, the former was most barbarously and inhumanely murdered by a rebel banditti on the evening of 23rd July 1803 the two latter died of the wounds they received on the same night.*

Erected in January 1804, it was unveiled by Colonel Donald Robertson, the commander of the regiment. It was restored in 1910 by the 2nd Battalion of the Royal Scottish Fusiliers.

There were two National Schools at the back of the church – one for boys and one for girls. The old girls' school was destroyed by fire in the early 1990s; a beautiful chestnut tree, still talked about in the area, was also burnt and destroyed around this time. The boys' school, with very distinctive architectural features, is now a local community resource facility where Dublin City Council and City of Dublin Education and Training Board run courses for both young and old; there is a small children's playground attached to the building.

A priority on the tourist trail in Dublin is the Cobblestone Pub, at 77 North King Street. A mecca for music lovers from around the globe, some of whom arrive with their instruments, it is one of the attractions on the official Dublin Tourist Trail. Traditional music is on offer every night from seven o'clock; in the early evenings it is popular with locals as a conversation pub and there is no television on the premises. Proprietor Tom Mulligan hails from Cabra Park; he took over the running of the pub from Laois man Gerry Power in 1988. Tom's father, also called Tom, in association with John Egan and Tony Conlon, ran St Mary's Music Club from a building next to Lavin's pub on Church Street; founded in the mid 1950s, it moved into the Cobblestone in 1988 and operated there for over twenty years. The club now meets on Tuesday nights in Hughes's Pub, beside the old Motor Taxation Office, another popular venue for music performers and music lovers; although the pub has a television set, it is turned off every evening after the six o'clock news.

At the corner of North King Street and Church Street, near the present-day Tap public house, is the spot where Kevin Barry was captured following his involvement in an attack on British army forces during the War of Independence on 20 September 1920. Three British soldiers were killed in the incident. Kevin Barry, an eighteen-year-old student, was later executed in Mountjoy Prison on 1 November 1920. With Kevin Barry on that day was his friend and fellow republican Frank Flood, born on 1 December 1901 at 6 Emmet Street. On 1 June 1920 he had taken part in a successful raid on King's Inns, where a large quantity of arms and ammunition was captured. He was arrested in early 1921 and executed for high treason in Mountjoy Prison on 14 March 1921. His body was exhumed, along with that of Kevin Barry and eight others, and reinterred in Glasnevin Cemetery following a State funeral on 14 October 2001. There is a plaque commemorating the incident on the wall of the Tap public house, called the Dardenelles by the locals for many years after the heavy casualties inflicted on British forces in the area during the 1916 Rising.

Red Cow Lane, between Brunswick and North King Street, derives its name from an old inn-sign. Bow Street, off North King Street, was once the site of a large pond called Lough Buoy, situated at the King Street end and connected with Channel Row and the Bradoge Water. A Night Shelter for the Homeless Poor was founded in 1838 at 8 Bow Street 'for the purposes of giving shelter during the night to persons destitute of the means of providing a lodging for themselves'. In 1910, lodgings were provided for a total of 34,736 destitute persons and in that year a Mr William Small was 'collecting subs at 8 Bow Street' for the upkeep of the shelter. In the old Jameson house on the corner of May Lane and Bow Street the Bow Street Academy for Screen Acting is located; the building formerly housed the Commercial Court, a Division of the High Court. Established in 2004, it sat here for the first time, with the Honourable Mr Justice Peter Kelly presiding. The Court's first Registrar was Kevin O'Neill. On the other corner of May Lane, surrounded by a protective railing, there is a bell on display dating back to 1761. The inscription on it can be clearly viewed by the passer-by.

The street is well known today through the charitable works of Br Kevin Crowley, who established the Capuchin Day Centre in 1969; he is highly regarded and respected throughout the city. The Centre provides a breakfast and dinner service, and distributes parcels for those in need, without question. Through his efforts and the commitment of those volunteers supporting him, he has helped many families survive the trauma and hardship of the post-2008 recession, when the numbers availing of the Centre more than doubled. The needs of the homeless and rough sleepers are prioritized; a medical and optical service and an advice and information clinic are also provided.

Muldoon's, 101 North King Street, circa 1925. Muldoon's fresh fish and poultry business has been trading in the area for over a hundred years. Sister and brother Helen and Hugo Muldoon have shops at 45 Manor Street and 36B Fassaugh Avenue, Cabra West. Their uncle Jimmy is the man in the centre of the photograph, and the boy in short trousers is Vincent, their father. The shop on North King Street, with its distinctive green front is almost 300 years old. It is one of the few remaining original buildings, now sandwiched between two modern apartment blocks. The Dutch-billy structure is best viewed across the road, where the style is more apparent to the eye. Turkeys were patently in demand at Christmastime during the early years of the twentieth century (Courtesy Hugo Muldoon)

11| The Quays, Church Street and Four Courts

Parkgate Street was the start of the old thoroughfare from Dublin to the villages of Lucan and Chapelizod and a ferry operated from a pier here to the southside. It was often the scene of late-night brawls among drunken passengers on the last ferry. The inn sign of the then nearby Royal Oak Tavern was much talked about due to the omission of one Colonel Careless from its illustrated inn-sign. Kings Bridge was designed by the London architect George Papworth (1781–1855), and was opened in 1828, despite much opposition by the ferry operators. It incorporates iron panels decorated with classical designs and was called Kings Bridge to commemorate the visit of King George IV to Ireland in 1821. It was renamed Heuston Bridge in 1966, in memory of the executed 1916 leader Seán Heuston. Sand Quay was afterwards renamed Pembroke Quay. It was rebuilt in the late 1800s and again renamed, to Sarsfield Quay. Towards the city, Gravel Walk Slip served as a docking area on the riverside where Blackhall Place joins the quays.

Parkgate Street has enjoyed a huge commercial revival following the opening of the Criminal Courts of Justice complex in January 2010; a popular and well-known pub here is Ryan's, which exudes Victorian character and charm. In the 1950s there was a pub on this street called The Drop-In. Its owner, John Francis

O'Reilly, was born in County Clare in 1916; he moved to London around 1938 and from there went to live in Jersey in May 1940, during the Second World War. Two months later the Channel Islands were occupied by Germany, and he then offered his services as a translator to the Nazis; he proved to be competent and was subsequently sent to Berlin to work as a propaganda broadcaster on the Nazi Irish radio service *Irland-Redaktion*. He used the pseudonym 'Pat O'Brien' for his broadcasts into Ireland. Sent to Bremen in September 1942 to train as a spy, in December 1943 he was parachuted into County Limerick, near Foynes, with a brief to spy and report on British shipping movements in Irish coastal waters. O'Reilly was arrested after just a few hours in the country and imprisoned in Arbour Hill. Ironically, he escaped from the prison on D-Day, 6 June 1944. He made his way to his father's home in Kilkee, County Clare, where his father Bernard reported him to the Garda authorities and collected the £500 reward for the arrest of his son.

He spent the rest of the war in Mountjoy Jail and was released on 12 May 1945. His father then presented him with the reward money, which he had invested on his son's behalf so he could establish himself in worthwhile employment. With this and the £300 the Nazis had given him to support his mission in Ireland, returned on his release, John Francis O'Reilly bought The Drop-In. The *Sunday*

Parkgate Street, early 1900s (Courtesy Seamus Kearns Postcard Collection)

Dispatch serialized his life story in the summer of 1952. He died while on holiday in London in 1971, victim of a hit-and-run. It is interesting to note that his father, a former Sergeant in the Royal Irish Constabulary, was the officer who arrested Roger Casement at Banna Strand, County Kerry, in April 1916. A collection of files relating to John Francis lies in the Irish Military Archives.

The pub was later named The Deerpark and in the late 1980s, together with the adjoining former post office, it was acquired by P.J. McCaffrey, proprietor of The Hole in the Wall pub on Blackhorse Avenue. The buildings were demolished. Jim O'Sullivan, a painter from the area, was commissioned to oversee the construction using recycled materials, and Nancy Hand's rose from the rubble. P.J. recalls the building works: 'The big front window came from the country house of an English lord; the stone came from a convent on the South Circular Road; the timber floors came from part of the old Guinness brewery, the windows and doors came from an old London pub called The Green Man and the staircase came from Trinity College, Dublin.' Jim added that the staircase featured in the film *Educating Rita*, recalling that at the time they 'also dug down 380 feet to a spring well; we had the water tested and it was found to be fine drinking water'. The bore was capped and is located on the footpath outside an entrance to the pub.

A view of the Esplanade, 1932 (Courtesy Neil Ward and *Garda Review*)

Ellis Quay is called after the family of Agar Ellis, Viscount Clifden, who retained a valuable leasehold interest from Dublin Corporation extending from Arran Quay to the Phoenix Park. Some of these leases dated from 1662 and the maps attaching to them show the Liffey as the southern boundary of the Ellis property. The apartment complex, built at the end of the twentieth century, is called Clifton Court. The Phoenix Cinema was located at numbers 7 and 9 Ellis Quay, now occupied by the furniture shop of Kings and Queens. It was opened by the Lord Mayor of Dublin on 3 December 1912 and could accommodate 750 patrons. Called 'the Feeno' by locals, it was famous for its Saturday afternoon 'penny rush' when it is said it often doubled its capacity. It closed down in 1958. Number 15 was the location of John Ireland & Son Ltd, well-known uniform, hat and cap manufacturers.

Ellis Street, originally called Cuffe Street and renamed Silver Street in 1772, got its present name in 1872. Under the name Silver Street it was the setting for the military street fight in *Belts*, one of the 'barrack-room ballads'. Bloody Bridge was an old wooden bridge that derived its name from a fatal pitched battle, or brawl, in 1671, the year after its erection, in which the proprietors of the former ferry service figured prominently. In 1704 the wooden bridge was replaced by a stone one named Barrack Bridge. In 1863 this was in turn replaced by a metal structure named Victoria Bridge after the long-reigning queen of England, linking Ellis Street to Watling Street. It is now called Rory O'Moore Bridge, after one of the leaders of the 1641 Rising.

Before 1675 there was only one bridge over the Liffey, called Dublin Bridge or the Old Bridge. Connecting Church Street to Bridge Street on the south bank of the Liffey, on old maps it is simply called 'The Bridge'. Built by King John in 1210, it was erected on the site of a previous crossing, for during construction traces of the foundations to an ancient Irish or Norse bridge were found. Rebuilt in 1385 by the Dominicans, who had an abbey on the site of the present-day Four Courts, a lay brother collected tolls from those crossing. The structure lasted until 1818 when it was replaced and named Whitworth Bridge. It was renamed Father Matthew Bridge in the last century. Next to the quays to the west of Old Church Street lay Gravel Walk, afterwards renamed Tighe Street, now part of Benburb Street. Ormond Quay, formerly called Jervis Quay, was embanked in 1770 and Upper Ormond Quay was built around the same time on the site of the Pill or estuary of the Bradoge River. The quays are dominated by two major historic buildings, the Custom House and the Four Courts.

Four Courts

The Four Courts is the renowned architect James Gandon's masterpiece. It houses one of our foremost institutions, the Law Courts and is situated on a site formerly occupied by the first Dominican monastery in Ireland. In 1316, when the all-conquering Edward the Bruce of Scotland camped at Castleknock, contemplating an assault on the city, the Lord Mayor of Dublin, Robert Nottingham, set about its defence. He razed the Dominican monastery to the ground and used the materials from the buildings to erect a fortified gate at Winetavern Street (St Audoen's Arch), and a considerable line of wall. Following reports of the defensive preparations of Dublin, Edward abandoned his siege, decamped from Castleknock and retired to Munster. In thanksgiving for the salvation of the city from military attack, King Edward II commanded the citizens of Dublin to rebuild the monastery.

In 1662 the Court of Claims, dealing with the land and property forfeitures following the unsuccessful rebellion against English rule from 1641 to 1650, was held on the site of the Four Courts. The rebellion culminated with the death in 1649 of Red Hugh O'Neill in County Cavan and the arrival of Oliver Cromwell at Ringsend the following year. The Dominicans were restored to possession of the property in 1685, but moved to Cook Street shortly afterwards. In 1689 King James II held Parliament on the site.

On 13 March 1786 the foundation stone for the Four Courts was laid. Based on an original design by Thomas Cooley, architect of the Royal Exchange and Master of Francis Johnston, James Gandon was subsequently assigned to execute the works. The project was completed in 1796 at a cost of £200,000; the Courts opened for business on 3 November of that year. This imposing building has a frontage of 440 feet and occupies most of the stretch of quay from Chancery Street to Church Street. Particularly striking are the dome and the entrance portico of six columns of the Corinthian order. Various additions were made through the years, the last being the administration complex of Áras Uí Dhálaigh, named after the former judge and President of Ireland, Cearbhall Ó Dálaigh. It was built on the site of the old Four Courts Hotel in 1986; a modern extension of the hotel, built in the early 1970s, was incorporated into the new office development.

Arran Quay

Arran Quay was embanked in 1717. It is called after the Earl of Arran, the son of the Duke of Ormonde, and was once a very fashionable address. Edmund Burke was born on 12 January 1729 at 12 Arran Quay. The son of Richard Burke, an attorney of the Court of Exchequer, and Mary Burke (*née* Nagle) of Ballyduff, County Cork, he entered Trinity College Dublin in 1744 and graduated in 1748. In 1750 he went to London and became perhaps the most scintillating and original thinker ever to sit in the British House of Commons. Influential in the Whig Party, he served as Paymaster-General of Forces in the Rockingham ministry of 1782. During his lifetime he was the object of much malicious criticism, much of it relating to his humble Irish background. In later years he advised William Pitt the Younger, Prime Minister of Great Britain. A noted writer, his most famous work *Reflections on the Revolution in France* (1790) was a forceful attack on the principles of the Revolution; although extravagantly expressed, it made him the international apostle of counter-revolution. Edmund Burke is regarded by many as a founder of the modern conservative tradition; he died on 9 July 1797.

William Haliday was born at 32 Arran Quay in 1788; his godfather was John Toler, Lord Norbury, the infamous hanging Judge. This Irish-language scholar and linguist was a founding member of the Gaelic Society of Dublin, established in December 1806, and he taught Irish to the artist George Petrie in return for drawing lessons. In February 1812 he married Miss Alder, a neighbour whose father, William Alder, ran a timber and bark business on Arran Quay. Haliday died shortly after his marriage in October 1812. The house, with others on the quay, was demolished in the late twentieth century. The present structure, offices of Sean Costello Solicitors, is aptly called Haliday House, its fine entrances to the front and side reminiscent of the Georgian houses it replaced.

William's younger brother Charles Haliday, born in 1789, was a historian and author who wrote the *Scandinavian Kingdom of Dublin*, edited posthumously by his friend, the historian John P. Prendergast, in 1882. Charles enjoyed a successful career as a banker, and was an active member of the Ballast Board, forerunner to the Dublin

Port Authority, and a director of the Bank of Ireland from 1838 until his death in 1866. Residing in Monkstown, his business address was at the family home on Arran Quay. His collection of tracts and pamphlets, numbering 35,000 and invaluable to the historian or curious researcher, was donated to the Royal Irish Academy by his widow Marianne in 1867. Of some architectural interest are the buildings at 35 and 36 Arran Quay, offices of Moran & Ryan Solicitors and the adjacent Bank of Ireland. A Carmelite convent once stood at the rear of 16 Arran Quay, in Pudding Lane, now called Lincoln Lane, where the offices of Dublin solicitors Michael Staines & Company are located. The Allied Irish Bank building, the former Smithfield branch of the bank, closed down in December 2012; its last manager was Bob Wallace.

Constituted in the year 1096, Halston Street and Arran Quay is the oldest parish in the city of Dublin. However, it has an ecclesiastical history dating back to the beginnings of the sixth century. St Paul's dates from 1835–37, was designed by Patrick Byrne, and is one of the most prominent buildings on the city quays. The foundation stone was laid on St Patrick's Day 1835 by the archbishop of Dublin, Dr Daniel Murray. The *Catholic Penny Magazine* published an engraving of the facade and a description of the church in its edition of 10 January 1835. Opened for worship in 1835, the tower was erected in 1843 and its peal of six bells were first rung on the Feast of All Saints in 1843. These joy-bells, as they were called, were popular with the citizens of Dublin, who came in their thousands to hear them rung for the first time, probably because they were the first bells to ring out from a Roman Catholic church in Dublin since before the Reformation. According to the *Catholic Directory* (1846) the bells were rung every Sunday and on special days 'by select and judicious persons chosen and adapted for that important purpose'. They were made by James Sheridan of the Eagle Foundry in nearby Church Street. James was so pleased with his work he placed an advertisement in the *Catholic Directory* describing the bells and the 'great delight and satisfaction of the assembled thousands who came to witness the reviving sounds of Irish Christianity'.

The first parish priest was Monsignor William Yore and he was instrumental in getting the bells installed, contributing some of his own funds towards them. This energetic and enlightened man petitioned the British authorities to permit Roman Catholic soldiers to be marched by an officer to attend Mass, in a manner similar to that of Anglican soldiers; he succeeded and the first soldiers to be marched to Mass at St Paul's left the church for the Crimean War in the winter of 1853. Few returned.

Dom Abbot Marmion, the noted Benedictine monk, served as an altar boy in St Paul's. Born on 1 April 1858, his father worked as a salesman with Vernon & Cullen, cornfactors on Arran Quay; the family lived at 57 Queen Street and moved to 2 Blackhall Place in 1863. Joseph entered Clonliffe College at fifteen and went to Rome for further studies from 1879 to 1881. He joined the Benedictines and entered the Belgium abbey of Maredsous, becoming a noted spiritual writer. He died at Maredsous from influenza on 30 January 1923. He was beatified by Pope John Paul II in September 2000. The marriage of Sinéad Flanagan to the former President of Ireland, Eamonn de Valera, and the baptism of Oliver St John Gogarty and his siblings, took place in St Paul's. The church community was revitalized by the arrival of Polish immigrants in the early part of the present century, with Mass celebrated in the Polish language. It is not presently in use.

From the late 1960s a sharp decline in the population of the area became evident following the general move to the outlying suburbs, although that decline has been reversed in recent years. A number of small-scale housing complexes were constructed by Dublin Corporation in Queen Street, Hay Street and Blackhall Place during the mid and late 1980s. Early this century improvements continued with the revitalization of the flats complex on Queen Street and the addition of further new homes. The building of private apartments along the quays and on Church Street in the mid to late 1990s has enabled the social renewal needed to make Arran Quay and its environs once again a vibrant, thriving district.

Catholic Youth Council

The former Catholic Youth Council headquarters at 20 Arran Quay once served as two presbyteries before Arran Quay parish was amalgamated with that of Halston Street in 1974. An unusual feature of the premises is the well-kept garden in the front of the house – the last building on the north quays to have one. The house was redecorated and refurbished in 1988. The Council was the Diocesan Youth Agency for the Archdiocese of Dublin and was founded in 1944. Originally located in Westland Row, it established its headquarters in Arran Quay under the Directorship of Fr John 'Fitzer' Fitzpatrick, well-known to many Dubliners through his leadership of the organization during the 1970s. When the Council moved to Arran Quay in 1974, it had a staff of six to cater for the needs of Dublin youth and by 1992 employed seventy-five and had developed its youth services nationally and throughout the greater Dublin area. The building is now occupied by Crosscare, who offer vocational classes, irrespective of means, at no cost. The Catholic Youth Council was subsumed into Crosscare, which continues to provide youth services, at its Drumcondra centre.

Church Street

Church Street gets its name from the presence of the ancient church of St Michan and is the oldest inhabited area of Dublin's northside. John Watson Stewart (1762–1822) lived at 1 Church Street and inherited his family's printing business; this included the publication of the *Gentleman's and Citizen's Almanac*, which ran from 1727 and was in continuous production for over one hundred years. Up to the end of the 1600s the portion of the city north of the River Liffey was small, comprising mainly Church Street and a few streets to the east and west of it. From the east side of the street to the sea lay a significant stretch of open country that formerly belonged to the Abbey of St Mary and the Dominican Priory, suppressed by Henry VIII. At this time the sea ran from Clontarf to Ballybough to present-day North Strand Road and Amiens Street, around by Beresford Place and down to Strand Street and Grattan Bridge at Capel Street, formerly called Essex Bridge.

Church Street provides a dramatic insight into the terrible living and social conditions that existed in Dublin in the early twentieth century. The following words of Jim Connolly in early 1913 proved to be prophetic: 'Ireland is a country of wonderful charity and singularly little justice, and Dublin ... a city famous for its charitable institutions and its charitable citizens, should also be infamous for the perfectly hellish conditions under which its people are housed and under which its men, women and children labour for a living.'

On Tuesday 2 September 1913, at about nine o'clock at night, two houses in Church Street collapsed without warning, burying the occupants. The buildings were four storeys high, with shops at ground-floor level. The sixteen rooms over the shops were inhabited by ten families, over forty people in all; seven died in the disaster and numerous others were injured. Many of the victims had been standing in the doorway and street outside when the front wall of the houses suddenly collapsed. Rescue parties worked throughout the night, digging out people from beneath the rubble. A Mrs Maguire, who occupied a room in one of the houses that collapsed, described the scene: 'I was standing in the hallway of the house, looking at the children playing in the streets. Other women were sitting on the kerbstone so as to be out in the air. Suddenly I heard a terrible crash and shrieking. I ran, not knowing why, but hearing as I did a frightful noise of falling bricks. When I looked back, I saw that two houses had tumbled down.'

Many were shocked that such a disaster could occur but some were not surprised. Mr Pilkington of the Dublin Citizens Association Committee on Housing wrote to the *Irish Times* stating, 'the mass of the citizens are in ignorance of the real wants of the city ... we have evidence to show that (owing to dilapidation) what recently happened in Church Street may occur in other parts of the city'.

As a result a Committee of Inquiry was set up by the authorities to study Dublin housing, which bore out Pilkinton's remarks. The Committee reported its findings in 1914 and presented a picture of appalling poverty in tenement areas. The tenements, situated mainly in the city centre, once housed the wealthy, who vacated them to live in fashionable new abodes such as those in Fitzwilliam Square and Merrion Square. The Committee defined tenement houses as 'houses intended and originally used for occupation by one family but which, owing to change of circumstances, have been let out room by room and are now occupied by separate families, one in each room for the most part'.

At that time over 400,000 people lived in Dublin; of these, 87,300 lived in city-centre tenements –nearly 25 per cent of the population. More alarmingly, 80 per cent of the tenement families occupied just one room. An anonymous poet of the day, writing in *The Irish Review*, contrasted the sheer squalor of life in the city slums with the beautiful countryside only a few miles away. These idyllic pastures might as well have been on the moon:

> And children, faring to far fields forlorn
> Forget her squalor for a single day
> To break great branches of the blossoming thorn
> Or strip, and in the cooling water play
> Or gather cowslips till at dusk, footworn
> Returning home, each court and narrow way
> Is fresh with flowers from the meadows borne -
> But in the stifling slums they soon decay.
>   – 'Dublin', by 'N'.

The foundation stone for the Capuchin church of St Mary of the Angels was laid by Cardinal Cullen in 1868 and completed in 1881. The Capuchins came to Ireland in 1615 and established themselves on Church Street in 1689, where The Tap public house now stands. In 1720 a small Mass House was erected on the site of the present church; enlarged in 1796, it became known as Church Street Chapel. There is a distinctive rose-shaped stained-glass window in its east front and it has fine timbered ceilings. James Pearce, father of Pádraig and Willie Pierce, designed and built the high altar. During the upheavals of 1916 to 1923, the Capuchins often put themselves at risk ministering to the condemned, the injured and the imprisoned; they acted in the belief that men of good faith and in danger of death were entitled to spiritual comfort. Friars Albert, Aloysius and Augustine attended to the leaders of the 1916 Rising prior to their execution. The apostle of temperance, Fr Theobold Matthew, often celebrated Mass at St Mary of the Angels. The offices of Threshold, which offers housing and tenant rental accommodation advice, was founded in the late 1970s by Fr Donal O'Mahony in one of the church buildings; it is now located at 21 Stoneybatter.

The Father Matthew Hall was built in the late 1800s and it may have been the first cinematic venue in Dublin. Advertisements mention pictures being shown here as early as October 1909. However, the Volta Cinema in Mary Street, founded by James Joyce in that same year with financial backing from Italian investors, is credited with the status of being the first Dublin cinema. An advertisement in the *Evening Telegraph* of Saturday 13 November 1920 reads:

> Tomorrow (Sunday) at four o'clock Sessue Hayakawa in *The Great Horizon*. Splendid new seating accommodation has been installed and in the reserved portion plush-covered tip-up seats are available.

The Hall served as the Headquarters of the 1st Battalion under Commandant Ned Daly during the 1916 Rising, a fact commemorated by a plaque on the front wall of the building.

Church Street takes its name from St Michan's, which was founded in 1095. It is the oldest building on the city's northside and is the second-oldest after Christ Church Cathedral, established just a few years previously. Although St Michan's was rebuilt in the 1680s, the tower dates from the fifteenth century. Handel is said to have used the Renatus Harris organ in the church during his visit to Dublin.

The vaults are celebrated for the quality of the air that for centuries have preserved the dead they shelter. Experts attribute this to the dryness arising from the yellow limestone walls.

Brothers Henry and John Sheares began practising law from their office and home on Ormond Quay in 1789; in 1796 they moved their lucrative practice to Baggot Street. Active in the United Irishmen and charged with treason, their trial was prosecuted by the notorious Lord Norbury. They were convicted of treason and executed on 14 July 1798, beheaded and buried in the vault of St Michan's.

William Jackson, an Anglican clergyman ordained in London, met Wolfe Tone and others in Dublin in an effort to secure French military assistance in Ireland; following this he was betrayed by John Cockayne, a London lawyer. The meeting had been arranged by Leonard McNally, himself an informer for the British authorities, probably as a result of damning information on his own treasonable activities relayed to them by Cockayne. Rev. Jackson was tried for high treason on 23 April 1795. Just before being brought up for the delivery of judgment by the court on 30 April, he took poison and later died in the dock.

Oliver Cromwell Bond was born in Donegal, son of a Presbyterian minister. He moved to Dublin in the early 1780s to trade in woollen goods at 54 Pill Lane, present-day Chancery Street, and joined the United Irishmen, becoming a member of its national leadership. He later moved to 9 Lower Bridge Street where his business prospered. Oliver Bond was arrested in 1798 and he died in Newgate Prison in unexplained circumstances on 6 September. Oliver Bond and Rev. William Jackson are buried in St Michan's churchyard.

Maguire & Paterson

The first recorded mention of the humble match is found in China around 1000 AD, when they went under the name of 'fire sticks'; their introduction into Europe was chronicled by Marco Polo in 1270. In 1827 an English chemist called John Walker invented the first match, called chemical friction lights. These were flat cardboard slivers with antimony sulphide and potassium chlorate heads. They were ignited by pulling the chemical tip sharply over sandpaper. The invention put an end to precarious fire-making. Modifications continued and in 1855 the safety match, marketed under the name 'Congreaves', was invented.

The manufacture of matches in Dublin began in 1882, when Paterson & Company started production in Hammond Lane just off Church Street, upriver from the Four Courts. In 1922 they amalgamated with Maguire Miller & Company, Liverpool, to form Maguire & Paterson. Northern Ireland buyers boycotted the company's product and this led to the formation of Maguire & Paterson (Belfast) Limited in April 1923; by agreement the Dublin company was precluded from selling matches in the six counties of Northern Ireland and in the border counties of Cavan, Donegal and Monaghan.

The company brand names became familiar throughout Ireland and these included Bo Peep, Buffalo, Cara Safety Match, Irish Gem, Parnell Match, Pilot Match, Rotary, Solus, Superior Wax Vestas and The Friendly Match. At the height of demand for matches, up to the end of the Second World War, the company employed 250 people. The terms under which Maguire & Paterson commercially operated were strictly controlled, as the following letter dated 22 July 1929 from the Revenue Commissioners bears out:

> I am directed by the Revenue Commissioners to inform you that they have granted final approval in respect of the structural alterations to your match factory at Hammond Lane, Dublin, which were provisionally approved by the Commissioners letters dated 16 August and 14 December 1928. I am further to inform you, in reply to your application of the 26 January 1929, that the main door to your match factory may remain open outside the ordinary working hours, in the absence of an Officer of Customs and Excise, provided that all finished matches produced in the course of each day are placed under revenue lock in the secure compartment in the factory, and that no matches are manufactured during night hours.

The match factory at Hammond Lane continued in production until 1989, when Maguire & Paterson closed its manufacturing plant and began to import its matches from Liverpool. In 1992, when the company operated an office and warehousing facility at Hammond Lane, there were only four match manufacturing plants in Western Europe, excluding Russia, which then had 150 entities. By the mid-1990s even the small operation on Hammond Lane was being scaled back, and the company later closed the facility. The factory was subsequently demolished. The site underwent archaeological excavations, revealing post-holes and firepits of earlier Viking settlements; details of the survey can be viewed on www.heritagemaps.ie. The factory site has yet to be developed and in 2016 it appears as a large hole in the ground, surrounded by a protective hoarding running alongside the light rail track of the LUAS and the footpath on Church Street.

Hammond Lane itself was formerly called Hangman's Lane, which over the centuries, became corrupted to Hammond Lane. It appears in early eighteenth century maps of Dublin as Hangman's Lane and finds reference in the poetry of Jonathan Swift.

The Pawn Shop

The first pawn lender was founded in 1452 by Franciscan monks in Perugia to combat usury. The Monte dei Paschi di Siena, which claims to be the world's oldest bank, originated in the pawn business and still operates a pawnbroking division. Many Italian banks are engaged in the activity and in 2006 Sanpaolo-IMI, based in Turin, had five pawn businesses and held auctions every two days; it then had €45 million worth of pawn loans on its books. Pawn shops once dotted the Dublin landscape; in 2016 only three registered pawnbrokers remained, Breretons of Capel Street, Carthys of Marlborough Street and Kearns at 69 Queen Street, Dublin 7.

An observer of social conditions in Dublin in 1912 wrote that 'the number of articles pawned in Dublin is very large. From inquiries I made some years ago, I ascertained that, in a single year, 2,866,084 tickets were issued in the city of Dublin'. Pawning articles in order to manage from week to week became an ingrained aspect of city living and was a fact of life in Dublin for a great part of the twentieth century. In the Cabra West that I grew up, many a woman pawned their husband's suit on Monday mornings, to be redeemed on the following Friday or Saturday, praying that her husband didn't have to attend a funeral during the week. It was a common practice until the late 1960s, when the birth and growth of the Credit Union movement, coupled with economic expansion and a rise in living standards, significantly reduced the dependence of many on 'the pawn'.

Pat Kearns resides in the district and his family has run the Queen Street pawnbrokers for over one hundred years; until the late 1960s the majority of transactions involved clothing. In the 1980s this changed to jewellery, sports and camera equipment, musical instruments and electrical goods. Items over £10 in value had to be redeemed within four months; items under £10 could be redeemed within six to twelve months. For a loan of £50, a client had to pay £52.50 on redemption, plus an interest charge of one pound per month. Regular auctions are held of unclaimed goods on hand. In 2016 most transactions involve jewellery and loans issue for sums of €200 and upwards; interest is charged at the rate of 2 per cent per month. Four people are employed in the business, which is governed by the Pawnbrokers Act 1964 as amended and regulated by the Department of Consumer Affairs; Pat's licence has to be renewed on an annual basis.

Queen Street and Environs

Queen Street is identified on Dublin street maps from 1687; the street and the bridge at its riverfront end were probably named after Catherine of Braganza, consort of Charles II. The bridge was renamed Queen Maeve Bridge after the Connaught queen of legend. Built in 1776 and replacing a 1683 structure first called Arran, then Bridewell Bridge, it is the oldest existing city span on the River Liffey. The street fell into a state of decay during the 1970s and today it is dominated by the furniture outlet of Bargaintown. Thundercut Alley, a laneway off Queen Street and next to North King Street, was boarded up during the 1980s, and its metal place-name sign only disappeared during 1992. The laneway was not allowed to disappear, however, and was incorporated into the apartment development at Smithfield.

One of the most celebrated residents of Queen Street was the architect George Semple, born in 1700. He acquired land on Queen Street, in the area of Oxmantown, in 1754 and constructed a number of houses, including his own. He also built some houses on Capel Street. He undertook the rebuild of Essex Bridge at Capel Street, now Grattan Bridge, completed in 1753 at a cost of £20,661, after two years and eighty days of continuous construction. It closely resembled Westminister Bridge in design, with the use of a process incorporating coffer dams for laying the foundations. Such was the quality of the work that his foundations were retained when Grattan Bridge was built during 1873 and 1874.

George Semple designed St Patrick's Hospital and was the supervising architect for the construction of Newbridge House, Donabate. Completed in 1749 as a country residence for the extremely wealthy Charles Cobbe, Church of Ireland Archbishop of Dublin from 1743 until his death in 1765, this fine house, part of the

A view of Queen Street taken from Bridgefoot Street, 1930
(Courtesy Neil Ward and *Garda Review*)

Newbridge Demesne, is a popular local and tourist attraction owned and managed by Fingal County Council. It was designed by the renowned Scottish-born, London-based architect James Gibbs, and George Semple meticulously followed his designs and plans and visited the great architect on numerous occasions in London during construction. It is not known whether James Gibbs ever visited Ireland. George Semple lived on Queen Street until his death in 1782.

Blackhall Street, off Queen Street, was built in 1789 and was named after Sir Thomas Blackhall, Lord Mayor of Dublin in 1769. Irwin's *Guide to Dublin*, published in 1853, describes Blackhall Street as 'the part of Dublin enjoying a most mild and genial climate, in gardens here the grape and fig ripen in the open air'. Georgian buildings, demolished in the 1970s, were replaced by redbrick local authority houses, which have blended in with the environment created by this unusually wide street.

Facing Blackhall Street, on Blackhall Place, is the landmark building housing the Incorporated Law Society of Ireland. This was the former King's Hospital School: also known as Bluecoat Boys' Hospital or Bluecoat School, deriving its name from the dark blue, brass-buttoned cutaway coat that formed the uniform.

Founded in 1669 'for educating, maintaining, clothing and apprenticing the sons of reduced citizens of Dublin', it was called The Hospital and Free School of King Charles II. Originally located on Dublin's Queen Street, in the then southeastern corner of Oxmantown Green, it was granted a Royal Charter by the King in 1670. The Irish Parliament was convened in the school during 1729, the same year the foundation stone was laid for the new Parliament House in College Green.

King's Hospital School moved to its new address on Blackhall Place in 1783, the foundation stone having been laid by Lord Harcourt in 1773. It was designed by Thomas Ivory, a Cork carpenter, and the school boardroom contained a ceiling executed by the celebrated plasterer Charles Thorp between 1778 and 1780, for which he was paid £72. Parts of this ceiling are reproductions following a fire in the early twentieth century. The building also possesses a good example of stained-glass art, carried out in 1935 by the noted Dublin-born Evie Sydney Hone (1885–1955). A distinguished former pupil was the artist James Reily; born around 1735, he attended the school between 1745 and 1748. He came from modest family circumstances. He took up the brush as a young adult and excelled at miniature portrait painting. Two of his signed works are on display in the Victoria and Albert Museum, London and the National Gallery of Ireland, Merrion Square, Dublin. His first studio was in Capel Street, and he later moved to premises in Grafton Street, where he died in 1780.

In 1806 King's Hospital School had a complement of 120 boys and the Rev. Allen Morgan was the chaplain and schoolmaster; in the middle of the last century it incorporated Mercer's girls' and Morgan's boys' school, Ashtown, a move that contributed to steadily increasing numbers. This in turn created a need for additional space, and it subsequently moved out of the city centre to a spacious eighty-acre site at Brooklawn in Palmerstown where a modern, purpose-built school was established on the banks of the Liffey. A portrait of the founder, King Charles II, which formerly hung in the dining halls of the school when it was in Queen Street and Blackhall Place, now hangs in the dining hall at Palmerstown. The Incorporated Law Society took possession of the building in 1970. The playing field at the back of the building is the last surviving portion of Oxmantown Green.

The Gaelic League Hall was situated at 5 Blackhall Place and was the meeting place for both the Gaelic League and the Colmcille branch of Cumann na mBan. Called Colmcille Hall, the Volunteers first paraded here in December 1913 and the following extract from the *Irish Times* of 8 February 1916 provides an interesting insight into their activities:

> The Irish [Sinn Féin] Volunteers were active on Saturday night in Dublin. About 11 o'clock a large number of them, uniformed and carrying rifles with bayonets, gathered in Blackhall Place, where there is a volunteer hall. From that hour until two o'clock on Sunday morning they took part in what appeared to be a representation of street fighting. The operation aroused many people in the neighbourhood, and many police assembled. It is reported that an altercation took place between one of the volunteers and a policeman who accused the former of pointing his rifle at him.

Members of the 1st Battalion, Dublin Brigade mobilized in the hall prior to the Easter Rising under the leadership of Commandant Ned Daly.

Paul & Vincent were fertilizer and feeding stuff manufacturers and were located at 9 to 13 Blackhall Place; they also made binding twine and other necessities for the agricultural industry. In recent years the building was converted into apartments; the facade has been preserved and the company name, set in mosaic tiles in the wall, reminds the passer-by of the previous occupier. The Dublin Prison Gate Mission was located at 40 Blackhall Place; it was established in 1876 for 'the reclamation of released female prisoners and of others on the verge of being absorbed into this class'. It admitted all denominations without 'controversy or inducement'. During the early 1900s the complement averaged around one hundred females and the yearly running costs totalled £3000. Women worked in the institution's laundry or at needlework. Two thirds of the running costs of the Mission were met from earnings derived from the laundry and needlework; the other third came from public subscriptions.

Hendrick Street is off Blackhall Place, and connects it to Benburb Street. An orphanage was established here in the late 1700s. Founded and run by Maria O'Brien with help from her father, Denis Thomas O'Brien, a wealthy Dublin merchant, she later transferred it over to the care of the Poor Clare nuns in 1806.

Benburb Street

Benburb Street, formerly called Barrack Street, after the Royal, now Collins Barracks, is located off Blackhall Place. The area in front of the barracks is called

The Esplanade. Following the ruthless suppression of the 1798 rebellion against English rule by General Lake, the executed remains of slain rebels were displayed on public view here, beside the banks of the Liffey. There is no record of the number or names of those interred in this site of mass burials; their bodies lie beneath the neatly-kept grass in the enclosed memorial:

> No rising column marks the spot
> Where many a victim lies
> No bell here tolls its solemn sound
> No monument here stands – Robert Emmet, 1800.

The park has been redeveloped in recent years and a simple Wicklow granite rock, with a bronze plaque, is a fitting memorial to those who died for Irish freedom in 1798. Further up from the Esplanade, at Heuston Bridge, Dublin Corporation opened a beautiful, enclosed park as a memorial to those who gave their lives for Irish freedom. Opened in 1984 and called Croppies Memorial Park, it won a Bord Fáilte/Royal Town Planning Institute Civic Award in that same year. A quiet haven in a traffic-congested, noisy city intersection, its small pond and fountain offer a tranquil repose to the passer-by or tourist. 'Anna Livia', a sculpture by Sean Mulcahy and Eamonn O' Doherty unveiled in the city centre for the millennium year, was relocated to this more tranquil setting in recent years; Dubliners variously nicknamed it the 'Floozie in the Jacuzzi', the 'Mott on the Pot' and the 'Hoor in the Sewer' during its early sojourn on O'Connell Street.

Thomas Lambert Synnott was born at 61 Barrack (Benburb) Street in 1810 and in 1835 established himself as a grocer at number 61. He was appointed Governor of Grangegorman Female Prison in May 1848, a position he held until his dismissal in 1865, which may have resulted from his favourable treatment of Margaret Aylward during her controversial incarceration there in 1860/61.

Benburb Street was referred to by John D'Alton as 'the suburra of Dublin'. Some of those women who turned to prostitution out of necessity or coercion operated on Benburb Street. Practitioners of the oldest profession were traditionally associated with army bases throughout the garrison towns of Ireland. Called 'Pavement Hostesses' by Detective Sergeant Jim 'Lugs' Branigan, a legendary Dublin Garda, many operated on the street during the 1960s and into the present century.

St Mary's Abbey

Parallel to Capel Street and running off Mary's Lane is Meetinghouse Lane, home to one of the oldest and least-known of Dublin's historic buildings, St Mary's Abbey, a name as old as the Magna Carta. St Mary's Abbey is in the OPW portfolio of ancient buildings and is surrounded on all sides by warehouses. A six-foot drop to the chapter house floor shows how the ground level of the city has risen over the centuries; built around 1180, it is forty-five feet long by twenty feet wide. It has a vaulted roof similar to one in the chapter house building of a Shropshire abbey dating from the same period. The chapter house is the scene of the defiance of Lord Thomas Fitzgerald, better known as Silken Thomas, a name given to him as a result of his love of fine clothing. While acting as Lord Deputy and chairing a meeting of the Supreme Council in 1534 he heard a false rumour that Henry VIII had had his father executed. He drew his sword and flung it onto the table in front of the Council, renouncing his allegiance to the Crown. His rebellion was suppressed and he surrendered in 1536 and executed at Tyburn, London, on 3 February 1537.

St Mary's Abbey was the largest building on the northside of the Liffey in pre-Reformation Dublin. The Benedictines founded an abbey here in the tenth century, with some sources stating 908 as the foundation date. In 1156 the Cistercians settled here and having exercised a huge influence on the life of Dublin over nearly four centuries, the abbey was dissolved by Henry VIII in 1539. The land attaching to the abbey stretched to Ballybough in the east and Grangegorman in the west and is mentioned by Haliday under the title 'St Mary's Abbey de Ostmanby'. The buildings covered present-day Capel Street, Little Mary Street, East Arran Street and Mary's Abbey.

The Bank of Ireland, established by an Act of Parliament, first opened in St Mary's Abbey on 25 June 1783. The National Eye Infirmary opened in October 1814 in St Mary's Abbey; according to *Thom's Directory* in its first nine months it treated 800 people, which included 'fifty-eight persons restored to complete vision, among whom were five cases of cataract, two of closed pupil and four of gutta serena'. It was supported entirely by public subscription. The names of streets and lanes in the immediate neighbourhood derive from the abbey.

Chancery Street and Environs

Chancery Street, formerly called Pill Lane, once stood at the edge of the estuary of the Bradoge River. In September 1896 the name of this once-famous thoroughfare was changed to Chancery Street following a petition to the Paving Committee of Dublin Corporation from all but one of the residents in the lane. The name change was not welcomed by the City Engineer of the day, Spencer Harty, who stated that 'the Pill is a very old historic name in Dublin, and it is a pity to have it wiped out now. If, however, the Committee so desire, there is no objection to Chancery-street.'

Bridewell Garda Station, Chancery Street, 1933 (Courtesy Neil Ward and *Garda Review*)

The Bridewell Garda Station and former Custody Courts of the Dublin Metropolitan District Court dominate Chancery Street, at the rear of the Four Courts. This is where the passer-by of yesteryear would often hear requests of those in custody on remand, shouted out to their loved ones outside through the bars of the cells: 'Ma, gerrus a few fags.' Construction of the Bridewell began in 1901 and finished in 1906; first rated in 1910, it was a familiar location as a result of media attention during celebrated or landmark criminal cases, as it was in the Dublin Metropolitan District Courts – called the Custody Courts – that the first appearance on foot of criminal charges was made. In January 2010 the criminal business of the Bridewell custody courts transferred to the new Criminal Courts of Justice at the corner of Parkgate Street and Infirmary Road.

Many famous Gardaí have been stationed at the Bridewell, including Tom Langan, Mayo Senior All-Ireland championship medalist in 1950 and 1951. Tom joined the Gardaí in 1944 and served in the force up to his untimely death in 1974. From Ballycastle, County Mayo, he was named 'best full-forward of the century'. Greg Maher and Eamonn 'Junior' McManus, who played on the Mayo and Roscommon Senior County football team respectively, were stationed at the Bridewell in the early 1990s. One of the most successful Garda boxers of the late 1900s, Willie Cooper, served in the station for many years; he was Irish National Senior Heavyweight champion in 1974.

River House stands on the corner of Greek Street. It was formerly home to the Dublin Corporation Motor Taxation Office and is on the site of Donnelly's pub, owned by the celebrated Irish boxer Dan Donnelly. Born in Townsend Street, Dublin in 1788, he staged exhibitions at the Donnybrook Fair in 1815. Afterwards, he refused offers to return to the ring and established a public house. He died there on 18 February 1820 after a sudden illness, brought on by the 'rigours of a hedonistic lifestyle'. Greek Street was formerly called Cow Lane. One of the pubs in the vicinity, Hughes, was referred to by Circuit Court Judge Charlie Conroy as 'the bail office' – anyone having difficulty securing a bailsperson for a defendant in custody on criminal charges during the 1960s and 1970s could, for a fee based on a sliding scale relative to the amount of bail fixed, obtain a suitable bailsman 'at the bar'.

Henry Jackson, a member of the United Irishmen (1750–1817) is listed in the *Dublin Directory* from 1768 as an ironmonger in Pill Lane and from 1787 as an iron and brass founder in Old Church Street. In addition he had mills for rolling iron in Phoenix Street. A Presbyterian, his house in Pill Lane was often used for clandestine United Irishmen meetings; three of his brothers and his son-in-law Oliver Bond were also United Irishmen.

Chancery Place was formerly called Mass Lane after a Jesuit church that opened there during the reign of the King James II. It was closed after his defeat by Williamite forces in 1690, becoming a meeting house for Huguenots, French Protestant refugees then newly arrived in Ireland, escaping pogroms in their native land. Renamed on two occasions during the 1700s, to Golblack Lane, then

Lucy's Lane, it received its present name of Chancery Place in 1825. The Alfie Byrne, renamed The Legal Eagle in the mid-1990s, was once popular with anyone doing business in the Courts. For many years it was run by the Boland family; in 1914 the premises were valued at £20 per annum in the name of Nicholas Boland. In that same year P. Doyle, cabinet maker, operated from number 8; Robert Maxwell, a boot-maker and J. Flanagan, edge-tool manufacturer, from number 10, and William McCune, solicitor, from number 11.

MacGinley's Solicitors operated from number 3; Maoilíosa MacGinley moved into offices and home here in the 1940s and ran a busy practice in malicious injuries claims; this was a time when acts of vandalism, arson and other damage involving property were compensated through claims against the local rating authority – Dublin Corporation and Dublin County Council in the case of the city and suburbs of Dublin. Through his virtual monopoly of the business he was called 'Malicious MacGinley', a pun on his Christian name Maoilíosa. When he died in 1986, his wife Roisín (*née* Gavin) oversaw the practice.

Their daughter Deirdre qualified as a solicitor in 1974; following the post-2008 economic downturn, she retired from practice and opened up a legal services business called Orca Print Ltd. The postal address of the practice was 3 Inns Quay, Chancery Place; this is as a result of the building originally fronting onto the quays, and it was the one-time headquarters of the Dublin Pawnbrokers Association. Deirdre recalls a large billiards table on the upper floor of their home, which the Association left behind when they sold the premises. For many years a billboard on the side of the building advertised the Burger King chargrilled hamburger. It was the subject of a legal action, which lasted for two days in the High Court, under the Local Government (Planning and Development) Act 1963. The case centered on whether the billboard came under the provisions of that Act (as it was a pre-1963 billboard, it was considered exempt). 'Imagine listening for two whole days to a load of waffle about a bloody hoarding advertising a hamburger' was the wry comment of the Court Registrar rostered for the case, Robert 'Bob' Flynn.

From the 1940s to the 1960s a popular Dublin solicitor, Liam Trant McCarthy, practised from number 4 and was noted for his lively courtroom banter and wit. Number 4 is now the office of Mel Christle, Barrister at Law; over his nameplate outside the premises a brass plaque bears the inscription 'Boxing Union of Ireland'. Mel Christle comes from a famous boxing family and was Irish Light-heavyweight

Champion in 1977. In 1980, the year he was called to the Bar, he and his brothers, Terry and Joe, established a unique record by winning the Irish middleweight, heavyweight and (newly created) superheavyweight titles on the same evening.

Ronnie Ringrose was one of the most prominent solicitors on Chancery Place and in the 1960s and early 1970s had the biggest criminal practice in the city. Many a young barrister was given his first assignment with a 'Ringrose Special', generally a road-traffic matter before one of the District Courts in the Bridewell or outlying courts such as Swords, Dundrum or Lucan. During a lecture delivered at NUI Maynooth in February 2009, the late Mr Justice Paul Carney recalled being the recipient of Ringrose Specials as a young barrister; these were generally cash-in-hand transactions.

Beresford Street nearby was called Phrapper Lane. Luke Fagan, born around 1656, served as the Roman Catholic Archbishop of Dublin from 1729 to 1733. He died at his home on Phrapper Lane on 10 November 1733 and left directions for his burial in a Church of Ireland burial plot in St Michael's churchyard; there is no evidence of any tombstone today.

Mary Frances Clarke was born beside Phrapper Lane around 1803, eldest child of Cornelius Clarke, a leather dealer, and Catherine Clarke (*née* Quartermas), daughter of an English Quaker. She was educated at a nearby penny schoolhouse. During the cholera epidemic of 1831 she met four other women while helping the sick and the following year they founded a school, Miss Clarke's Seminary, for girls unable to pay for or afford convent education fees; it was located on the corner of North Ann Street and Cuckoo Lane. In 1833 a visiting American priest persuaded them to transfer their charitable work to the USA, and there they founded the Sisters of Charity of the Blessed Virgin Mary. Mary Frances Clarke was elected the first Mother of the congregation and died on 4 December 1887 in Iowa. During her fifty-four years in charge she oversaw the foundation of forty-four parochial schools in the USA, the last of which was St Brigid's parish school in San Francisco (1887), and nine boarding academies. She was inducted into the Iowa Womens' Hall of Fame on 27 August 1984, in recognition of her work in the education of the American frontier.

St Michan Street, previously called Fisher's Lane as far back as 1390, received its present name in 1890. In the opening years of the eighteenth century it was the seat of three Dublin convents, the Dominicans of Cabra, the Poor Clares of

Harold's Cross and the Carmelites of Ranelagh. Bounded by St Michan's Street, Chancery Street, Arran Street East and Mary's Lane is the Dublin Corporation Wholesale Markets, one of the most architecturally striking Victorian structures in the city. It was completed in 1892 and opened on 6 December of that year. It was designed by Parke Neville, Dublin City Engineer from 1851 until his death in 1886. He was succeeded in the post in 1887 by his understudy Spencer Harty, who carried out Parke Neville's plans with modifications. The iconic building boasts ornate wrought-iron gates and distinctive polychrome brickwork. Most interesting are the terracotta carvings of fish, fruit and vegetables; in her book *Dublin – Buildings of Ireland* Christine Casey states that these 'were supplied by Henry Dennis of Ruabon, though the template has been attributed to CW Harrison'. The facades are mostly in red brick, with yellow brick lining the arches and providing contrast in patterned blocks. Behind the screen of brick arches the roof is supported by structural ironwork and rises in a series of pitches, with glazed north-facing portions providing light without glare. It still serves as the central fruit, vegetable and flower market for the city. Dublin City Council mooted proposals to turn it into a more retail-oriented upmarket showpiece, although it still appears to be business as usual with wholesale produce and flowers on sale to trade buyers and the public.

Dublin Fruit Markets, Little Mary Street, 1950s (Courtesy Howard Keogh)

The Dublin Wholesale Market replaced a warren of small markets in the surrounding streets; these were in old buildings and conducted in unsanitary conditions. The former Newgate Prison in Green Street was let on a seventy-five-year lease for use as a fruit market in August 1875 at a rent of £140 per annum to Messrs Patrick Moran, J. Flanagan, Patrick O'Hanlon, J. Halpin and W. Byrne. The Dublin Fish Market was also nearby; it was recently demolished and is now a temporary car park.

Halston Street and Environs

Originally called Bradoge Lane, from the river that flowed past, the name was later changed to Halston Street. St Michan's Roman Catholic church was constructed in 1817, commemorated by a simple plaque at the back of the building. It is known on the northside simply as Halston Street church; it originally fronted onto Ann Street North, but in the late 1800s the architect George Ashlin was commissioned to create a more prominent entrance on Halston Street, complete with an imposing and unique castellated cut-stone tower. The first Irish branch of the Society of St Vincent de Paul was established here in 1844, just eleven years after the foundation of the movement in Paris. O'Keeffe's printers, at 3 Halston Street, printed bulletins of the *Irish War News* issued from the GPO during the 1916 Rising. Cuckoo Lane nearby was the home of the Jameson and Pim Distillery and a lease dated 1715 shows that part of the site incorporated a previous brewery called Hassard's.

Cuckoo Lane leads to George's Hill Presentation Convent, the order's oldest Dublin convent. A school was established on this site in 1794 by Teresa Mulally and was the first legally permitted Roman Catholic school of its day, following the repeal of a provision in the Foreign Education Act prohibiting 'papish' schools. Teresa Mulally was born in October 1728 at Pill Lane (Chancery Street) and while still young her father Daniel, a provisions dealer, retired and moved to nearby Phrapper Lane. Teresa established a successful millinery business but lost interest in it after the death of her parents in 1762 and retired to devote the rest of her life to caring for the poor. It is possible that she acquired her interest in philanthropy from her mother Elizabeth, who assisted the poor of the neighbourhood during successive severe winters in 1740 and 1741. In 1766 she rented a three-storey house in Mary's Lane and founded a charity school, providing education for up to one hundred girls; five years later she opened a boarding school and orphanage nearby.

Aware of the frailty of her health, she entered into correspondence over a two-year period with Nano Nagle, founder of the Presentation Sisters, hoping the latter would take over the running of the school. Her efforts continued after Nano Nagle's death in April 1784, and to this end she purchased a disused glassworks at George's Hill, rebuilding the premises and making it ready for use as a convent in August 1789. She was eventually successful and in April 1794 the Presentation Sisters took over the school. A chapel, completed in 1802, was built on the site.

It was thought that Teresa might take holy vows; she never did and moved into the orphan house located beside the school, from where she looked after the school finances. She was independent-minded and not always in agreement with the religious community, particularly when religious exercises conflicted with the efficient running of the school. She died there on 9 February 1803 and is buried in a vault of the convent chapel.

In 1965 the school catered for 800 pupils and the religious community then numbered twenty-five; in 2016 160 pupils attend the National School, and the current principal is Aileen Finnegan. In 1992 the Presentation nuns handed over a new housing development on their site at George's Hill to Focus Ireland, who provide accommodation for individuals and families in need. There are seventy-two apartments within the complex, with nuns occupying nine of them. Several Focus Ireland staff live locally, including Anna Sullivan and Linda McGrane, who both attended the school as children.

Green Street

The area between Green Street and Halston Street was formerly called Little Green, which belonged to St Mary's Abbey and was the site of a cemetery for monks. In the late 1700s the need for new prisons became apparent and a committee of Dublin Corporation recommended the Little Green as a suitable site. The foundation stone for a new prison was laid on 28 October 1773 and in 1781 the first prisoner was received. Called Newgate Prison after the old prison in Cornmarket on the south-side of the city, it was built on a design by Thomas Cooley, an English architect practising in Ireland. Thomas Cooley died in 1784, aged just forty-four, at his home in

Anglesea Street. The prison building cost £18,000, of which £2000 was contributed by a parliamentary grant with the balance footed by the city taxpayer. Lord Edward Fitzgerald was incarcerated in the prison, where he died of wounds in 1798.

In its early days Newgate Prison was notorious for robbery, assault, rape and murder, all committed within its walls. Prisoners were robbed by fellow inmates, often with the encouragement of the guards, or turnkeys, who shared in the plunder. If a prisoner died it was not unusual for relatives to be charged a bribe to secure the release of the body. In one documented case a family was charged £50 for the head of a deceased relative after they already had paid for the release of the body, they then discovered that the head was missing. Prisoners were crammed into ground-floor cells, apparently to spare prison staff the exertion of going up numerous flights of stairs for inspections, and in one such ground-floor cell, measuring twelve feet by eight feet, ten to fourteen women were held. These abuses came to an end after a visit by the Commissioners for Inspecting Gaols in Ireland in 1808, and their report to government was followed by an Act of Parliament in 1810. The same visiting committee, after an inspection in 1812, reported that they had found a 'great reformation having taken place ... and all floors occupied' and 'great improvements carried out thereon'.

Built on a restrictive site measuring 170 by 127 feet, Newgate functioned as a prison until 1863, and lay idle until 1875, when it was let for use as a fruit and vege-table market. This was demolished in 1893 and the site converted into small public park, incorporating a renovated handball court. It is now a well-used, popular inner-city park managed by Dublin City Council. The walls were levelled to three feet above ground and the enclosed space filled in to the same height. The outlines today are indicated by the two semi-circular entrances to the park at the corners of Little Britain Street with Green Street and Halston Street. The knocker on the door of the prison was on display in the foyer of Green Street Courthouse at the time of the closure of the venue as a functioning court in 2010.

Sheriffs Prison

A City Marshalsea and Sheriffs Prison were also built by Dublin Corporation on the Little Green. The Sheriff's Prison was completed in 1794 and the City Marshalsea completed in 1798. The Marshalsea cost £2174 and built to a design by Sir John

Trail. By 1808 it was in a state of disrepair. The prisons replaced the 'Sponging Houses', where people arrested for debt were detained by a bailiff until bailed out by friends. These sponging houses were more often the homes of the bailiffs and got their name from the extortionate charges for the enforced accommodation provided. The Sheriffs Prison held those imprisoned for debts exceeding £2, and the Marshalsea held the lower class of debtor, with debts of £2 and less. Weekly accommodation charges for the Sheriffs Prison were set at 10/= (64 cent) for a furnished room on the landing, unfurnished rooms 3/= (19c), with four persons usually to a room. Rooms in the wings, all unfurnished, cost 1/6d. (10 cent) and the lowest class of prisoner was held in the basement at a charge of 9d. (5 cent). These charges were quite high for the year 1800. New prisoners, called 'new fish', had to pay a fee to their fellow inmates, which would be spent on a good night's feasting and drinking. New fish were welcomed by the inmates with the following chorus:

> Welcome, welcome, brother debtor,
> To this queer but merry place
> Where no bailiff, dun or setter
> Dare to show his murky face.

In the late 1700s the inmates would have arranged the purchase of their food and drink from the Bordeaux Wine Cellar around the corner in Mary's Lane. This was run by Leonard McNally, who graduated from being a young grocer to a lawyer and informer in that order. He betrayed Lord Edward Fitzgerald and other leaders of the 1798 rebellion. Debtors were allowed to beg at the gates of the jail and to even advertise for donations. The following petition appeared in the *Dublin Journal* of 3 June 1788:

> The insolvent debtors in the City Marshalsea that are entitled to the benefit of the Insolvent Act, inform the public that their long confine-ment has rendered them unable to procure their liberty and whose wives and children are entirely dependent on their industry, are now in a deplorable condition, most humbly request that the charitable and humane will take their distress into consideration and grant them relief.

With a change in the law relating to insolvency and debt recovery the Sheriffs Prison and Marshalsea were closed down in the mid-1800s and used as stores for Newgate Prison nearby. They were purchased from the Corporation by the government in June 1864 for the sum of £1000. The buildings were then adapted and handed over to the Dublin Board of Guardians for use as a hospital at the height of a cholera epidemic in 1865. During the Fenian trials in 1867/8 they accommodated the heavy British guard on security duty at the courthouse. The building was then adapted in 1869 for use as boarding quarters for the Dublin Metropolitan Police; it continued in such use for many years and served as a quarters for members of An Garda Síochána until the 1940s. In 1992 the building underwent renovation for proposed as emergency accommodation for the homeless. Access was through a small gate in the wall of the yard on Halston Street, beside the court.

Green Street Courthouse

Green Street is dominated by the courthouse, known throughout the land as the former venue of the Special Criminal Court. Designed by the architect Richard Johnston, construction began in 1792 and was completed in 1797. Located between Halston Street and Green Street, it has an entrance on each thoroughfare; the stepped entrance on Halston Street is the more imposing of the two. From the late 1950s until the early 1970s a resident caretaker lived in the building: Charlie was a colourful character and his wife used to cook dinner for the juries there. The main course never changed – every day it was mashed potatoes, corned beef and cabbage. When I revisited the courthouse around 2005 for the first time in over twenty years, I could still get the smell the corned beef and cabbage in my nostrils. The courthouse is immortalized in Irish history as the place of trial of Henry and John Shears (1798), Robert Emmet (1803), Charles Gavin Duffy, John Mitchell and William Smith O'Brien and other Young Irelanders (1848), the Fenians (1867) and Invincibles (1883). In the late 1900s it was used to process terrorist crimes with the passing of the Offences Against the State (Amendment) Act 1972. The building ceased to be a functioning courthouse in January 2010 after the transfer of the business of the Special Criminal Court to Parkgate Street. However, it reopened in 2006 and now houses the Dublin Drugs Court.

South of Green Street is Little Britain Street where Arthur Griffith, founder of Sinn Fein and signatory of the 1921 Treaty, was born on 31 March 1872. He attended St Mary's Place and Great Strand Street schools. A journalist (he was editor of the *United Irishman* journal) and patriot, he served as President of

Ireland from January 1922 until 12 August that year, when he died in St Vincent's Nursing Home, Leeson Street, worn out by the stresses of Civil War.

To the north of Green Street lies Yarnhall Street, at the top of which the imposing gateway to the former Linen Hall still stands. The hall was built in 1716 and was destroyed in the Easter Rising. Memories of the trade survive in the area through the names of Coleraine, Lurgan and Lisburn Streets, northern towns with which the Linen Hall did much trade. Bolton Street College of Technology now covers the site of the Linen Hall. In pre-railway days the stage coaches to Derry, Dundalk and Newry set off from numbers 1 and 2, Bolton Street.

Not far from Yarnhall Street is Henrietta Street, with its magnificent facing terraces of early Georgian houses. Number 15 is the headquarters of Na Píobairí Uilleann, the Society of Uilleann Pipers, founded in 1968 when there were fewer than one hundred uilleann pipers in Ireland. Following restoration and renovation, the building was unveiled as the official home of the pipers in January 2007.

Envoi

Dublin 7, although artificially created to facilitate the postal service, is in some ways an area naturally constructed over a period of time to form an organic existence of its own. While part and parcel of the city of Dublin, it has its own unique blend of village and town life, from Ashtown and Cabra West to Phibsborough, Stoneybatter and Smithfield.

The particularity of the district, and indeed of Greater Dublin, is long celebrated in the writings of Swift, O'Casey, Joyce, Clarke and other famous sons and daughters of the city; it is a quality which is embedded in a sense of community, deep, strong and enriching. From wedding grushees to Kennedy's bread, from pawn shops to credit unions, and from poverty and deprivation to home ownership and cars, over the years Dublin 7 has seen vast changes in living standards, income, education and opportunity. Such progress has not diminished the values and norms of community life. The sheer number of voluntary groups, bodies and associations throughout the neighbourhood bear testimony to this. A visitor to the area, standing at a bus stop or sitting in a coffee shop, would have no difficulty striking up a friendly conversation with a local standing or sitting beside them.

History is made every day in Dublin 7 and now a younger generation will fashion and record such history for posterity. In May 2015 Irish social history was made with the passing of the Marriage Equality referendum. Olivia McEvoy, Chair of the National LGBT Federation, lives in Stoneybatter and spearheaded the Dublin 7 YES campaign. Her efforts, and those of hundreds like her, helped to transform the lives of those once marginalized within Irish society.

Younger people are setting up businesses in the area, such as Cayeleen Caulfield, who established The Fabric Centre on the corner of Brunswick Street and Stanley Street; many new Irish are also stamping a mark on the fabric of Dublin 7 and have helped, in their own unique way, to revitalize the district. Alfie Garcia from Angola established Carlito's Store in Manor Street, which traded for a number of years during the early 2000s. The present hairdresser's premises on the corner of Stoneybatter and North King Street is run by Mr Luky from Burundi; this and other retail outlets in the area are a focus for the African community. Sylvia Wojtczak established the Polonia Pharmacy in Unit 4 of the North King Street complex in January 2015 and does a thriving trade with both the Polish community and the older residents of the district. Their stories, and those of countless others, have yet to unfold and await the pen, or keyboard, of the future chronicler.

As Dublin 7 constantly evolves and changes, one has only to look at the present light-rail LUAS works that will connect Liffey Junction in Cabra West to the Broadstone Railway Station and the city centre, and merge with the LUAS lines to Tallaght and Sandyford. These announce a future of closer links with communities throughout Greater Dublin. But while an extended LUAS network constitutes a new dawn, it also incorporates an older one with the track from Broadstone to Liffey Junction replacing that first laid out 170 years ago in 1847. The conjoining of communities past and future – all one, each individual – collectively make up a unique Dublin 7.

Sources and Bibliography

An Cosantóir, The Irish Defence Journal

An Leabharlann, December 1930 and June 1937

Archives Office, Dublin City Council

Barracks and Posts of Ireland (*An Cosantóir*)

Ball, Francis Erlington, A *History of County Dublin*

Behan, Anthony B., *Our Lady Help of Christians Navan Road Celebrating 50 Years*

Bishop of Canea, *Short Stories of Dublin Parishes*

Book of Survey and Distribution, Public Records Office, Dublin

Cabra Library

Catholic Directory

Catholic Penny Magazine

Cobbe, Alex, and Friedman, Terry, *James Gibbs in Ireland Newbridge House Villa for Charles Cobbe Archbishop of Dublin* (Cobbe Foundation/Irish Georgian Society 2005)

Collins, James, *Life in Old Dublin* (1913)

Connell, Joseph E.A. Jnr, *Dublin in Rebellion* (Dublin 2009)

Conradi, Peter J., *Iris Murdoch A Life* (London 2001)

Constabulary Gazette, The Royal Irish Constabulary Magazine (July 1916)

Culloty, A.T., *Nora Herlihy Irish Credit Union Pioneer*

Curriculum Development Unit, CDVEC, *Divided City – Portrait of Dublin 1913*

D'Alton, John, *The History of the county of Dublin* (Dublin 1838)

Dillon Cosgrave, *North Dublin City and County* (1909)

Doyle, Oliver & S Hirch, *Railways in Ireland 1834–1984*

Dublin Builder (various volumes)

Dublin Civic Museum, South William Street

'Old Dublin Society', *Dublin Historical Record* (various volumes)

Encyclopedia Britannica, 15th edition

Evening Herald

Evening Mail

Evening Press

Evening Telegraph

Flood, *Dominican Convent, Cabra, Annals Review*

Freeman, Dr Edward, *Mater Misericordiae Hospital 1861–1961*

Garda Review (various volumes)

Glazier, Michael (ed.), *Encyclopedia of the Irish in America* (1999)

Hardiman, Mr Justice Adrian, 'Law, Crime and Punishment in Bloomsday Dublin' (paper delivered to the Irish Legal History Society, 2007)

Harvey, *Dublin* (Batsford 1949)

Igoe, Vivien, *James Joyce's Dublin Houses* (Dublin 2007)

Irish Builder (various volumes)

Irish Independent

Irish Railway Record Society

Jenkins, Raymond and Simms, George, *Pioneers and Partners* (Dublin 1985)

Johnston, Francis, letter to J.N. Brewer, 1820

Joyce, Patrick Weston, *Irish Local Names Explained* (Dublin 1870)

Joyce, Weston St John, *The Neighbourhood of Dublin* (Dublin 1913)

Kiely, Commandant E. (ed), *A Short History of McKee Barracks* (2000)

Leas Coimisnéir P. Ó Cearbhailm 'Notes for a History of Police in Ireland', *Garda Review*, September 1961

Lysaght, Moira, *A North City Childhood in the Early Century* (Dublin Historical Record, Vol. XXXVIII)

MacDonald's Irish Directory and Gazetteer, William MacDonald & Company Ltd, Edinburgh

McCready, Rev. C.J., *Dublin Street Names* (Dublin 1872)

McDermott, Frank, *Tone and His Times* (Dublin 1969)

McLoughlin, Adrian, *Guide to Historic Dublin* (1972)

Moore, Peter, *Insurgent Wheels* (1990)

Murray, K.A., *Dublin Railways* (Dublin 1976)

Myler, Walter Thomas, 'St Catherine's Bells', *Dublin Historical Record*

National Library of Ireland, Kildare Street, Dublin 2

Neary, Bernard, *The Candle Factory* (Dublin 1998)

Neary, Bernard, *Lugs – The Life and Times of Garda Jim Brannigan* (Dublin 1985)

Northside People

O'Beirne, Kathy, *Kathy's Story: A Childhood Hell Inside the Magdalen Laundries* (Edinburgh 2005)

O'Brennan, Lily, 'Little Rivers of Dublin', *Dublin Historical Record* (Volume III)

O'Donovan Rossa, Jeremiah, *My Years in English Jails* (New York 1874)

Paul Hamlyn Library, British Museum, Great Russell Street, London

Pearse Street Library

Purcell, Mary, *The Story of the Vincentians* (1973)

Railway Magazine (various volumes)

Regina Coeli Hostel Information Booklet

Reid, Tony, *Bohemians AFC, Official Club History 1890–1976* (Dublin 1977)

Reynolds, Joseph, *Grangegorman Psychiatric Care in Dublin* since 1815 (Dublin 1992)

The Ryan Report

St Joseph's School for Deaf Boys, *Centenary Record 1857–1957*

Saorstát Éireann Official Handbook, Bulmer Hobson (ed.), (Dublin 1932)

Stephenson, Patrick J., *Dublin Historical Record* Vol. XIII

Story of Church Developments at Phibsborough, Vincentians 1902

Sunday Dispatch

The Church Review, Dublin & Glendalough Diocesan Magazine (Church of Ireland)

The Economist

The Illustrated London News

The Irish Press

The Irish Times

Valuation Office List of Primary Valuations, 1850

Warburton, J., Whitelaw, Rev. J., and Walsh, Rev. Robert, *History of the City of Dublin* (London 1818)

Wright, G.N., *Ireland Illustrated* (London 1831)

www.heritagemaps.ie

www.historyireland.com

www.thejournal.ie

Acknowledgments

Dublin 7 incorporates my previous, earlier local histories, entitled *A History of Cabra*, *A History of Cabra and Phibsborough* and *Dublin 7*, published in 1976, 1982 and 1992 respectively. In completing that trilogy of work on the sprawling Dublin 7 area, I was greatly indebted to the following, many now deceased, who in their own unique way passed on a living oral history for future generations: Garda Allen (Garda Museum), Robert Ballagh, Derek Brennan, Fintan Brennan, Willie Buckley (National Library of Ireland), Jimmy Campbell, Mrs E. Canning, Bobby Charlton, John Clarke, Mary Clarke (City Archivist), Michael (Mick) Coogan, Fintan Corrigan, Victor Craigie, Mrs Dixon, Fred Duffy, Jack Ennis, Fr Patrick Farrell, Cosy Finnegan, Fergus Fitzgerald, Tom Flanagan, Andrew Flynn, Brother Con Foran, Mr Hegarty, Bobby Hudson, Leonard Hynes, Archdeacon Jenkins, Mr Jones (Ranks Mills), John Kavanagh, Pat Kearns, Seamus Kearns, Barney Kelly, Christopher Keogh, Mr Lenihan, Frank Lyons, Ciaran and Gerry McGowan, Mick McGuinness, Alan McGurdy, David McKeon, James McKeon, Fr McMorrow, Larry Maher, Peter Martin, Edwin Mitchell, Gerry Moore, Sean Moyles, Dr Moynihan, Matt Mulhall, Agnes Neary, Willie O'Callaghan, Tom O'Connor, Coleman O'Donovan, Rose O'Driscoll, Kevin O'Loughlin, Joe Reid, Dorothy Reid, Tom Reilly, Hubert Richards, Br Riordan, Henry Segrave, Ned Slane, Mark Swords and Tommy Thornton.

For this expanded work published by The Lilliput Press I would like to thank the contribution of the following, who helped make the present work possible:

Des Abbot, Andrew Barry, Lar Boland, Bríd Brophy, Áine Broy, Tom Burke, Stephen Byrne, Anne Cadoo, Patrick Campbell, Martin Cannon, John Condon, Kevin Conlon, Captain Sharon Crean, Aideen Delaney, Kathleen Delaney, Paul Ferguson, Dr Dermot Fitzpatrick, Johnny Forbes, Gertie, Jim Grant, Meredith Greiling (Curator, Windermere Jetty Museum of Boats, Steam and Stories), Audie Healy, Tommie Hodnett, Jackie Hurley, Josephine, Nigel Kavanagh, Jennifer Kenna, Marie Kenny, Peter McCormack, Danny McCormick, Pat McGilloway, Bryan McGovern, Marion McLoone, Peter Maguire, Andrew John Malone, Seamus Meehan, Stephen Meehan, Gladys Mooney, James Mooney, Martin Mooney, Na Píobairí Uilleann, Lilly O'Brien, Lily O'Neill, Síle O'Neill, Pól Ó Murchú, David Pierpoint, John 'Johnny' Quirke, Susan Richardson, Shane Ryan, Commandant Andrew Shinnick, Margaret Smyth, Martin Sneyd, James Sweeney, Nancy Taylor, Alan Tormey, Edel Vaughan and Djinn von Noorden. Thanks to Denis Burns for the tour of 30 Mountjoy Street before its refurbishment in 2010.

Maps marking the opening of each chapter are as follows: 1, John Speed 1610; 2, John Taylor 1816; 3, 4, 6, 7, 8, 10, 11, Ordnance Survey 1943; 5, John Rocque 1756; and 9, William Duncan 1821. All courtesy Trinity College Dublin.